PEP'S CITY

THE MAKING OF A SUPERTEAM

'The Treble made them immortal . . . this is their origin story'
THE ATHLETIC

'A great read'
PEP GUARDIOLA

'As an insight into the inner workings of a modern top-level football club, there's not much around to match it'
MALACHY CLERKIN, *IRISH TIMES* SPORTS BOOKS OF THE YEAR

'A nuanced, access-all-areas study'
FOUR FOUR TWO

'A stunning insight into the Guardiola era at Manchester City. Brilliant access and superbly told stories'
DANIEL TAYLOR, *THE ATHLETIC*

'Excellent'
PAUL HIRST, *THE TIMES*

'Fascinating'
JAMES DUCKER, *THE TELEGRAPH*

'Brilliant'
JONATHAN SMITH, *GOAL.COM*

'Fascinating'
JAMES ROBSON, *THE STANDARD*

'Explains the tactical and human elements of City's success'
SAM LEE

PEP'S CITY

THE MAKING OF A SUPERTEAM

POL BALLÚS

&

LU MARTÍN

BACKPAGE

POLARIS
PUBLISHING

This edition first published in Great Britain in 2023 by

BACKPAGE PRESS
and
POLARIS PUBLISHING LTD

www.backpagepress.co.uk
www.polarispublishing.com

First published in 2019

ISBN: 978-1-909430-60-0
eBook ISBN: 978-1-909430-41-9

Parts of this book were first published in Spain in 2018 by
Malpaso Editorial as *Cuaderno de Mánchester: De cómo y con quién Pep Guardiola conquistó Inglaterra*

British Library Cataloguing-in-Publication Data
A catalogue record for this book is available on request from the
British Library.

Designed and typeset by Polaris Publishing, Edinburgh
Printed and bound by CPI Group (UK) Ltd, Croydon, CR0 4YY

CONTENTS

This book is dedicated to all the victims of the Manchester Arena attack, including their families, friends and anyone who somehow suffered the consequences of that horrible night. And to Cristina, Maria and Valentina for being so brave.

FOREWORD

I first met Pep Guardiola – *El Señor* – on May 26, 2016, at the City Football Academy. I'd been asked to interview him for the club website, and there were half a dozen people in the room as we waited for him to turn up.

None of us had met him before, so let's just say we were all a bit . . . not nervous but . . . y'know?!

When he arrived, he immediately put everyone in the room at ease. He shook everybody's hand, asked their name, and what they did.

Over the next 45 minutes, he proceeded to tell us, quietly, confidently, what he hoped and expected to happen over his initial period at the club.

What he expected from the players, the supporters, the staff.

How he was looking forward to experiencing the weather.

How he was going to work *and* live in the city centre.

He looked like one of us.

He spoke like one of us.

He dreamed like one of us.

And as he left the room and the door closed behind him, I vividly remember the rest of us collectively blowing out our cheeks, looking at each other and saying: "Wow!"

My friends – most of whom are blues – were straight on the phone to me, asking: "What's he like? What did he say?"

I assured them that our ridiculous little football club had pulled off the masterstroke of all masterstrokes in getting him to Manchester.

I've hung out with him many times since in both victory and defeat. Always calm but intense, always focused but fun, always demanding yet sympathetic, he must be a joy to play for.

We've never witnessed this kind of magic, not in my lifetime anyway.

P.S. He was lying about the weather!

Noel Gallagher

INTRODUCTION

The first time I saw Pep Guardiola he had a ball at his feet and was training with FC Barcelona's first team. I looked at him and thought, 'Boy, he's skinny'. Thirty years on and now the man's in charge of Manchester City – and somehow he's managed to maintain that figure, no matter what he eats.

The first time I spoke to him was on December 16, 1990, a few days after his debut at the Camp Nou against Cádiz. I was working for the Spanish football paper *Sport* at the time and myself and the paper's photographer, Fernando Zueras, had agreed to meet Pep at the stadium at 8am. The three of us then piled into Fernando's old Renault 11 and raced across the city at breakneck speed to get a snap of Pep standing in front of the statue of the Drummer of El Bruc. Legend has it that the drummer, a young boy from Santpedor, Pep's hometown, helped defeat Napoleon's troops in the battle of El Bruc in 1808. The sound of his drumming echoed round the mountains, giving the impression of a much larger force than actually existed. These days, for the people of Catalonia, he's an important symbol of national pride. A local hero. Much like Pep.

Since then I've had the good fortune to follow and report on each stage of Pep's career. I had the honour of assisting him (with fellow journalist Miguel Rico) in writing his book *Mi Futbol, Mi Gente* (*My Football, My People*), in which he talked about his experiences as a player. I saw him play for Spain and for clubs in Italy, Qatar and Mexico and was there when he came back to Barcelona as coach, first in the mini-stadium, in charge of Barcelona B, and then in the Camp Nou. For four unforgettable years, until his last day in charge, I chronicled the daily ups and downs, triumphs and defeats of that extraordinary team and then did the same during his successful time at Bayern.

Over the years we've developed a solid friendship, which now includes Pep's wider circle of friends and family to the extent that these days I'm probably closer to his wife Cristina than I am to him.

The city of Manchester has always been close to my heart. As a young man I fell in love with its music and visited the city for the first time in the 90s to dance several nights away at the legendary *Hacienda* night club – basically inspired by my love for The Happy Mondays. It changed my life, and my love for the city, its people and culture has only grown over the years. Which is why, when I heard that Pep was taking over at Manchester City, I didn't think twice. To get the chance to cover Pep Guardiola whilst living and working in the city that produced the Hollies, the Smiths, the Happy Mondays and Oasis was the stuff of dreams. After 13 years writing for *El Pais* it was time to move on. So I packed in my job and moved to Manchester.

The first thing I did when I arrived in October 2016 was to meet Pep and Cristina in their Deansgate apartment. I wanted their blessing for the book I was planning. "I'm not sure yet exactly how I'm going to approach it or what I'll focus on, but I want to tell this story," I explained.

Pep was a bit doubtful. "But what if I mess up? What if nothing interesting happens?"

"Well, I'll write about that," I told him. "But I don't think there's any chance – you're going to ace this."

"Okay. Do what you need to."

We toasted our new 'joint venture' with a gin and tonic on the terrace.

So, I had a book to write. I already knew Ferran Soriano from his days on the Barça board and my relationship with Txiki

Begiristain dated way back to his playing days at Real Sociedad. They were both a huge help to me from the start, as were all the staff at the City Football Academy (CFA). Their support and friendship was invaluable to me as I adapted to my new life in Manchester and I will be eternally grateful to them.

I spent that first season planning the structure of my book. Over the years I've written thousands of articles about Pep. We've probably done more than 100 interviews and I'd followed him and listened to him talk football from Barcelona to Munich, via New York. Was I a bit too close to my subject? I decided that I needed a fresh pair of eyes and a different perspective. And found them in Pol Ballús.

Pol had moved to Liverpool in 2014, shortly after graduating with a degree in journalism. Initially getting work waiting tables, he was appointed as *Sport's* Manchester correspondent soon after Pep arrived at the Etihad. We first met in the press room at the CFA the day before Pep's first derby at Old Trafford. Since then I've come to hugely respect him as the kind of journalist I would have loved to have worked with back in the day, when news desks really were news desks. Over the last three years we've worked together, travelled the length and breadth of the country and spent many long, happy nights talking football over drinks in more than one Manchester bar.

During one of those chats, I suggested we work together on this book and, to my surprise, he agreed. Since then we've followed Manchester City at home and away, witnessed daily life behind the scenes at City and discovered the secrets of Pep's inner sanctum at the CFA. It's been an amazing adventure and a real education and, I'm sure Pol would agree, we've both grown in the process, as journalists and as people. Getting him to come on board was vital.

It's been a hell of a ride. Living in Manchester, following Pep and working with Pol has been one of the best experiences of my life.

This book is a tribute to Manchester, to its music and its energy and to Pep Guardiola's City. The humble offering of two journalists who love football and love City.

We hope you enjoy it.

Thank you Pep, for this opportunity.

And thanks to you too, Cristina, for all the coffees, dinners and gin and tonics. And for being there.

Lu Martín

PROLOGUE

"THIS IS OUR YEAR"
THE ROAD TO ISTANBUL

As he entered the jubilant winners' dressing room in the immediate aftermath of the 2023 FA Cup final, Khaldoon Al Mubarak was looking for Pep Guardiola. The chief executive of Manchester City has a close relationship with the club's emblematic head coach. The two men speak at least once a week. Now, after Ilkay Gundogan's goals had won an all-Manchester final against United, Khaldoon's mission was one of reassurance.

Victory at Wembley on June 3 secured a domestic double, but it also started a countdown to the final of the Champions League, in seven days' time. That trophy represented the overarching ambition of Guardiola's City. So far, it had given them not glory but agony – time, after time, after time.

Khaldoon knew that Guardiola would already be thinking about Inter and Istanbul, and he pulled his manager aside as the players partied, to reinforce his belief that the ultimate objective was within their grasp. He was taken aback by the response.

"Don't worry!" replied an exuberant Pep. "It's meant to be! We're going to win the Champions League. I can guarantee it. This is our year!"

***

It was a sense of certainty upon which City and their manager travelled from Manchester to Istanbul.

It was there, shared by a less-celebrated member of the City staff, on the eve of the final, on the terrace of the JW Marriot Marmara Hotel, where the entire squad and staff had dinner. As soon as the meal was over, Pep stood up with the microphone and ordered Jorge Gutierrez onto the stage.

Chef Jorge was leaving the club after eight years spent preparing the first team's meals and occasionally cooking private dinners in the homes of staff and players. Pep wanted to express his appreciation on this, the Spaniard's penultimate day at the club. But he also used the opportunity to express his gratitude to all staff, at every level within the club, who played their part in getting the team to this point.

The Catalan paid tribute to the man he called "a culinary genius", thanking him for his service and the care and commitment he brought to the job. "You cook so that we can live. And sometimes we don't even say thank you. But it's your work, and the work of every single employee, that has got us to the Champions League final."

Jorge was almost too emotional to respond but thanked everyone for eight wonderful years and reminded them that, when he arrived in 2015, he'd come from Barcelona, who'd just won the treble under Luis Enrique. He insisted – there was no doubt in his mind – that he would see out his last day on the job watching City conquer the Champions League and win their own treble.

***

And that same sense of certainty was there on the morning of the match, when captain Ilkay Gundogan joined Guardiola for breakfast and started to share a recurring dream he had been having.

The two had worked together for seven years. They were even neighbours for a while, in the City Suites on Chapel Street, near the Cathedral. It was no big deal for Gundogan to flop down beside Pep and say: "Boss, just think, today might be the day I become the first Turkish player to lift the Champions League as captain."

"What are you talking about? You were born in Germany!"

Gundogan laughed. Pep was right. He was born in Gelsenkirchen, Germany. And he credits his birthplace with instilling the discipline and ambition required in elite football.

However, as he told Spanish newspaper, *El Pais*, his Turkish roots are also a fundamental part of his character. "I have a very Germanic mentality: train hard, be consistent and do everything to the very best of your ability. But my Turkish blood also makes me a passionate, emotional person. My roots, my family and friends – they mean the world to me."

Guardiola knew there would be more than a few of those family and friends in the Ataturk Stadium and told his captain to get ready for the biggest moment of his career: "Just go out there and enjoy the game. You'll be lifting that cup before the night is out."

***

A single phrase had been dragging Guardiola back to 1992. He was 21 years old and the defensive midfielder of Johan Cruyff's Dream Team – the Barcelona side that won the club's first European Cup with victory over Sampdoria at Wembley (with Txiki Bergiristain, the City director of football, on the bench). Cruyff's warning to his disciples that night was: "Italian clubs will never beat you. But you can *lose* to them."

Cruyff was on Guardiola's mind in Turkey. The Dutch genius not only changed football as a coach, but as a player, when he was indelibly associated with the No.14 shirt. Season 2022-23 was

Guardiola's 14th coaching at the top level. He won 14 trophies at Barcelona and had just celebrated the 14th anniversary of his first treble with the Catalan club. With the Premier League and the FA Cup already in the bag, a win against Inter would give him his 14th trophy at City.

As Manel Estiarte, the former world and Olympic water polo champion and Guardiola's trusted lieutenant (for the past 14 years) says: "I've never met a sportsman who didn't admit to at least one superstition."

In the days before the final, Pep told friends and family: "I wish I could share this success with Johan. I'd want him to know that a part of it belongs to him. He'd be proud of us right now."

Of course, lucky numbers and outright destiny aside, there are plenty of rational explanations for what Txiki Begiristain calls "the perfect circumstances for this win".

And there was no greater single factor in City finally taking the final step toward the greatest prize in club football than the recruitment of Erling Haaland in the summer of 2022.

Bergiristain recalls travelling to Monaco with Omar Berrada, chief football operations manager at City, to meet with the player's then agent, Mino Raiola – who died in April 2022 – and his dad, ex Man City player, Alfie Haaland.

From the start, City were focused on meeting the salary demands of the most sought-after footballer in the world (including his signing fee and commissions, he would end up costing the club around €100 million).

With the bar set that high, few clubs had the means to compete and only one – Real Madrid – had the will as well as the resources. Yet Haaland knew that Madrid were planning to hold on to Karim Benzema for another season and figured that they were also interested in Kylian Mbappe, who then seemed to be positioning himself for a move away from Paris St Germain. Haaland's father was in favour of a move to Manchester and Raiola had given Alfie the green light as far as the salary negotiations were concerned.

Before doing the deal, Erling and Alfie Haaland had a 30-minute video-call with Pep. The coach explained his vision and how he planned to realise it, telling them that this move offered huge opportunities for both club and player.

He couldn't offer Haaland guaranteed playing time but he did go into detail about how important the Norwegian could become to City. Guardiola's colleagues see this as typical of the Catalan's upfront approach: don't make promises that you can't deliver.

Haaland fundamentally understood he wasn't being bought as a 'trophy signing'. In the end, no huge sales-pitch was required. Given his father's playing history, Haaland had grown up with a fondness for the club and had been enjoying watching Pep's City. He understood their style well and felt that he knew what to expect.

For the striker, the decision was relatively straightforward. According to a senior executive, it was one based on Haaland's personal assessment of what the club had to offer – rather than the persuasive powers of his new manager.

In football terms, the arrival of Haaland pushed Pep's tactical philosophy to evolve even further. Those closest to Guardiola say the signing led to the manager 'reinventing himself'.

From the start at Barca, right up until the previous season at City, Pep's teams have played, won and scored copiously, largely without a traditional No.9. There had been totemic strikers such as Samuel Eto'o and Zlatan Ibrahimovic at Barcelona, Robert Lewandowski at Bayern Munich and Kun Aguero at City. However, Guardiola also used the false No.9 to great effect and most of his City teams had triumphed without an all-out centre-forward, with Ilkay Gundogan, Phil Foden, Bernardo Silva and Gabriel Jesus among those acting as mobile forwards.

And so there was much speculation about Haaland's signing. Would the arrival of the greatest No.9 in the world force Pep to change? Or would playing for Pep's City change Haaland? With typical precision, Guardiola himself can tell you exactly how long it took for his new signing to make it work: a little over 90 minutes. Essentially, the duration of the 2022 Community Shield match against Liverpool in Leicester, which City lost and in which Haaland failed to score.

In his next appearance, his debut in the Premier League, the Norwegian took West Ham apart, scoring two goals and silencing those who had already attempted to question his ability to make a success of his new role. By the season's end, he had scored 52 goals and registered nine assists.

Haaland is hugely popular with City staff. "He's always in a good mood and has a kind word for everyone," said one member. "He's made such a difference to the team and, when you think how famous he is, it's amazing he's still such a sweet guy. You'd expect that a player of Erling's status and physical size might be arrogant and demanding – a bit of a diva. But he's got a smile for everyone and is always happy to chat. He'll take the piss, too, but more importantly, he can handle a joke at his own expense."

Everyone, from the cleaning ladies to half the players in the dressing room, know from personal experience that almost no request for a signed shirt or photo will be rejected. The Norwegian can be spotted, most days, with a marker pen in his hand. As one coach told us: "He'll get sick of it sooner or later, but at the moment he never turns any request down. And believe me, he has to sign a *lot* of shirts!"

Those who have been with Pep since his Camp Nou days state with authority that even the great Leo Messi, back in his Barca heyday, didn't generate as many requests for personalised merchandise as Haaland currently does.

Although City's new striker initially planned to move outside of Manchester, on the club's advice he and his partner decided to live in a city-centre apartment block, 10 minutes from training, where his neighbours include Sergio Gomez, Ruben Dias, Julian Alvarez and Jack Grealish. Dias has assumed the role of big brother for the rest of the group, giving them a hard time when necessary but being supportive and encouraging too.

Haaland's closest team-mate is Grealish – the pair are inseparable. They insist on sitting together whenever the team flies to away games to the extent that it's become a superstition.

The humility with which Haaland accepted the limitations of his role within Guardiola's system was appreciated by the senior players. And his sense of humour became apparent early in the season when he turned up to the Halloween party – organised by Kyle Walker and Riyad Mahrez plus their wives – in full Viking regalia, his bare chest exposed to the freezing Manchester night air.

But Haaland is the prototype modern elite footballer – scrupulously dedicated to his preparation. He's particularly impressed City's management team with the care and attention he pays to his health and recuperation. He works very closely with the club's Italian physiotherapist, Mario Pafundi, who accompanies him on international breaks with Norway, a personal physio on City's payroll. The two have become close and meet for dinner most weeks.

He also believes that sleep is a fundamental part of the recuperation process. Every night, an hour before going to bed, he puts on blue-light glasses to protect his eyes. It means cutting short the Minecraft sessions he plays with his mates but it's worth the sacrifice for a good night's sleep.

Nutrition is also important and although he has his own personal dietician, he also follows the club's directives to the letter.

"Haaland's eating habits are the stuff of legend at the club, but a lot of it is exaggerated. He actually eats more-or-less the same as everyone else," one of the chefs explains. In fact, the main difference between Haaland's diet and that of his team-mates is the sheer quantity. The Norwegian is a big guy and, as the kitchen staff will tell you, "if you're double the height and weight of Bernardo then, logically, you're going to have to eat more than Bernardo".

What that means is that if, on match day, one player has 200 grams of pasta, Haaland will have as much as 350 to 400 grams. When you're that tall and that heavy, you need to eat a lot. One of his favourite foods is salmon and the club now sources the highest quality Norwegian salmon from a company Haaland himself recommended, and which only deals with the most exclusive clientele, including the Norwegian royal family.

"Signing Haaland has paid dividends financially and in sporting terms," Ferran Soriano, the club's managing director, tells us. "But beyond the role any one player has played, no matter how brilliant, the key to City's success is our consistency and resilience. We could have won the Champions League before now.

"In this business it's very easy to let the doubts creep in, so that you end up panicking and changing course. But you have to give it time. As long as you believe that you have the talent and that everyone is prepared to put the work in, both of which are true for us, then, in business terms, time is the one of the best investments you can make. It's about sticking with your model and keeping the faith."

At times that faith was sorely tested, not least in the competition that became their all-consuming goal. There was the elimination in the 2022 Champions League semi-final at the Santiago Bernabeu, after Madrid's incredible fightback, scoring three times after the 90th minute; the lost final in Porto, when City had entered April chasing an unprecedented quadruple; and a traumatic quarter-final elimination at the hands of Tottenham in 2019.

During the 2022-23 season there were moments when doubts began to creep in. "We were so far behind Arsenal [in the Premier League] that for a while it felt like we'd never catch up," recalls Soriano. "But Pep never lost faith."

"You can never point to one crucial moment, a single turning point that changed everything," is Estiarte's constant refrain. "You set off down a particular path and you have to follow it to the end. That's all there is to it."

There were plenty of bumps along the way. Perhaps the biggest was the end of Joao Cancelo's time with City. The instinctive and superbly talented full-back returned from the World Cup in January 2023 out of form and far from his brilliant best.

After a bruising World Cup which had seen Manchester United defender Diogo Dalot take his position in the Portugal line-up, Cancelo struggled to regain his rhythm on his return to City and lost his place.

Unfortunately, the Portuguese is the kind of footballer who deeply resents the loss of playing time and sometimes struggles to disguise his frustrations, something which doesn't go down well with Pep, who refuses to tolerate defiance or sulking from his players.

In Cancelo's case this kind of behaviour wasn't new. In 2019, just after signing for City, the defender threatened to leave if he continued to lose out to Kyle Walker.

In 2020, at the start of the pandemic, the assistant manager, Juanma Lillo, was tasked with trying to persuade Cancelo that it was in his own best interests – as well as the club's – to get his head down, do the work to improve his game and earn his place in the team.

There were several players out injured at the time and, at Lillo's insistence, Pep decided to try him out at left-back. It worked and Cancelo flourished in his new role, becoming one of the best wing-backs in Europe for two seasons. On February 1, 2022, he signed a lucrative new five-year contract with City. Unfortunately, everything was about to turn sour.

The start of the new season was bumpy for Cancelo, alternating between moments of sheer brilliance and horrendous mistakes – such as the one at Anfield on October 16, 2022, which led to the only goal in a defeat by Liverpool.

He refused to accept the loss of playing time after the World Cup and Pep was increasingly irritated by his behaviour during sessions and around the training centre. Neither was the Catalan impressed by the level of intensity Cancelo brought to games or his lack of attention in tactical meetings and team talks.

Pep decided to give Cancelo one last chance and started him in the Manchester derby at Old Trafford on January 14, 2023. City lost 2-1 and Cancelo turned in a lacklustre performance. It was his last official game for the Sky Blues.

The situation finally came to a head two weeks later, just before the fourth round of the FA Cup against Arsenal. A sullen Cancelo, pissed off when he learned he wasn't starting the game, was visibly disengaged throughout Pep's tactical talk.

It was the last straw for Guardiola and, en route to the Etihad, he spoke to his bosses, Begiristain and Soriano, to leave them in no doubt that the player had to go: "For the good of the team, Joao better be gone by the time the winter market is closed."

Soriano is more circumspect: "It's all about making the right decisions for the team as a whole. We came to this club determined to make good decisions and create a team with the right values and the right character. We had to maintain those standards."

Two days after the Arsenal game, Begiristain met Jorge Mendes, Cancelo's agent, to agree an immediate loan move to Bayern Munich.

For an illustration of the kind of character sought out by Guardiola, Soriano and the other architects of this City team, look no further than the story of another wing-back in the hours before the 2023 Champions League final.

When Pep announced the line-up in Istanbul, Kyle Walker was dismayed to discover that he was not a part of the starting XI, Manuel Akanji having taken his place on the right side of the defensive trio. However, Walker still had a job to do.

Pep wanted him to do the pre-game team talk in the dressing room – a reflection of his growing status as a leader and the trust Pep has in him. His speech referenced the fact that he was not starting the game – but that the journey they were on was a collective one, and that each of them had an important role to play.

For periods during the course of the season, Walker, like Cancelo, had been unhappy with a lack of game time. But while the Portuguese's relationship with Guardiola broke down terminally by the end of January, Walker remained an influential figure all the way to Istanbul – including signature performances versus Vinicius Junior in both legs of the semi-final against Real Madrid.

Even when an approach from Bayern Munich came in the summer of 2023, Walker's relationship with his manager was the key factor in his decision to stay. Over a private dinner at Japanese restaurant Musu in Manchester, Pep underlined his value both in the dressing room and on the pitch. That September, Walker agreed a two-year contract extension.

"I remember thinking that I'd never seen Pep as calm as he was on the morning of the game in Istanbul," recalls Pere Guardiola, the coach's brother and co-owner of Girona, one of City's satellite clubs. "Not when he was in charge for those two Champions League finals at Barca and certainly not before playing Chelsea in Porto."

Just before he boarded the bus to go to the Ataturk Stadium, Pep bumped into his final lucky charm. The Spanish film director and writer David Trueba had come to support his buddy. Trueba, one of Guardiola's closest allies, has been by the coach's side across all the pivotal moments of his career.

But this time, Trueba cut his arrival a little fine. Everyone outwith the club (the official party had a police escort through the traffic) would soon leave for the game and Pere Guardiola suggested Trueba go straight to City's hotel, where he could cadge a lift in the minibus taking the Guardiola family to the stadium.

As the film director arrived at the hotel, he bumped into Pep, who handed him the key to his room: "I'm in 1004 on the 10th floor. Go up and wait for me and I'll join you when I'm finished. I've got a bit of time and we can catch up."

"I don't remember much about the room itself but the view over the Sea of Marmara was amazing," said Trueba. "I also remember how relaxed he was compared to the Wembley and Rome finals with Barca. He said that it felt like the culmination of everything he'd done and that he was pretty relaxed about the game.

"I told him that hard work and perseverance win out in the end and I was sure that this was City's day. It turned out, of course, that he didn't need any reassurance. 'Don't worry David,' he said, 'we've got this!'"

Later, Trueba is in exactly the right spot in the Ataturk Stadium – right in line with the goal where, in the 68th minute, Rodri slams home the strike that will change the history of the club.

Inside the Marriott Hotel after the game, the privileged few were greeted at the door by staff who handed them a gold wristband and access to the most sought-after post-match party in the world.

The party filled the hotel foyer, through three more rooms and on to the spacious terrace and bar. The champions of Europe were footing the bill – a free bar for all.

There was a dancefloor and a DJ to keep it busy, and there was a stage and three pedestals for the trophies, which arrived with huge fanfare, after a few words from Ferran Soriano and ecstatic cheers from the attendees.

In attendance was the former City captain, Fernandinho, who himself was so close to lifting the Champions League trophy in his last two seasons at the club, and Juanma Lillo, at the end of his brief hiatus between two spells as assistant manager, but never less than a constant influence on Guardiola, whose ideas on football he has helped shape since they met in 1998.

The drinks flowed and celebratory cigars were handed out, courtesy of Josep Maria Orobitg, Pep's long-term personal financial adviser, and Joan Palau, an old friend of Pep's who produced a box of Cohiba 50 Aniversario, the Catalan's favourite.

Jack Grealish strolled in still wearing his match-strip, and proudly informed his coaches that he'd not be washing for a week. Erling Haaland and Kyle Walker arrived alongside him, with the latter making a beeline for the DJ to talk through his tracklist.

By 4am the party was well underway but the one person who hadn't yet made an appearance – and whom everyone was looking for, including his friends, assistants and even his family – was Pep. "I was up in my room chatting to Khaldoon," he said. "I can't even tell you exactly what we talked about. Probably how happy we were, how he deserved this success more than anyone."

Guardiola has nothing but praise for a president who has shown him unwavering support and trust, even in the bleakest of moments. Mansour bin Zayed Al Nahyan joined them and the three men savoured the moment in Pep's luxurious suite, whilst the party continued downstairs. Sheikh Mansour, as he is better known, had just witnessed City triumph in only the second club match he had attended since buying City in 2008.

Those closest to Pep underline that City's victory will go some way to rid Pep of the most painful 'stone in his shoe' – the memory of an agonising loss in the Jose Alvalade Stadium in Lisbon on August 15, 2020.

That night, Olympique Lyon beat City in the quarter-finals of the Champions League, the competition having only just restarted after the COVID pandemic; a shock defeat which nobody predicted.

For Guardiola, the pain of that defeat endured. More than Monaco in 2017, more than Liverpool in 2018, more than Tottenham in 2019 and even more than Real Madrid in 2022.

He knew he approached that match with the same attention to detail as ever. But, on the night, his 3-5-2 had been powerless against the French onslaught – a night when they were deadly in front of goal.

Irrespective of any extenuating circumstances, Pep has always blamed himself. He considers that defeat as one of the turning points in the modern history of Manchester City.

"It was one of those make-or-break moments," a senior executive told us. "Pep blamed himself and I think he might have offered to resign if Khaldoon hadn't intervened. He came down to the dressing room immediately after the game where everyone was sitting, utterly gutted after their shock defeat, and said three things: 'Don't worry, it's been a tough night, but we'll come back from this. This isn't our year but our time will come as long as we don't let it knock us sideways. Right now, we need to believe in ourselves more than ever before.' Pep was stunned."

Guardiola finally made it to his own party just after 5am and was immediately surrounded by family and friends. Several former colleagues were also there, including ex-assistant Domenec Torrent.

"Pep was so happy and I remember him telling me that, in football, you're only as good as your silverware. I actually don't think I've ever seen him as happy as he was after winning the Champions League," David Trueba recalls.

And it's Trueba who – after Pep's wife Cristina and the family headed off to their rooms to pack before heading out to the airport – joined Pep in his bedroom for a final glass of champagne and a good cigar.

Then Trueba himself departed and Pep was finally alone, silently gazing at the Sea of Marmara.

He could hear some of his players, still partying and singing at the top of their lungs.

Back in Manchester the fans were waiting.

Pep finished his cigar and took a deep breath.

He had done it.

***

The pages that follow these will explain how Pep Guardiola constructed what is arguably the best football team England has ever seen: certainly the greatest Manchester City side in history.

ONE

A DAY AT THE OFFICE

Pep Guardiola once said that it is the early risers of this world who make their country unstoppable. He gets up at around 7:30am. Not that early, really.

He greets his family with good morning kisses and heads to a window to look out at the city below, and to see whether or not it's raining. It usually is.

After breakfast with the kids, he sends them off to school, gets dressed and has a look at the press. Then, schedules permitting, he and his wife, Cristina, will head down to one of the trendy cafés close to Manchester Cathedral to have their first coffee of the day.

Then to work: The City Football Academy (CFA). En route to Clayton Lane he listens to Ràdio Cataluña or another Spanish station, RAC. He needs to hear the news from home.

He arrives as HQ is still stirring into life. He greets Stacy, the receptionist, and jogs up the 28 steps to the office he inherited from Manuel Pellegrini. On the wall is a maxim Pep wrote the day he moved in:

Primer és saber què fer.
Després, saber com fer-ho!
First, you have to know what to do.
Then, you have to know how to do it.

Beneath it, Maria, his eldest daughter, has added:

Maria was here!
Good luck!
I love you!

Pep prefers to be in close proximity to his team and since taking over he has had this area completely redesigned. As well as redecorating his own room, he added an office for Ana Leyva, director of football Txiki Begiristain's secretary, and working spaces for Carles Planchart (head of analysis), Mikel Arteta (assistant coach), Xabier Mancisidor (goalkeeping coach) and the first-team operations manager, Marc Boixasa (next door to Manel Estiarte).

The football analysis suite also occupies a far bigger area now and Pep will always pass technical staff already hard at work by the time he reaches his office and his own day starts.

Pep first visited City's training ground back in March 2016, during an international break, and then again on June 3. City CEO Ferran Soriano and Begiristain demanded those visits be kept as quiet as possible and only three other staff were involved: Joan Patsy, Begiristain's right-hand man, plus David Quintana (in charge of player care) and Begiristain's secretary Amaia Díaz – a characterful Navarran who was key in helping them prepare the arrival of their visitor, codenamed 'The German'.

The last two have both since left the club. Díaz escaped to San Domingo, looking for adventure and a new direction in life.

Quintana was forced to leave because of ill health. The player liaison manager, who had key responsibility for supporting new arrivals, was a particular loss for the club. As Begiristain's trusted lieutenant he was key to Guardiola's successful adaptation to his new city and it was Quintana who set out, in the early hours of

March 16, 2016 (the day after Bayern eliminated Juventus from the Champions League), on a top-secret mission to Germany.

"Go to Munich but tell no one," Begiristain ordered him. "It seems we've got a problem with The German."

They did indeed. In Munich, the Guardiola family had lived in a spacious mansion on Sophienstrasse. Pep demanded accommodation of a similar standard in Manchester and the issue was in danger of becoming a deal-breaker. Quintana and Pep met over a leisurely three-hour lunch in a local Vietnamese restaurant. Cristina, Pep's three kids, plus his agent, Josep María Orobitg, and Orobitg's wife Núria were also at the table. Lunch was spent discussing key elements of the club's organisation, infrastructure, players . . . but the issues around the Guardiolas' new home remained unresolved.

An anxious Begiristain demanded a full debrief on Quintana's return.

"So, what did you tell him?"

"The plain truth: that there basically isn't anything like that in Manchester."

The problem was that Pep was refusing to live anywhere but the city centre and there just wasn't the right kind of property there to suit him. It didn't exist.

Begiristain could see all his plans going up in smoke. The deal to bring Pep to City was under threat. Quintana, though, was still upbeat.

"I just told him, 'No worries; if we have to, we'll build you what you want. It might take a few more months, but we'll make it happen.'"

And so it was that the Guardiola family ended up renting a luxury apartment in the Deansgate area of Manchester while they waited for the building work on their new home to be completed. It took a little longer than predicted, but eventually they were able to move in.

At least once a day, Pep talks to Manel Estiarte. He'll then pop into his office, kick off his shoes before strolling down to the cafeteria in his socks, chatting to people on the way.

Today Silvia Tremoleda, a former triathlete and City's respected sports nutritionist, is there, supervising the day's menus. She usually gets to the club around 7am so that she can use the gym before work.

Pep grabs a hot chocolate and heads back to his office, where he starts taking notes on some match footage he has on his computer. He needs to speak to Begiristain but is told that he's not back from a scouting trip yet. He's due any minute though.

This morning Pep is in relaxed mode. City's next game isn't going to be too complicated. They're already well prepared, the team's playing well – everyone here is pretty chilled.

Pep is having a laugh on the phone with David Torras, an old friend and the director of communication at Girona, the Spanish club part-owned by City Football Group.

Pep hangs up when Planchart appears with some reports on the opposition. The pair are clearly in agreement about the kind of football they're likely to encounter. Planchart, Pep's chief performance analyst, isn't worried. "We don't need to take a lot of time over the analysis this week. They are a pretty predictable side – they don't hold any surprises for us."

Next up: a meeting with the club doctors. One of the players has a knee injury and Pep wants to know if an operation is needed. He knows that if they continue to play him, the problem could get much worse. Pep has already consulted the Barcelona-based doctor, Ramón Cugat, who is an expert in knee injuries. He's also discussed the player's situation with fitness coach Lorenzo Buenaventura on his daily tour of the CFA.

The medics know that they have to be on the ball. "He'll hit you with the most unexpected questions," says one member of the medical team. "Like today, he asked me if we'd compared the current scans with the ones we did at the start of the season."

"I know bugger all about whether it's a good idea to compare scans," Guardiola laughs. "It was Loren [Buenaventura] who gave me that tip. But if it makes me look good, so be it."

The injury is no laughing matter and Pep wants to avoid jeopardising the player's participation in the upcoming World Cup. He'll have a chat with the player and they will make the decision together.

One by one, the technical team arrive for the pre-training planning session. As they take their places around the meeting table, Estiarte hands the coach a pile of shirts for signing. Pep is a patron of the Johan Cruyff Foundation and this is one of the ways he supports them.

First item on the agenda: have all the players arrived? As usual, everybody except Yaya Touré. Pep knows exactly who the early birds will have been: Fernandinho, Gündoğan and Brahim Díaz are always first in. Then David Silva or Kun Agüero. Benjamin Mendy will have strolled in at the last minute, without a care in the world, and asked the receptionist for some jelly beans.

Everyone is rushing about. Players sprint up and down stairs from the gym to the cafeteria for breakfast, and from there to a session on the massage table. Meanwhile, Pep casts a beady eye over today's weigh-in results. Every player has been given detailed instructions regarding diet and weight, carefully calibrated by the club dietitian according to height and muscle mass. Pep's a stickler in this regard and there'll be no mercy for anyone who has failed to stick to the agreed parameters.

Over in the main hall, the Amazon team are setting up their cameras. The club has granted full access to a documentary crew who will tell the story of Guardiola's second season at the club, to be released on Amazon's own streaming service. The guys from the in-house media team, City TV, are waiting for Gündoğan, who's doing some promo work today.

Soriano is typing feverishly on his tablet and simultaneously talking on the phone when Begiristain arrives and heads straight up the stairs to greet Pep, who is outside his office having a laugh with Arteta, his assistant coach.

Txiki's got news: "Joan [Patsy] arrives tonight. Let's have dinner. We need to talk."

"That might be a problem. I've got tickets for the theatre with Cris and the kids. Maybe I could cancel that. They'd kill me though."

"No, don't cancel. It'll wait till tomorrow."

"You're a lifesaver. Let's do breakfast then."

"Breakfast it is," says Txiki. "I've loads to tell you."

Today is a light training session. It is the final stretch of Pep's second season and the championship is assured. However, it's been a long haul and Buenaventura focuses on short, intense toning exercises which won't overtire the players. Pep and Domè Torrent, then his assistant manager, have already run through exercises to practise bringing the ball out from the back. Arteta has some specific work to do with Leroy Sané and Raheem Sterling, while Mancisidor gives the keepers a more demanding session.

As always, training is closed to anyone except key personnel: the physios, medics, kit men, coaches, Estiarte and Begiristain. Pep does make an exception on Saturdays and Sundays, when he will sometimes bring his son Màrius along. The coach will also consider requests to attend the first training session after a match, although he's much more welcoming following a win. The Scotland rugby coach Gregor Townsend has already visited this year. He was initially allocated just ten minutes, but ended up spending an hour with Guardiola.

Pep always leaves his office and involves himself in training to one degree or another, no matter the weather; today there's a biting wind whipping round the training round.

Pep is out there on the pitches even when he's resting his key players. "The players that don't tend to get a game actually need more attention," he says. "You have to work even harder to make sure they're okay."

As he comes down to training today, Pep catches sight of some unusual activity on one of the side pitches and realises that it's the City disability team. When he calls his players over for the *rondos*, he tells them: "Today we're going to do something a bit different. Let's go over and watch these youngsters play. They're amazing. We should be giving thanks for our own good fortune."

The City dressing room is oval. Pep wanted it designed like that so that the players are able to interact easily. The layout means that they're much less likely to huddle in small groups (as they did in the Barça dressing room, which is divided into sections by columns and where players can end up almost completely cut off from each other).

A line from one of Tony Walsh's poems is written across one of the walls. "Some are born here, some drawn here, but we all call it home." Another Pep touch. However, the coach never goes into the dressing room, except on matchdays. "It's for the players. It's sacred."

Team talks happen in a mini lecture room on the first floor, beside the cafeteria.

At the end of training Buenaventura and the club doctor check out the data garnered by the apparatus which measures the players' biometrics and the physios get on with the obligatory massages.

Reggaeton booms out of the dressing room, where the kit men make a valiant attempt to tidy everything away while the players laugh and joke around them. Bernardo Silva, frequently, is the butt of the jokes.

Pep takes himself off for a shower and a change of clothes and grabs the chance to call his wife.

Over lunch Pep chats with his staff about the training session: what worked, what didn't, who caught on the fastest and mastered the new tactics.

The one trait that Pep appears to seek, or develop, in those around him is leadership. Begiristain sees this as one of his friend's main strengths. "He surrounds himself with people who are not scared to disagree with him, to give their own point of view. After that he does what he wants anyway, but he always asks for their input first."

Over lunch, Buenaventura's data helps settle an argument over a player who is showing great promise.

"The lad nearly killed himself at training today."

"Really?" says Pep.

"I told you," exclaims Torrent.

And with that, the unsuspecting player is one step closer to becoming a regular starter.

If there are no burning issues to discuss and lots of work piling up in the office, Pep will have lunch at his desk. Something simple, like a slice of tortilla followed by a glass of hot water (somebody once told him it aids digestion). He'll make his notes, pore over his computer screen. If he's got a lot to catch up on, especially on the eve of a game or when it's too cold to go outside, he'll put on some music, light an incense stick and shut himself up in his office for the rest of the day. The players are long gone.

His staff are hard at it too (getting kit ready, sorting injuries out, preparing reports on the upcoming opponent), but by 5pm everyone else is packing up, ready to go home. Pep works on, with the incense still burning and his music (Oasis, Manel or Carla Bruni) in the background.

The walls of his office are kept white so that ideas can be

scribbled on them. In the centre of one wall there is a caricature of Noel Gallagher and a verse from his song, *Rock 'n' Roll Star*.

Pep doesn't keep a lot of personal things in his office, but one of his prized possessions is the Cruyff statue (a gift from the Johan Cruyff Foundation) on his desk. Other than that, there are two computers, pencils, piles of paper and, to the left of his chair, a wall chart displaying the week's plan of work. It's all about the next game. Just beside it, he's taken a black marker pen to the white wall and scrawled out Marcelo Bielsa's words:

The moments in my life when I have improved are closely related to failure; the moments in my life when I have regressed are closely related to success. Being successful deforms us as human beings, it relaxes us, it plays tricks on us, it makes us worse individuals, it feeds our egos. Failure is the complete opposite, it forms us, makes us more solid, brings us closer to our convictions, makes us more coherent. I was happy when I was involved with amateur football, I was happy when I matured into the job that I love. I have a deep love for football, for the game, for the corner kick, for the narrow space, for the long line on the pitch, for the football itself. Yet I despise all the rest. Let me be clear. The joy that comes with winning lasts about five minutes and what's left is a gaping void and a loneliness that's hard to describe. Never allow failure to affect your self-esteem. When you win, understand that praise and accolades are deceptive for they feed our ego and deform us. When you lose, the opposite happens. What really matters is the nobility of the resources at your disposal.

The day after a game, Pep usually goes home to eat with his wife, but if the weather's good or there's a lot on, he'll stay in the office until late. On grey winter days, when it's dark by 3:30pm, he'll head home as early as possible, sit down at his dining table, switch on the computer and have a glass of white wine or a bottle of beer. Then he'll get back down to work.

Today he's behind the wheel of his black Mercedes by 6pm. Guardiola has a reputation from his Barcelona days of being a hapless driver, and this is the fourth car he has owned since coming to Manchester. His wing mirrors don't survive for long, and he's also managed to fill a diesel Range Rover with petrol and mangle a silver Bentley.

The drive home is just 15 minutes. Tonight he is off to see the musical *Shrek* with Cristina and the kids. The family make the journey to the theatre on foot and talk about how many homeless people they see. It's incomprehensible to them.

On the way home they have a bite to eat in a Spanish restaurant, Tapeo & Wine. They enjoyed the show. The title is almost in the bag. The family are all okay. Pep's had a good day at the office.

TWO

CI SIAMO

In the ruthless world of professional football, it is rare, if not unheard of, for a transfer of personnel between two elite clubs to be described as straightforward – much less amicable. Yet that is exactly how Txiki Begiristain, Manchester City's director of football, breaks down the process of signing Pep Guardiola.

"We always felt that if Pep wanted to come to the Premier League, we'd end up working together. We're good friends and when the time came, things just kind of happened naturally."

It was precisely that friendship which made Manchester City's offer so irresistible to Guardiola. "I picked this club because of Txiki, [Joan] Patsy and [Ferran] Soriano. They're all good friends and I was keen to work with them again."

Like Ferran Soriano (who was on the Barcelona board when Guardiola was manager), Begiristain (who had played with Guardiola and was his director of football at the Camp Nou) and Patsy (who worked under Johan Cruyff at Barcelona), Manel Estiarte has history with Pep. The two are close friends and Estiarte has been Guardiola's lieutenant at Barcelona, Bayern Munich and now in England.

Estiarte agrees that City were always going to be Guardiola's top Premier League choice. "Put it like this: Pep called me out of the blue during his year in New York and said, 'Are you sitting down? It's done. We're going to Munich!' But three years later, at the end of his time at Bayern, he didn't have to tell me where we were going next. We all took it for granted."

Pep had spent his post-Barcelona sabbatical year in New York, living in an apartment overlooking Central Park. Friends and colleagues from the world of football were regular visitors and it was on one such trip that Guardiola gave Soriano disappointing news. He'd already met with the Bayern Munich president, Uli Hoeness, and had made up his mind. Munich, not Manchester, would be his next destination.

Back in England, Begiristain reverted to Plan B. Negotiations began with their alternate choice and before too long the Etihad was echoing to chants of:

Sheik Mansour went to Spain
in a Lamborghini.
Brought us back a manager:
Manuel Pellegrini!

Soriano continued to hope, reassured by Begiristain: "Don't worry. We'll get our chance. Sooner or later, we'll have another go."

Patsy, the football director's right-hand man, was even more optimistic: "He'll stay at Bayern for three years and then we'll get the call. He'll come to us first."

Then, one day after a preseason friendly in Munich, Pep told Soriano: "If Pellegrini decides to leave, you'll let me know, won't you?"

First though, they'd have to make him an offer he couldn't refuse, and timing would be crucial. In July 2015, Patsy placed a call to Begiristain. "This is Pep's last year at Bayern. We need to get the ball rolling."

Patsy has known Pep since he first caught a glimpse of the talented midfielder in the Barcelona youth academy. In July 2015

Patsy was in Buenos Aires, looking after City's South American operations and, although he was in regular contact with Pep, there was no way he could know for sure what the Catalan's plans were. But his gut told him the time was right.

It was enough for Soriano to plot his next move. As usual, he would be spending the month of August in his Costa Brava holiday home and this seemed the ideal opportunity to invite Pep's brother Pere round for a chat. Pere is a football agent who, whilst not Pep's official representative, undoubtedly has his brother's ear. He joined Soriano over breakfast one August morning. The two men chatted casually for a while until inevitably the conversation turned to Pep.

"So, how's he doing?" Soriano asked casually.

"Well, his contract's up but he's not really said anything to me yet, so if you guys are interested ..."

The whistle had sounded. The ball was in play.

Soriano immediately started working on the contract and, over the next six months, the details were negotiated. The contract itself was pretty standard: a guaranteed salary plus performance bonuses and 20 per cent of image rights revenue. There was also a confidentiality clause, preventing details of the contract being made public.

Meanwhile, Begiristain began to look for players. He'd spent the last 20 years talking football with Pep and knew exactly what the new coach would want. "It's easy. If I like the look of a Dutch player, I ask Koeman; if it's a Dane, then Michael Laudrup's my first port of call, and so on. I have a lot of friends in football so there's always someone who can advise. When I was thinking about Leroy Sané, it was Pep I consulted."

In December 2015, with the coach having already informed Bayern of his departure, Pere and Pep's accountant met with Soriano and one of the club's lawyers at Pere's house in Barcelona and the deal was done.

Two weeks later, Soriano received the call he'd been waiting for. "As they say in Italy, *ci siamo*," Pep told him. "It's a done deal."

Soriano immediately called the Manchester City chairman, Khaldoon Al Mubarak, to share the good news. The task of informing Manuel Pellegrini fell to Txiki.

The press were given the news on February 1, 2016, just after the pre-match press conference before a Premier League game against Sunderland. City were in second place, three points behind Leicester. Pellegrini had requested that the announcement be made.

"I've talked to the club and have been released from my contract," he told reporters. "I still have one year left, but there's a clause which allows either party to unilaterally break the contract. City have been completely up front with me, but the rumours and speculation were becoming a real nuisance, so a couple of weeks ago I decided that the players and the press should be told. That's why we've announced it today."

Four weeks after that press conference, Willy Caballero saved three penalties to win a shoot-out against Liverpool in the League Cup final. City ended the season in fourth place as Leicester held out to claim a historic title. They reached the semi-finals of the Champions League, but lost to a Fernando own goal against Madrid at the Bernabéu.

The new coach's contract was signed by City's lawyers and Pere Guardiola, as Pep's representative, at the end of February, in London. When Pep arrived in Manchester on July 3 to be presented by the club, he admitted that there were several key documents still awaiting his signature. He got round to completing the task on the day that France beat Germany in the semi-final of the European Championships. That night he joined friends and colleagues at the Gaucho restaurant in Manchester. It was July 7, the first day of the running of the bulls at Pamplona.

THREE

FERRAN AND TXIKI: THE ODD COUPLE

May 20, 1992.

São Paulo, Brazil. A young executive is desperate to follow the progress of his team, FC Barcelona, who are playing Sampdoria in the European Cup final. He is alone in an enormous office with no internet. He decides to improvise and calls some friends who he knows will be watching the game. He asks them to hold the phone up to the TV so that he can hear the commentary.

"That's how I heard the game – in hands-free mode," laughs Ferran Soriano. "It all felt a bit ridiculous until [Ronald] Koeman's free-kick [which secured a 1-0 win for Barcelona]. I heard my mates roar and I knew that had gone in."

Twenty-four-year-old Soriano then tracked down a hotel with the TV channel which was about to rerun the entire game. "The receptionist was obviously a bit taken aback when I told him I'd only need the room for two hours, but once I explained, he understood."

Wembley Stadium, London, England. Twenty-seven-year-old winger Txiki Begiristain rushes on to the field to greet his friend and teammate Pep Guardiola. The winger, an unused substitute against Sampdoria but a key figure in Johan Cruyff's Dream Team, envelops the young midfielder in a bear hug as they join the rest of their teammates in celebration of Barça's first European Cup triumph. Sampdoria 0 FC Barcelona 1. A scoreline heard around the world.

It is the evening of Sunday, July 8, and Txiki Begiristain arrives at the CFA, having just sent a message to a friend: *Only Ferran would think of calling a board meeting on San Fermin! The guy never stops.*

Begiristain, director of football at Manchester City, will often be seen at Pamplona's running of the bulls festival, decked out in the traditional white costume, having a few beers and enjoying the festivities. Such shenanigans would be anathema to Ferran Soriano, the club's CEO.

They are completely mismatched personalities, yet the pair have created the most successful executive partnership in the Premier League. Three things unite them: a passion for football, devotion to Pep Guardiola and a love of economics.

As a young man, Soriano was both ambitious and intellectually inclined. While he was racking up one business degree after another, his future director of football was trying to work out a way of combining his job as a winger for FC Barcelona with a part-time degree in economics. In the end, the demands of the Dream Team displaced those academic ambitions.

They both joined Barça's board in 2003 when Joan Laporta took over. Begiristain was director of football and Soriano vice-president (finances). Since moving to Manchester in 2012, Soriano has managed the club's complex finances, while Begiristain has successfully spearheaded the recruitment operation that has built one of the most successful teams in the history of English football.

Soriano recalls talking to a senior Barcelona executive just after Laporta's election win. The process of transferring powers to the new board had begun and he was about to take over the club's finances.

"He said to me, 'Son, I'll give you one piece of advice. Don't come here thinking you're going to use fancy management techniques or even basic common sense. All the business nous in the world won't work here. This is football and it's different. It's all about whether the ball goes in the back of the net or not. When it does, everything's good. When it doesn't, it's a disaster and none of your preparations will help. It's purely a question of whether luck's with you or not.'"

Soriano disagreed. "It's just not true and certainly not over the long term. It's imperative to apply common sense in football just as much as in any other area of life."

The two friends hail from very different areas of Spain. Soriano was born in Barcelona, Begiristain in Goverri, the highlands of the Basque Country. Like many sportsmen, Begiristain places great value on his rituals and superstitions. Soriano detests irrational belief systems and lays out his pragmatic approach to sports management in his book, *Goal: The Ball Doesn't Go In By Chance*. The book opens with the 2008 Champions League final between Manchester United and Chelsea and the potentially decisive spot-kick which John Terry misses when he slips as he strikes the penalty which could win the trophy.

Soriano cites this game as part of his argument that, while luck can be a factor sporadically, in the long run success in football or any business enterprise will flow from resource management. You must have the resources to attract the best players and then you must manage those resources intelligently. Just like any successful business.

Begiristain sees things very differently: "You can say what you want but I never take off the watch that Albert Perrin gave me the year Barça won six trophies. I have two lucky shirts, one is for business and I wear it with a tie, the other is for less formal occasions. And I always have the four-leafed clover [a memento from his days with Urawa Red Diamonds in Japan] and a lucky one-peseta note with me. Just in case."

Soriano prides himself on meticulous organisation, which is perhaps the only way he can navigate his hectic schedule. If he tells you he has five minutes at 3.30pm on Thursday, then you better be ready to start talking at 3.29. No matter where he is, however, he never misses the Thursday management meeting and he expects all present to have done their homework.

One day he's in Abu Dhabi, the next New York and a week later he's off to China. "In football, as in everything, luck doesn't come into it. Success comes from working hard and being effective," he says.

They may disagree on the importance of good fortune and superstition in football, but both Begiristain and Soriano agree on the hard work part, and both men have their personal signatures on the success of the Guardiola era at City. This team would not exist if Khaldoon hadn't appointed Soriano, who then appointed Begiristain, who persuaded Guardiola to take the job.

When this project began, Soriano waited nearly a year before accepting Khaldoon's offer. It's not that he wasn't keen. Exactly the opposite. He'd been trying to save the airline Spanair when Khaldoon first got in touch. He was desperate to leave, but Spanair was in trouble and he was working on a deal to sell it to Qatar Airways.

During that first meeting, Soriano became convinced that the City project was not the sudden whim of a rich sheik who fancied adding some famous footballers to his collections, but he was in the midst of his rescue operation.

In the end he couldn't save the airline and Spanair ceased operations. He immediately renewed contact with Khaldoon, who was waiting patiently for the man several recruitment consultants had identified as the perfect fit to head up his football operations.

Once the deal was done, Khaldoon bought into his new chief executive's bold idea that City should become the first football multinational, with bases in Manchester, New York, Yokohama, Melbourne, Girona and Montevideo.

Soriano's key appointment, Begiristain, has been a key architect of some of the most successful and influential teams of the modern era. He put together Frank Rijkaard's Barça (they won the club's first trophy for six years, two La Ligas and Barça's second Champions League title) and provided the basis of Pep's Barça (14 trophies in four seasons). He also built Pellegrini's City side (having inherited the team of Roberto Mancini).

Pep Guardiola: "Txiki is the key to all of this. When nobody else would take a risk on me, when maybe three per cent of the people at Barça believed in me, he was the one who insisted on my appointment to the first-team. None of this would have been possible without him."

FOUR

PEP'S NO.1 PROBLEM

As he arrived in England, Pep Guardiola knew that his transformation of the style of football played by Manchester City had to start with his goalkeeper. It would not be a bloodless revolution. It was clear to the incoming coach that Joe Hart did not fit the profile – a goalkeeper who was comfortable with the ball at his feet, capable of recycling possession and even initiating attacks.

Pep's demands of whoever has the jersey have remained constant. And, after a frustrating start, the goalkeeping coach, Xabier Mancisidor, and director of football Txiki Begiristain tuned in to the coach's requirements in relation to the position.

Mancisidor, who usually has 99 per cent of the say on goalkeeping matters, proposed several names for the No.1 spot, none of whom fitted the bill. Begiristain had even suggested sticking with Hart, Pellegrini's first choice in his final year at the club and a firm favourite with City fans. The incoming coach insisted they keep looking for alternatives.

The news was broken to Hart during his very first meeting with the new coach. Guardiola detailed the way he wanted his keepers to play out from the back, starting attacks and being available to receive possession from defenders when they were under pressure. From that moment, it was clear that, as soon as there was a replacement, Hart would no longer be City's No.1.

After a miserable pre-season in China, Hart decided it was time to leave.

The close season of 2016 had initially brought some good news for Pep. Marc-André ter Stegen was interested in coming to City. His partner had applied for a place at Manchester University and it looked like a deal could be done to bring him from Barcelona, where he had been sharing goalkeeping duties with Claudio Bravo. All hopes were dashed, however, when Manchester University declined her application and Barcelona steadfastly refused to part with their German goalkeeper.

The next option considered was Victor Valdés, who Pep had planned to pair with the younger, less experienced ter Stegen as the German's back-up keeper. This deal, and any idea of going with Valdés as a potential first choice, also foundered after the Catalan joined Aitor Karanka's Middlesbrough with the promise of guaranteed first-team football.

It was then that Claudio Bravo emerged as a possible recruit. Barça were willing to sell him in order to promote ter Stegen to outright No.1, and it seemed too good an opportunity to pass up. Guardiola and Begiristain were both convinced and the third party in the decision-making process knew more about their target than anyone.

Manchester City goalkeeping coach Xabier Mancisidor grew up in Pasajes, a pretty village in the Basque region of Guipúzcoa. As a youngster he started playing for the local football club, Trintxerpe, and from there moved to Deportivo Alavés. He became their keeper for five years, during which time they won promotion.

He finished his playing career at Mallorca, then in the second division, where he was in a squad which contained Tito Vilanova and Ernesto Valverde, two future Barcelona managers, the first of whom assisted Pep during the golden era of his team. Good company as far as Guardiola was concerned.

Upon retirement, Real Sociedad recruited Mancisidor as a fitness coach for their youth academy, with some responsibility for first-team keeper training. During 11 years at La Real, he worked under six different club presidents and at least a dozen coaches: José Mari Bakero, Bernd Krauss, Javier Clemente, John Toshack, Juanma Lillo, Periko Alonso, Roberto Olabe, Miguel Ángel Lotina, José María Amorrortu, Chris Coleman, Reynald Denoueix, and Jabo Irureta.

Mancisidor eventually set aside fitness coaching and concentrated on full-time goalkeeper training. The list of keepers he has worked with is equally long, but right at the top is Claudio Bravo.

The backstory: signing Bravo for La Real was initially the idea of Bakero (Guardiola's Dream Team midfield colleague) while he was director of football at Real Sociedad.

"I want you to go to Dublin and take a look at this Chilean guy I've heard good things about," he told Mancisidor.

Chile were playing Ireland in Dublin, with Bravo in goal, and La Real's goalkeeping coach was immediately impressed. "The Chilean kid was so good that I only had to see him perform during the warm-up to feel that we had to sign him."

Just as Guardiola was bedding in for his second season as Barça's first-team coach, Madrid appointed Manuel Pellegrini to try to arrest the *Blaugrana* domination. Jorge Valdano was then Madrid's director of football, and he sought a change of goalkeeping coach. Juanma Lillo, one of the great influencers of Guardiola's football thinking, recommended Mancisidor. In due course, he moved with Pellegrini to Málaga and later, in 2013, to Manchester City, where he remained even after the departure of the former manager.

These days Mancisidor oversees all of City's goalkeeping development, including the first team and academy

(Daniel Grimshaw, Angus Gunn and the promising Kosovo international Aro Murić have all figured in the first-team squad during his time in charge). He played an influential role in Hart's rise and was sad to see the England keeper leave, but the coming change in football philosophy required a change in goalkeeper. Enter Claudio Bravo.

The Chilean moved to Spain at the age of 23, after that spot of scouting by Mancisidor. He was 31 when he joined Barcelona, in 2014, having experienced relegation, promotion and eventually Champions League football with La Real.

"You need to be very special to make it at Barcelona, both in terms of your technical ability as a goalkeeper and your mentality," says Bravo.

"They don't want a keeper who stays in his box and restricts himself to stopping the ball. Barça want a goalie who can play outside his area. They have to be able to play the ball and work closely with the defenders and full-backs. At Barça, you're considered just one more outfield player."

His first few matches with Barça remain seared in his memory. He'd bring the ball down and then kick it the length of the pitch. Then this odd, insistent murmuring would echo around the vast Camp Nou: "They wanted me to play the ball out to the wing, to pass it to Piqué. They didn't want me thumping it long, getting it away as fast and as far as possible.

"By my second game, I was already getting my head round it. It really brought home to me how complicated a job Barça's keepers have. I took to it quite easily because I was good with my feet, but I still had to go through a process of acclimatisation. And under the critical gaze of about 100,000 people!"

Once in Manchester, the Chilean was alarmed to hear the same level of grumbling from City's supporters. This time for the opposite reason. Bravo had come to City knowing exactly what Pep would expect of him – he was here as just another outfield player and would be expected to use his feet to play a key role in the first stages of attack. But the fans didn't like it.

Bravo: "They hated the way I was playing. They didn't want me with the ball at my feet and they made their discontent very clear from the start. It really bothered people because in England they expect the keeper to control the ball and then hoof it 70 metres up the pitch. And if you don't control it too well but thump it 75 metres, then all the better! You just have to look for your tallest striker and hope he gets his head on it. City supporters definitely needed a while to adjust.

"I had to lead the way. This was a completely new style of play for City and I just had to put up with the reaction. It was a process I had to get through because we were creating a whole new kind of football. You almost never see it here in England, although some teams in Germany and Spain have a similar game.

"We've proven you can still score goals without resorting to kicking long balls right down the park. We train hard for this style of play because it's Pep's formula."

Another considerable difference Bravo had to cope with is the respect offered to keepers in England in relation to high balls into the goalmouth: namely, none at all. Bravo watched English football and tried to prepare himself for the difference between the interpretation of the rules in England and Spain. But some things can't be learned in theory alone. He gives an example: "You'll have an opponent pulling at one arm as you jump, meaning you don't catch well. A keeper has to leap with both arms extended otherwise it's pretty impossible to catch and hold the ball."

Bravo hit a rough patch in his first season at City. The club's supporters were unimpressed with their new goalkeeper. By the end of January 2017, Bravo had conceded 16 goals from 24 shots on goal, including every single one of the last six shots he had faced.

No keeper in the division had a worse save percentage. Enough was enough. Pep had a word with Mancisidor and decided to drop his keeper. He explained his reasons to the player and Willy Caballero took his place.

Bravo: "Pep had been watching Willy and was impressed. He told me that since things weren't going well for the team, that we needed a change. It happens in football. If the team's doing badly, the keeper's the one to take the fall. It's an easier choice than replacing seven outfield players."

Bravo describes "nearly killing myself to turn the situation around". By season's end he had played 30 games and conceded 34 goals. Caballero conceded 26 in 27 appearances, with 10 clean sheets.

After the arrival of Ederson from Benfica in 2017, Bravo was relegated to the bench for most of season 2017-18. However, he was perhaps the key figure in the capture of the Carabao Cup, Guardiola's first trophy in England. He made saves in two thrilling penalty shoot-outs, against Wolves and Leicester, and then earned a clean sheet in the final against Arsenal in February 2018.

It was the reverse of his first season. "I played less than I did the first year but in more difficult matches. This is a very different job if you're not getting a game. It's much harder to maintain your competitive edge."

After the shoot-out win over Leicester, Pep sought out the keeper for a celebratory hug and Bravo appeared to rebuff him. It was interpreted as evidence of a deterioration in their relationship, but the Chilean insists the situation was misread.

"That's not what happened. There have been lots of stories about problems between him and Cesc Fàbregas, too, and then you see them together looking like they're on the best of terms. And people still claim that there's bad blood there. The working relationship is one thing, but it shouldn't end up creating bad feeling."

Bravo will be 37 when his contract expires in the summer of 2020. He lives in Wilmslow, outside Manchester, and if he has had mixed fortunes professionally since arriving, his life there has given him a perspective that is relatively uncommon among elite footballers.

"It takes me more than two hours a day to get to and from training but we couldn't find anywhere in the city centre that was suitable for a family of six plus a dog.

"Football is my job, it's not the thing that makes me happy. My home life is the thing that brings me most contentment. Accumulating trophies, winning matches, these are the things we work so hard for in football, but seeing your kids hanging out with their pals, speaking fluent English – that's the most satisfying thing of all."

The transition from Bravo to Ederson has to have been painful for the Chilean, but he, too, can appreciate the performances of the latest incumbent.

"I've tried to give him as much support as I can, to help him settle in," says Bravo. "Ederson has played brilliantly since he arrived and the team has done well. It would be pretty self-indulgent of me not to recognise that, not to acknowledge everything I've learned in my time here. I've always tried to be as professional as possible and would never go about looking miserable or stop speaking to someone over a work thing. It's just not the right way to behave.

"He's great with his feet, a perfect example of the modern goalkeeper. And he's adapted brilliantly to the style of football we play. We talk about this from time to time, the world-class keepers who couldn't handle it here, even guys who are at the top of their game. There are keepers that would get eaten up and spat out if you put them in the Camp Nou and you passed them the ball as part of starting the build-up."

When Bravo first arrived at the Etihad, the boos were all about him not getting rid of the ball fast enough. Now they cheer when Ederson plays like a full-back. Things have changed at City.

"I know I told him it's up to him what he does out there, but sometimes he does go a bit too far," jokes Guardiola about his Brazilian keeper.

The club had followed both Ederson and Bernd Leno, of Bayern Leverkusen, for a year as they evaluated which one they would pursue. "They both fitted the bill. One was more expensive to buy, the other required a higher salary. I left it up to the coaches to choose," explains Begiristain, who at the time was looking for a young player who would be able to adapt to Pep's ideas and who, above all, had the potential to improve. He wanted someone who would work and learn alongside Claudio Bravo.

Benfica sold Ederson to City for £35m, making him the second most expensive goalkeeper of all time, £12m less than Juventus paid for Gianluigi Buffon. "Cheap at the price," smiles Soriano, who renewed and improved Ederson's contract at the end of the Brazilian's first season, at which time Leno, City's other target in summer 2017, joined Arsenal.

Ederson Santana de Moraes started out as a full-back for Champions Ebenézer FC. That explains a lot.

On December 18, 2017, City destroyed Tottenham at the Etihad. Ederson gave a masterclass, not in acrobatic saves or one-on-one dominance, but in passing and control. He had a pass completion of 78.9 percent (higher than Dele Alli and Christian Eriksen) and those passes included medium and long-range balls, as well as high-risk passes to beat a press.

As City lifted their first league title under Pep in 2018, the stats told the tale of the upgrade at No.1. Pass accuracy, from Hart to Bravo to Ederson: 52.6 per cent, 72.6 per cent, 84.8 percent. Long balls played: 72 per cent, 42 per cent, 31 per cent. And no matter his talent with the ball at his feet, he also has a better save ratio: 68 percent compared to 56 per cent for Bravo and 66.4 per cent for Hart.

In training, the Brazilian added another laurel to City's glorious season in 2017-18. The club invited the *Guinness Book of Records* to measure his place kicks and after a couple fell short, Ederson smashed one 75.3 metres for a world record.

The Burnley manager Sean Dyche described what it's like to face a player of his calibre: "It's like they've got Ronald Koeman in goal. The ball comes to him and he moves it expertly round the pitch, in line with the game plan. He neutralises the opposition's game completely."

As a kid, while still a full-back, his coach told him: "Either you go in goal or you don't play at all."

Starting out at his local club in São Paulo, he took free-kicks. Later, in Benfica's youth academy (he left Brazil aged 16) he'd often be asked to go into midfield in training sessions if someone was missing.

The Brazilian arrived in Manchester with ready-made dressing-room connections. Bernardo Silva had been a teammate at Benfica, Ederson knew Fernandinho from the Brazilian national team and Gabriel Jesus from their participation at the Olympic Games. He endeared himself almost immediately to the rest of the squad, who even tolerate his occasional eccentricities.

City were in Nashville, Tennessee, as part of their preseason tour of the United States and Ederson was still new to the squad. The team travel with three security guards and one of them, Okon, is particularly enormous. The squad were in the dining room for a meal, with Okon keeping watch, when out of nowhere the new goalkeeper rushed the security guard, taking him down with a rugby tackle. No explanation was ever offered.

Ederson is a powerhouse, a physical as well as a technical marvel as a goalkeeper, at a muscular, heavily tattooed 6ft 2ins.

His robustness was evident after a sickening collision with Sadio Mané of Liverpool in September 2017. Ederson was carried off on a stretcher and in a neck brace, and later posted images of two stitched wounds on his face. It seemed like that was the last City fans would see of him for weeks, if not months. Seven days later, he was back in goal as City beat Watford 6-0.

FIVE

MIKE SUMMERBEE'S HAT

Hats are back in fashion. In particular, the flat caps worn in *Peaky Blinders,* Steven Knight's between-the-wars drama about the Shelbys, a family of Birmingham gangsters. Much of the hit show's fourth series was shot in Manchester's old industrial areas.

Until the 1930s, the flat cap was a common sight on the streets of Manchester, worn by working men employed in the heavy industries. In an era when an umbrella was a luxury item, the flat cap was practical and inexpensive, often handmade from offcuts by the women of Manchester.

The flat cap is emblematic of the working classes and Pep Guardiola, proud of his own working-class roots, has fond memories of his father and grandfather wearing them.

Saying nothing to Cristina (the undisputed authority on fashion in the Guardiola household) Pep tracked down the finest tailor in Manchester and a few days later debuted his new look as he arrived home after work, wearing one flat cap and with two spares in a bag.

Prior to his shopping trip, Pep sought the advice of Mike Summerbee, the Manchester City legend (and one of the stars of the classic Second World War / football movie *Escape to Victory*) who now acts as an ambassador for the club. Summerbee, something of a *fashionista* himself, has been wearing a flat cap for years. He recalls chatting to the Catalan coach post-match on a cold mid-January day. "Pep told me that he liked my hat. It reminded him of the ones they wear in *Peaky Blinders* and I said I knew just the place he could get one."

Summerbee is an iconic figure in City's history. Born in Preston in 1947, he played for the club for 10 seasons. He was an old-school winger who took players on, again and again, and crossed with brilliance.

He was also a lifelong friend of George Best. Summerbee says Best was in the process of picking up a girl in a coffee-bar when they first met. The two mavericks played on opposite sides of Manchester's football divide, but they connected immediately and were soon sharing a flat. They opened a clothes shop together. "We didn't ever really sell very much," recalls Summerbee. "It was basically just a way to meet girls."

And just as Summerbee and Best found a connection, Guardiola and Summerbee clicked on their first meeting. Pep's first words to Summerbee: "I need someone for the right wing."

However, Summerbee does not share the coach's relentless focus on the game, and when they talk, business is rarely on the agenda.

"I don't have much to do with the football, although occasionally he's got a particular query I can help with," says Summerbee. "Pep's immersed in football 24 hours a day and that's not for me. I suppose our chats give him a bit of light relief. I've gradually got to know him well and we get on like a house on fire, but we talk about everyday things. About life."

Summerbee calls for Pep at the coach's home, and the two men set out on their mission. The tailor's shop is tucked away on Chapel Street, behind a small church. Here is the Black Lion, a pub where the two Georges, Orwell and Best, are said to have been regulars. Nearby is Lupo Caffè Italiano, the tiny Italian restaurant that has become the most famous in Manchester in the two years since Txiki Begiristain's wife, Mara, fell in love with it. Around here is also a former police station, now converted to an architect's office. This neighbourhood is in the process of gentrification and its skyline is dominated by construction cranes. Gabriel Jesus, İlkay Gündoğan, David Silva and Leroy Sané all have homes here.

Only an old-fashioned black sign with white lettering gives you any clue as to the shop's function. It's close to impossible to find, not least because the façade bears the shop's original name, Thomas Silk. In Manchester, everyone knows it by the surnames of its founders: Williams & Gill.

David Williams and his partner, Jonathan Gill, have run this place for 40 years. They specialise in bespoke tailoring.

Williams picks his tape measure out of a pile of offcuts and measures Pep's head: 60.5cm. His team work in the next room, one eye on the new customer.

"I never thought for a second that I'd end up doing this for a living," says the tailor. "Back in the 70s, business was great. We had a factory here in the city and we had 20 people making shirts all day."

The company produced shirts for the most exclusive retailers in the north of England, and took orders from aristocrats, actors and footballers – including Johan Cruyff.

"Mike Summerbee introduced me to all the big names, and not just in Manchester. We'd end up in the dressing room at Chelsea or Tottenham or even at whatever ground the England team were training at. We'd watch the match or training and then we'd measure the players up for their suits or shirts. I remember the only one who didn't come off the pitch all sweaty was Cruyff."

The Dutchman joined Williams & Gill's list of high-profile clients before the 1975 European Cup semi-final between Leeds and Barcelona, at Elland Road.

"It was the day of the match and the players had been training," recalls Williams. "Mike and I went down to the dressing room to do the usual measurements. He just told me it was 'another footballer', without saying whom. But it was Cruyff and I'll never forget that moment.

"When I started to measure him, I realised immediately that he didn't have a drop of sweat. Not a drop! It was really weird."

Pep's caps were £75 each. When he returned to pick them up, Williams suggested a bespoke price for his wealthy customer. Pep, joked the tailor, could afford to pay £1m for his new headgear.

"Fine," said Pep. "I'll just take the one."

SIX

LORENZO BUENAVENTURA: PEP'S FIRST SIGNING

As soon as Pep Guardiola finished his coaching badges in Madrid, he promised Lorenzo Buenaventura, who was one of the staff tutors at the Spanish Federation: "When I take my first job, I'm going to call you to join me." Buenaventura didn't really believe him. He'd heard all this before from other departing students. But the instant Pep took over Barcelona's first-team, the call came. They're still in harness today.

"The first contract I negotiate when I'm moving to a new club is his – always. Loren's the best," Pep explains about his fitness coach.

Lorenzo is Pedro Buenaventura's son. Pedro, for years, was pretty much 'Mr Betis' having been their coach, match delegate, technical secretary and director of football.

His son Lorenzo was born on January 1, 1963, and schooled in Sevilla but left to study physical education in Madrid. Once qualified, he was about to return to his native city to combine coaching for the Betis youth academy with a job teaching PE at a local school. The Cádiz president, Manuel Irigoyen, happened to be looking for a first-team fitness coach and mentioned it to his opposite number at Betis.

"Talk to Pedro Buenaventura's boy," Irigoyen was told.

So, aged 24, Loren suddenly found himself charged with getting Cádiz in shape.

"Football's full of such lucky coincidences on and off the pitch," Buenaventura points out now. "The ball hitting the post can turn a whole match around or, as in my case, a casual chat can affect your entire future."

He married his girlfriend, Isabel, and they moved to Cádiz. Two kids followed, his daughter, now 25, and Loren Jnr, 20, of whom Buenaventura says: "Everyone has an angel in their lives and he's ours."

There are very few things Buenaventura loves more than a gentle wander along the waterfront back home with his wife and children, yet he is living alone in the centre of Manchester. His family remain back in Puerto de Santa Maria, because Loren Jnr is autistic and requires stability and consistency in his daily life.

Lorenzo is very tight with Mikel Arteta, who also lives on his own, and nearby, in the city centre. They've known each other for 15 years.

"We're a long-established couple," Arteta jokes. "He possesses two qualities which are fundamental in a fitness coach. The first is the chemistry he has with the playing group. He transmits boundless energy and has a real trust-confidence relationship with the men. He'll say, 'Listen, we train this way here but if you've just arrived from, say, Portugal or France and bring different ideas then we'll help you adapt and understand gradually. We want you to feel comfortable and at home.'

"But he also has this innate ability to match the team's fitness preparations to whichever tactical and physical approach Pep has planned for the next game."

Before signing with Guardiola, Lorenzo's boots had trodden half the training pitches in Spain: six years with Cádiz, then Valladolid, Espanyol with Marcelo Bielsa (who also took him to the 2002 World Cup with Argentina), and five years at Atlético (he jokes that he worked under more coaches there than during the rest of his career). Across his working life he's been a personal coach to a long list of elite footballers because, aside from his talent as a fitness coach, he's a rehab expert and physio.

The sabbatical year in New York, when Pep recharged his batteries, learned German and improved his English, is the only period since they took over at Camp Nou when the two have not worked together. Buenaventura still had a contract at Barça back in 2012 but, out of loyalty to his friend, left when Pep did. They were together at Bayern and in 2016, Pep brought him to Manchester.

Buenaventura's team produce post-match reports which contain an exhaustive analysis of the team's performance. The data includes the distance run by each player, and the number of times they've made a light sprint (categorised as one metre per second) or a power-sprint (between three and six metres per second). These parameters are also studied during training and are a key part of the fitness planning process. They measure how much effort each man puts in on matchday or at training.

"We study the data, but we don't go crazy over the details – it's a help rather than an absolute indication of anything. Occasionally your initial impressions can misguide you," says the fitness coach.

He mentions a game in Germany which Bayern won away from home, 7-1. "It looked like a stroll in the park if you simply take in the scoreline, but the analytics told a different story. You look at the data and suddenly realise, 'Bloody hell, look at the intensity our guys showed – look how they ran the other side off their feet!'

"A similar thing happens when we play Arsenal. You'll have 67 minutes of flat-out football when the ball's been in play a lot. Against most opponents you can expect a maximum of around 50 minutes like that and it looks like you're deploying much more energy because you're being blocked more. The reality is that against Arsenal you have to play more, concentrate more and the physical outlay is much greater."

Individual monitoring of players shows their effort levels and the results tell you a story about who goes to their limit across a series of training sessions and matches. There are also custom-made warm-ups for players based on this constant monitoring. It's an additional touch that wasn't used at Barça or Bayern and was already in place when Buenaventura arrived at City.

"The warm-up is like a biological clock. Take Kyle Walker and David Silva, for example. They need completely distinct intensity exercises as they prepare to play. We were impressed by this approach when we got here and decided to keep it going.

"In our second year we also designed a special programme for new players, tailor-made for each man and based on their anatomy and biology."

At City there is a fundamental maxim when preparing training: Buenaventura must adapt to the specifics Pep requires for a particular game.

"Playing Stoke at home is not the same as playing away at Chelsea," explains Buenaventura. "A big pitch like the one at West Ham is a completely different prospect from a much tighter one like Selhurst Park."

Lorenzo's initial discussions with Pep focused on how City were going to play, and from there he began to identify the challenges they might face in the Premier League. Buenaventura breaks these down into three broad areas.

"Firstly, Pep wants his footballers to play with a really high tempo and training has to be planned accordingly. Secondly, he has a very specific vision which underpins everything we do, every day – the physical, the tactical and the technical. England has been a big change from Germany, for all of us. In Germany the players run with the ball much more, there's a lot of racing up and down the pitch with and without the ball. Here in England there's more physical contact, so there has to be an element of that in training.

"Pep's very shrewd, very intelligent about how best to blend his specific tactical and technical demands with the football culture here.

"The third factor is that, here, we don't have as many free training days to work on upcoming matches, which means we have to be ultra-efficient in blending the physical work, which is so vital when you play in England, with Pep's tactical plan for the upcoming game."

The point is that a team which is less physically powerful, less strong in the contact moments of a match, needs to pass the ball quicker so that clashes with bigger, more aggressive opponents can be avoided as much as possible. This means that Pep's players must be able to think fast and training at City therefore always includes mini-games where one side will be forced to play with one player fewer. They also do speed drills in which players apply their explosive technical skills in small spaces. For example, a player will race against a teammate, controlling the ball while sprinting, and finish by tucking it away into a small net.

"We make the best of the fact that there's not a great deal of time to train and plan and teach strategies. Every minute of every session is aimed at the players understanding the tactical specifics of the next game, but also the fundamentals of how Guardiola wants his football played. Sometimes he'll demand: 'I want more play inside.' So from the warm-ups onwards in training we'll invent some drills which emphasise inside movements [as opposed to width]."

And the plan can be adapted at short notice. As Buenaventura explains, the boss can throw something in out of the blue, opening up an entirely new avenue.

"He'll see some move in a game – made by either team – and say, 'I liked that'. We'll then try to incorporate it in training because we know that he's already thinking of using it in his own tactical planning and we need to be ready when he does."

In Spain, Germany and England, Buenaventura has experienced the enormous demands Pep makes first of himself, and then of those around him. "He gifts you a lot of personal responsibility and always acknowledges the work we do. He's a very supportive boss and can be very affectionate. So it is his absolute right that occasionally we'll all get a telling off. We all bear the brunt when he thinks someone's messed up.

"Pep looks at every last tiny detail, but I'm different. He'll say: 'The centre-halves played far too close to each other when they were trying to bring the ball out from the back today.' Meanwhile I'm thinking: 'Fucking hell Pep, today we started playing out from the back about 836,000 times and we lost possession just once, the opposition didn't score and they only managed to earn two corners against us! We've done brilliantly today! Let's go have a beer!'"

SEVEN

STONES, OTAMENDI, LAPORTE: BUILDING FROM THE BACK

March 15, 2017. Monaco.
City have just been eliminated in the last 16 of the Champions League, losing 3-1 in the Louis II Stadium after a 5-3 win in the first leg. No Pep Guardiola team has ever been knocked out of the competition at such an early stage. In the away dressing room, Pep is incandescent, ripping into his players for a perceived lack of passion and their failure to play 'the City way'. His explosion at half-time – with Monaco 2-0 up – had been even more volcanic.

However, by the time the City party is back at the hotel, the manager's mood has changed. All the backroom staff are having dinner together. The atmosphere is sombre. Then Pep arrives and immediately apologises to all of his staff. "I wasn't at my best. It's my fault we're out."

If City's style of play and subsequent success under Pep is built on ball-playing defenders, then Monaco was a crucial turning point. City kicked off with Nicolás Otamendi and Vincent Kompany on the bench. John Stones and Aleksandar Kolarov played at centre-back, with Bacary Sagna and Gaël Clichy in the full-back positions. Pep's reflections were stark.

"Why the fuck didn't I play Otamendi, given the year he'd had? Why the hell didn't I even put him on? An ultra-competitive central defender who can bring the ball down and play! Or

Kompany, who I also left on the bench. It was the Champions League!"

The Monaco result crystalised Pep's efforts to find the perfect mix at centre-back, whatever the demands his team faced.

Central defenders have a crucial role in Guardiola teams. The players who fill these positions do not have it easy. In the words of Txiki Begiristain, a man who has dedicated many hours to finding exactly the right kind of player for these positions: "You've got a bastard of a job if you're a central defender in this team."

The list of defenders on City's payroll changed over the first two seasons of Pep's reign. Guardiola started out with Stones, Otamendi plus a recycled Kolarov, whose brilliant passing as he brought the ball out convinced the coaching staff to include him in their plans.

Injury prevented Kompany from being a regular starter right up until the April of Pep's first season. However, in 2017-18, his return to fitness saw him clock up 600 more minutes of football. His key impact in several of City's biggest games re-established the Belgian as an indispensable member of the defensive line-up, and the team's natural leader.

In July 2017, Kolarov left for Roma as part of the overhaul of Pep's options for the wing-back positions, ending seven years in Manchester. Then in January Aymeric Laporte joined City's defence. For the technical staff he was the ideal player to complete the line-up of central options with Stones, Kompany and Otamendi. The recruitment strategy had produced a central defensive roster that combined different skill sets and experience levels, giving Pep's staff options in the short-term and potential for improvement beyond that – if they could continue to adapt to the particular demands this coach places on his centre-backs.

Mikel Arteta: "Our style of game is high-risk – defenders have to play the ball out. Their first job is to defend well, maintain our offside line (because we always play with a high defence), communicate well, anticipate. You have to know where the spaces are, who's pressing you and where the gaps are. After a mistake, you've just got to do the difficult thing again – no hiding."

Nico Otamendi went from being an unused substitute at Monaco to becoming, for much of Pep's second season, the best centre-back in the Premier League.

Mikel Arteta: "Nico's progress was incredible. People didn't believe he could play at this level. He's played while he was injured. He's played every other day, or having just come back from Argentina on only three hours sleep – whatever the circumstances."

Pep's technical staff analysed Otamendi before Guardiola joined City. The report concluded that he was a similar player to Barça's Carles Puyol: forceful, good in the air, ready to give everything all the time. What hadn't been spotted was that he enjoyed the challenge of playing out from the back. The change in his game had surprised City's coaching staff.

Domènec Torrent, then assistant manager to Guardiola: "What brought about this change? It's because Pep makes things so straightforward for them. He tells them: 'They'll press you here, then this other guy will come at you and try to close you down. You'll have two options for your pass. You choose which to go for.' That quality of information helps the players a lot."

Otamendi cuts an intimidating figure on the pitch. "He goes after every ball as if it's the last one he'll ever kick," adds Arteta.

This pugilistic attitude may be a hangover from his other great passion: boxing. In 2008 he almost changed course completely to dedicate himself to the ring. Otamendi was 20, and training just as hard in the boxing gym as he was with his club in Argentina,

Vélez Sarsfield. But as fifth-choice centre-back, he was starting to think he had a better shot as a boxer than a footballer. All that changed in 2009.

One centre-back broke his hand; one was away on under-20 international duty; another was suspended after a red card in a reserve game. Otamendi got his chance and never gave it up. Within three months, he was a full international with Argentina. A year later, he starred at the 2010 World Cup. After that he moved to Porto, then to Valencia before signing for City.

Otamendi organised the team's pre-match playlist, having taken over from the now departed Clichy, whose musical tastes were not universally applauded ("Clichy being in charge was a fucking nightmare," remembers one player). Now it's Reggaeton – mostly Daddy Yankee. But he caters for all tastes, and has continued the tradition of playing Oasis. *Don't Look Back in Anger* (a favourite of Pep's) can still boom out whenever the team has secured an important victory.

As City competed in the closing stages of season 2018-19, Otamendi's game time dipped. The Argentine played all of the Carabao Cup final in May 2019, but only two of the final seven games of the league campaign. He was absent for the crucial second leg of the Champions League quarter-final against Spurs and watched the FA Cup final from the bench.

However, his stats for his landmark season of 2017-18 are phenomenal: he led the team in passes (3,074), and was second in the entire league. He led the team in successful tackles (48) and clearances (122).

The Argentine didn't miss a single league match through injury that season, just one through suspension and one or two more as a result of squad rotations – a singular achievement given his numerous transatlantic trips with his national team. Forty-six matches played across all competitions, five goals scored – more than in any of his previous seasons in England.

It was Otamendi's goal that won the Old Trafford derby in December 2017, a game in which he was partnered by Stones.

Domènec Torrent: "Together, John and Nico were outstanding – one of the best defensive partnerships in the world."

John Stones arrived in Manchester during Pep's first preseason, with a £47.5m price tag – the second most expensive defender in the world. No pressure, then. He took time to adapt to City's playing style, and during that process he faced a barrage of criticism. He was signed as a ball-playing centre-back, a reputation earned at Everton. But in his first months at City, his use of the ball was questioned – as were his defensive abilities. Nor were his errors only on the pitch.

A turning point came in October 2016. City were about to play West Brom and Stones was in the CFA when his agent called. Stones had been snapped by paparazzi sneaking into a Manchester hotel with a girl who was not his girlfriend of 12 years, Millie Savage.

The scandal broke, hitting the young defender and his girlfriend hard. Stones' agent gave it to him straight: "You need to decide right now – either you change your ways or you go ahead and destroy all your potential."

Stones looked to friends and colleagues for advice, including Pep, and eventually he and Millie got back together.

With harmony restored in his personal life, Stones' performance on the pitch took a giant leap forward, enhanced further by the arrival of one of his best friends in football, Kyle Walker. Since the two Yorkshiremen teamed up, they have formed an almost unbreakable partnership off the pitch.

Stones was back on track, and started learning Spanish – a pursuit he has maintained, using Claudio Bravo and Nico Otamendi as his sounding board. But just as he recovered the form that won him his move to City, injury halted his progress.

Stones played back-to-back 90 minutes for England in November 2017 friendlies against Brazil and Germany, and during the following league game, against Leicester, he tore his hamstring and was out until the New Year, a lay-off that saw Guardiola recruit Aymeric Laporte, a rival for Stones' primary position at centre-back.

With fewer injury problems, Stones clocked up more minutes during 2018-19, but like Otamendi he was a casualty of the Laporte-Kompany pairing favoured by Guardiola down the stretch. He was on the bench, a late substitute or absent entirely for all but two of the final eight league games, plus both Wembley finals and the Champions League quarter-final ties against Spurs.

The two big reasons for Pep's new look in defence? A welcome run without injury for Kompany in his final season at City. And the emergence of a player who, during this season, became first among equals on Pep's roster of centre-backs.

Training is done for the day and Aymeric Laporte goes home to his city centre apartment, dumps his stuff and heads straight down to Grindsmith, a trendy coffee pod in the heart of Manchester. He had his lunch at the CFA, now he just wants a good cup of coffee and a game of *pocha* with his friends and whichever teammates decide to join him today.

Grindsmith is a home from home for City's central defender. The staff are friendly and they serve a damn fine cup of coffee, maybe the best in Manchester. Here the Frenchman can relax, play cards and put the world to rights. The subject of the weather comes up a lot.

"It's the only drawback about living in Manchester," he says. "But then, I didn't come here for the sunshine.

"The city's changed since I first arrived – there's constant construction work, new buildings going up all the time. It's like this great industrial city is getting a modern facelift."

'Ayme' came to Manchester in January 2018, 18 months after he jilted them at the altar. In summer 2016 City had agreed to pay the buyout clause in Laporte's contract with Athletic Bilbao. Terms had been agreed between the English club and the defender. They shook hands on the deal on a Friday. On Sunday, Laporte renewed with Athletic and City diverted to sign John Stones.

The following summer, once again on the look-out for a centre-back, the club had their sights set on Southampton's Virgil Van Dijk. Saints had other ideas however, rebuffing the overtures of both City and Liverpool. By the time the winter market opened, Southampton's position had changed. They were willing to let the Dutchman go for £75m. The decision-makers at City described the price as "ridiculous".

Laporte's name resurfaced and this time it was the Frenchman who made the first move. He called Txiki Begiristain to say that he was now ready to come to Manchester. City could get him for £60m, signed and sealed, or continue to pursue Van Dijk, in competition with Liverpool and with an outcome that was far from certain. City had no doubts and Laporte had been convinced by frequent conversations with Benjamin Mendy, a teammate through France's age-group teams.

Laporte arrived in the UK on Tuesday, January 30, and played against West Brom the following day. City won 3-0.

"I remember everything about my debut," he says. "My mum, loads of my family and friends had come to watch, and I played well. I remember doing the post-match interviews and then heading into the dressing room. The lads gave me a huge welcome, people were hugging me – it was brilliant."

Laporte joined the club halfway through Pep's second season. He played 13 times and ended the season a Carabao Cup and

Premier League winner. The following season, 2018-19, he was Manchester City's best defender and only Ederson racked up more minutes on the pitch. He missed just two games through injury, aided by Didier Deschamps' decision to ignore Laporte every time he selected a France squad. The 25-year-old centre-back, despite becoming an indispensable player for Guardiola, is yet to make his international debut at the time of writing. Pierre Mankowski, an assistant to Deschamps, told *L'Équipe* that the coaching staff of *Les Bleus* view Laporte as "a good individual, who does not integrate well into a group".

To begin with, his lack of English meant that he was closest to the French speakers – Kevin De Bruyne, Riyad Mahrez and Bernardo Silva – and those who spoke Spanish. He is a friend and neighbour of David Silva, with whom he spends time away from the club, and part of the club's Fortnite fraternity – those who spend time on the most popular video game in the world. "To be fair, I'm not City's best Fortnite player. Phil Foden's the top performer but then he does dedicate a lot of time to it."

In 2018-19, Laporte led his team in successful passes, clearances made and aerial duels won, and scored five goals, three of which proved critical: his header against Wolves to earn City a vital point on August 25; opening the scoring against Everton away on February 6 and giving his side the lead at Brighton on the final day of the season, as City came from behind to win the league. His place in the PFA team of the year – alongside Fernandinho, Bernardo, Raheem Sterling and Sergio Agüero – was inevitable and a source of no little pride for Laporte.

"It was the same at Athletic. I started just after Christmas and had made it into the team of the year by the end of the following season. I gave everything to my performance because it's a brilliant feeling to know that you're a vital part of a champion side. It's great to have your work recognised like that, although every individual's success is the result of the hard work of the whole team."

Laporte is an ideal fit for Guardiola's philosophy. Before his arrival the squad lacked a left-footed centre-half who could lead the team as they played out from the back. His passing range makes him a weapon when his team is in possession, and when they lose the ball his speed is vital in negating counter-attacks.

Like many new recruits, Laporte was briefed personally and at length by his new coach when he arrived at City. The message: play my way and you don't need to worry about mistakes – that will be on me.

"He explained how he envisages my position and his whole approach to football. He made everything clear."

In his first full season, Laporte made a giant leap forward. Off the pitch, first-team operations manager Marc Boixasa saw him integrate fully into the squad, most importantly learning English. And on it, he emerged as the most important defender on Guardiola's roster.

"If you're driven by a huge work ethic then you continue to develop and improve," he says.

The Frenchman thrives on the kind of pressure elite-level games bring. "It was like this in Spain too – relentless pressure at Athletic, where the fans are very demanding. It's gone up a level now I'm at City but that's mostly because I put so much pressure on myself. I came here to win as many trophies as possible."

"He's got balls of steel," says Mikel Arteta, who sees something of the famous Basque toughness in the player. "He may have a French passport but it's like he was raised in Bilbao. He's got the Basque mentality – rock hard. He never backs down. You tell him he's got to go toe-to-toe with Mo Salah at Anfield and it's no bother to him. He simply doesn't care who he's up against."

Less than a year after joining the club, Laporte was called in to see Ferran Soriano and Txiki Begiristain, who offered him a contract renewal with improved terms. In February 2019, an extension until 2025 was announced. City now value their French centre-back far higher than the £65m they paid for him.

EIGHT

MARC BOIXASA: THE FIXER

Destiny. Fate. Serendipity. Call it what you like. Some people just seem to end up exactly where they're meant to be.

Take Marc Boixasa, for example. Born in Barcelona, he now lives on the former site of the iconic Manchester nightclub, *The Haçienda.* Today he is first-team operations manager at Manchester City, working under Pep Guardiola.

As Guardiola assembled his staff at City in the summer of 2016, he decided to retain as many incumbents as possible.

He reflected: "Ernesto Valverde drew on his own experience at Olympiacos and explicitly advised me: 'Don't turn up with 40 of your own guys when you take over at a new club. It's much better to rely on the expertise that's already in place.' And he was absolutely right. That's why only Loren, Carles, Domè and Manel went to Munich with me. There was a lot of talent in place already and it made sense to trust in the established staff. That was even more true here at City. And of course, Txiki was in post and already knew that Marc was the dog's bollocks."

Boixasa was one of the first Catalans to join City's staff, in 2012. His journey to a place on Guardiola's title-winning staff in England began in 2007 as an intern at FC Barcelona, where he spent 12 character-building months refining his photocopying skills before eagerly taking a job with Sevilla.

Marc fell in love with the Andaluz city and the club from the red-and-white half of Sevilla. In professional terms it's where he cut his teeth and he's still an avowed *Sevillista* who follows them from England and visits the Andaluz capital as often as possible.

After a stint as an external consultant to Girona (2010-11) Boixasa made the move to the Premier League. A round of discussions with Sunderland, Manchester United, Chelsea and Tottenham left Spurs very close to appointing him, but fate had different plans.

In October 2012 he joined City's commercial department in London. For the next couple of years Boixasa was centrally involved in the organisation behind the club's summer training tours around the world, plus the running of City's various youth training schools.

At Begiristain's suggestion, Boixasa was appointed general manager to the youth squad in May 2014. "There were quite a few foreign players in the team (from France: Seko Fofana, Olivier Ntcham and Thierry Ambrose; from Spain: Pablo Maffeo, Angeliño and Manu García), so my languages [Boixasa speaks Catalan, Spanish, English and French] came in handy."

That facility for languages meant his remit quickly expanded to include first-team duties. Boixasa regularly translated for Pellegrini at press conferences, as well as beginning to travel with the first team in a support role. He looked after the logistical aspects of their travel, dealing directly with the FA, the Premier League and UEFA and had responsibility for ensuring the club didn't contravene any match-day regulations. In his increasingly limited free time, he'd head back to Barcelona or Seville.

A soon as Pep took over, Boixasa transferred to full-time first-team duties and his first task was to plan how and when the squad would be reunited in time for preseason training (many of City's stars had just competed in Euro 2016).

He began reporting to Pep via email and remembers the surreal feeling of corresponding with a coach he'd yet to meet. The two finally met just before the squad's calamitous 15-day tour in China. Day-to-day organisation of the preseason tour fell to City's newly promoted team manager – an unwelcome inheritance. For Boixasa, the experience proved to be a baptism of fire which nearly drove him mad. Across the two weeks he barely slept once.

"It was a fiasco. China's an awful place to work and everything was brutally difficult; we had to jump through hoops to get the right flight permits, our hotels were miles from the stadiums and because of the heavy rains the training camp pitches were waterlogged. We even had to abandon the game with United. It was a nightmare – a catastrophe from first to last. It was my first trip as team manager and it was a total flop. They hardly got any training done at all. I felt awful. But I just had to get on with it. I made sure that I listened closely to everything Pep said. I knew there were lessons to learn from a tour which had been organised before I was promoted."

Keeper Joe Hart wasn't so magnanimous and laid the blame at Boixasa's door in front of the whole squad.

Back in Manchester, Boixasa began to show his worth. Immediately after a game at Crystal Palace, when their plane from London to Manchester broke down, he somehow had to get them all transferred to a train. Or when they were hit by another plane breakdown, away to Southampton on the last day of the 2017-18 season, Boixasa spent the whole night trying to find an alternative and successfully produced a flight for the following evening.

"Late in that match it was still 0-0 and I was terrified that they'd think the cancelled flight had brought them bad luck and stopped them reaching their 100-point target! I reckoned I'd get it in the neck. When Gabriel Jesus scored, I went totally crazy," he confesses ruefully.

Boixasa is thick-skinned, having spent much of his childhood in his grandparents' pub, Bar Valldonzella, in Barcelona's Gothic Quarter.

"I'd go down there after school and sit and do my homework or just hang out. I love that neighbourhood and I knew all the regulars. My gran did the cooking and my grandad was behind the bar. Sometimes it got so late that I'd lie down on the floor and go to sleep." The son of a nurse and an economist, the young Boixasa would go back to Taradell, his grandparents' village, in the summer holidays. Once there he'd hang out with his cousins and watch matches at the local football club, Manlleu. So he has a penchant for underdog clubs. Which explains why, since coming to England, he's made a point of going to watch the likes of Bury, Oldham and Rochdale play. This is a guy who never misses Channel 5's Sunday programme, *Goal Rush*, for all the action out of England's lower leagues.

Boixasa has a trip down memory lane planned for this new group of Manchester mates – Loren, Edu, Eva, Álvaro, David, Brandon, Pep et al – around the old streets of Barcelona's *Barrio Gotico*, where he spent his formative years hanging around his grandparents' place. Bar Valldonzella is long-sold to new owners, of course. But what did they decide to call it? Bar Manchester.

It was right there, at the long wooden counter in Bar Manchester that Boixasa drank a *caña* of beer to celebrate Manchester City's 100-point title win.

NINE

GÜNDOĞAN AND FERNANDINHO: THE CENTRAL PILLARS

It's April 2016 and Pep Guardiola is in Munich, approaching the end of his third and final season at Bayern. Over in Manchester, City executives plan their assault on the summer transfer market in preparation for the Catalan's arrival. Meanwhile, in Amsterdam, a shadowy figure is smuggled into a city centre hotel via the kitchens.

The fugitive in question is Txiki Begiristain and he's here to meet the representatives of Borussia Dortmund's İlkay Gündoğan. Unfortunately, the word is out and Begiristain has gone to extreme lengths to avoid the predatory attentions of the paparazzi. His chauffeur, Rob, has spent hours driving all over the city to shake them off.

Happily, everything goes to plan and a deal is done. The first signing of the Guardiola era.

"I didn't need to talk to Pep. It was enough just to know that he wanted me in his team," the German midfielder would say later.

The impetus for the Amsterdam deal came from Guardiola's time at Bayern. He'd been impressed (and frustrated) by the midfielder's superb passing ability during the historic clashes with Jürgen Klopp's Borussia Dortmund. "I loved watching him, although he drove me nuts every time we played against him in Germany."

Behind the scenes, the Catalan made no attempt to hide his appreciation of the young German's skills and would often seek him out post-match. But by the time Guardiola was preparing to leave for Manchester, Gündoğan would become the first subject of a rivalry that would become a central part of Pep's reign: Guardiola v Klopp; Liverpool v Manchester City.

Klopp, already in charge at Liverpool, was keen to be reunited with his former protegé and was talking with Gündoğan about a move to Anfield. Klopp had been hugely influential in Gündoğan's career and the two remain close. But one factor gave Begiristain the upper hand.

"Knowing Pep was taking over at City changed everything," says Gündoğan.

Gündoğan arrived in Manchester on crutches, meeting the press on the same day that Guardiola was first presented. He had dislocated a knee with Dortmund, an injury that kept him out of Euro 2016, and he wouldn't play for his new club until September 14 that year, in a Champions League game against Borussia Mönchengladbach. He recorded his first assist in that game and over the next few months his influence in the team and his popularity among the fans grew.

Sadly, however, there was more bad luck to come. A clash with Watford's Nordin Amrabat on December 14 ripped his cruciate ligaments and put him out for 32 matches. It was a crisis for the player, who remembers the response he received from his manager.

"Pep came into the infirmary and just enveloped me in this big bear hug, told me how devastated he was and that he wanted me back as soon as possible," said Gündoğan.

"That was a hugely important moment. It was the second horrible injury I'd had in a very short period, but Pep was massively encouraging and that gave me added strength to get through the long rehab."

The two men stayed in contact during the eight months Gündoğan was out. Pep demanded regular updates from Dr Ramón Cugat, who was supervising the recuperation, but Gündoğan remembers a necessarily different relationship to that between an active player and his manager.

"We kept talking, but the rehab took such a long time that I didn't expect him to see me every day or even every week. I wouldn't have wanted that, to be honest. When you're injured you want to be totally focused on getting back to full fitness as soon as possible. Pep and I would have a chat from time to time and we'd bump into each other in the rehab facilities or the staff canteen. But that was enough and our relationship stayed strong even though I wasn't playing."

Gündoğan is one of the players whose natural playing style most closely integrates with Guardiola's philosophy.

Mikel Arteta breaks it down: "The complete player in terms of the game we like to play. He's fast, intelligent, two-footed, shows for the ball bravely, breaks up the opposition's attacking lines and the late runs he makes towards the opposition penalty area – wow! He is blessed with a superb first touch, plays brilliantly in tight spaces, knows exactly where everyone is. He's the best at all of that."

Watching Gündoğan at training is a revelation – not only because of his apparently limitless energy, but for the efficiency with which he deals with every challenge. That goes some way to explaining his bursts of speed into the opposition box as well as his prowess as a defensive pivot.

He loves the coffee in Grindsmith, a tiny but popular café in Greengate Square, underneath his building. He lives on the edge of the city centre (on the border with Salford), the area of choice for many footballers. Inevitably paparazzi are a constant presence – hanging about, hoping to get a shot of a famous face leaving home. Or in Gündoğan's case, popping out for coffee.

Guardiola lives in the same building, another big target for the snappers. They are next-door neighbours. "Across a whole year I've bumped into him maybe six or seven times, which isn't a lot. Sometimes I see his wife and kids in the lift and we have a chat. He's a very quiet neighbour, as am I."

Gündoğan is dedicated to avoiding the limelight – a counterpoint to the many boisterous characters in the City dressing room.

"When he plays he's very different and can even lose it a bit if he's being booted around. Otherwise – he's a gentle, calm soul," confirms Arteta.

Family has shaped Gündoğan's personality and his decision-making. His grandfather, Ismael, was a Turkish immigrant who came to Gelsenkirchen from his home in Balikesir and worked in the Ruhr Valley mines. His father, Ifran, was a delivery man for Strauder beer, and his mum, Ayten was a cook. Today he employs his uncle, Ilhan, as his agent. It is a family tradition that all male names start with the letter 'i' (his brother is called Ilker).

Gündoğan is proud of his country's history of welcoming immigrants and grateful for the multicultural environment in which he grew up. "My best friends are Germans of Moroccan, Tunisian or Polish origin," he says. "We're a mixed bunch. I've always loved visiting and getting to know cultures that are different from my own."

As well as German and Turkish he arrived in Manchester already able to speak fluent English. When he was growing up, his parents were determined that he would not abandon his studies, regardless of his emerging talent with a ball at his feet. He believes that this philosophy was aimed at "insulating my brother and I from the problems on the street" as they grew up in Gelsenkirchen, as well as promoting their education.

Gündoğan's closest friend in the dressing room is Leroy Sané. In Germany they were on opposite sides of a fierce rivalry, playing for Borussia Dortmund and Schalke, respectively. The day City became champions in April 2018, after Man United's defeat at home to West Brom, both men were in Germany watching their former teams in the Ruhr derby.

After starting out with VfL Bochum and then Nuremberg, Gündoğan spent five years with Klopp in Dortmund before joining City for £21m in 2016. Injuries meant he played only 16 games during his first season. In 2017-18, as City smashed record after record, the Germany international played 49 games, sometimes as the midfield pivot, sometimes in one of the more offensive central positions – but coming off the bench in around half of those appearances, understudying David Silva and Kevin De Bruyne further forward, or Fernandinho at *pivote*.

His importance to City is borne out by one particular performance in which he claimed one of those Premier League records all by himself. On March 4, 2018, in City's 1-0 win over champions Chelsea at the Etihad, Gündoğan made 167 passes – surpassing at that point Yaya Touré (157 v Stoke City in 2011) and Arsenal's Santi Cazorla (154 v Sunderland in 2015).

At the end of the following season, Gündoğan had made almost exactly the same number of appearances, but his game time had rocketed and he was a virtually unmoveable starter. Meanwhile, the player who had so limited Gündoğan's participation in the first half of season 2018-19, ended it watching from the sidelines.

In this multinational dressing room, Fernandinho is ribbed for his 'British' punctuality. Rain or shine, when the clock strikes 9am he is in the first group at the academy, and on the training pitch.

The Brazilian is ultra-reserved in person. However, the truth is that he is one of this group's leaders and after five years at the club was named vice-captain to Vincent Kompany in 2018. Like the Belgian, Fernandinho is a senior statesman, commanding the respect of his peers and also willing to speak on their behalf when needed.

Shakhtar Donetsk have a unique import-export business going when it comes to Brazilian footballers. The Ukrainian club specialises in scouting and importing South American talent and Fernandinho is one of their many successes. He moved to Donetsk from the Brazilian Serie A club, Atlético Paranaense, in 2005, aged just 20. Blistering performances in the Champions League earned him international attention.

Txiki Begiristain approached Shakhtar in 2012, hoping to buy both Fernandinho and Willian, the forward now at Chelsea. City's football director met Willian at his home in Donetsk and then twice more in São Paulo. Negotiations ground to a standstill, however, when newly-wealthy Russian club, Anzhi Makhachkala registered their interest in the player. The club had recently been bought by multi-millionaire Suleimán Kerímov and having already bought both Roberto Carlos and Samuel Eto'o, they were intent on buying Willian. City would not match the astronomical amounts being offered and Willian signed for Anzhi. He lasted a mere six months there and then, just as the Russian club's financial problems were coming to light, he was snapped up by Chelsea for £30m in the summer of 2013.

Fortunately, City's negotiations for Fernandinho were much smoother and the £34m deal was signed in Curitiba, where Atlético Paranaense is based, 400km from the player's hometown of Londrina. By July 1, 2013, Fernandinho was a City player.

He continued to develop as a defensive midfielder, becoming more of a destroyer than a creator under Manuel Pellegrini, who used him behind the attacking midfielders to regain the ball. This perhaps explains why so many commentators questioned his ability to adapt to Guardiola's game. By the third season of the new era, he was widely viewed as the one player for whom there was no replacement in the starting XI.

As Pep closed in on his first Premier League title in 2018, he said: "Everything we've done so far we couldn't have done without him, no way. It wouldn't have been possible, on or off the pitch. He's a real captain. One of the big memories when I've left will be the pleasure of having been his manager in Manchester."

The Catalan had already stated that, in his current form, the Brazilian was one of the top three defensive pivots in Europe. Fernandinho is something of a wildcard for the Catalan – he has played as a pivot, a midfielder, on both wings and even as a central defender. It follows that a player with an understanding of Pep's system from all these perspectives is also one of the players with whom the coach spends most time discussing tactics.

As 2017 turned into 2018, City knew that Yaya Touré was on his way out of the club and that Fernandinho's importance was about to increase still further – and there was only a year left on his contract. Daisy Brandino, super-agent to several Brazilian footballers, knew who was in the power seat and initially refused to even negotiate. City got their man for a further two years, but, as one of the negotiators recalls, "We had to work our fucking arses off."

It was worth it. By the end of Pep's second season, Fernandinho had surpassed his game time from 2016-17. He finished the championship-winning campaign as the City player who won the most aerial clashes, made the most tackles and earned the greatest number of yellow cards.

Fernandinho will be 35 when that contract expires in the summer of 2020 and he carries the responsibility of a senior player comfortably. He speaks Portuguese and English and understands Spanish, and he makes sure he is there to help welcome new players to the club and help them to settle in.

TEN

THE BEST RESTAURANT IN MANCHESTER

By the time Pep Guardiola was presented as manager of Manchester City on Sunday, July 3, 2016, Txiki Begiristain had begun to build the technical team who would assist the new coach. Contracts had already been exchanged with Lorenzo Buenaventura (fitness coach), Domènec Torrent (assistant manager), Mikel Arteta (assistant coach) and Carles Planchart (head of performance analysis). Brian Kidd (co-assistant coach) and Xabier Mancisidor (goalkeeping coach), whilst not yet on board, looked sure to be joining the crack team. Manel Estiarte would be in overall charge of the player support team and Marc Boixasa would become first team operations manager.

And they were all set. Or were they?

One of Guardiola's biggest frustrations at Bayern Munich had been the club's choice of medical personnel and he was determined that history would not repeat itself. His hand-picked team at City consisted of the renowned Barcelona-based doctor, Ramón Cugat (external medical consultant), plus Dr Edu Mauri, a former player and close colleague of Cugat (chief on-site medic). Asturian physio Edu Álvarez also joined the team, having been enthusiastically recommended by David Silva.

However, there was one vital post they were struggling to fill: the team's dietician. For Pep, this was becoming a headache. "We needed a nutritionist. I can't think of a single top-flight club that doesn't prioritise nutrition – the players' eating habits can have a huge impact on their performance. It's like getting enough rest or the right physiotherapy. There are a thousand details that determine whether you win or lose and one of them is nutrition."

Eventually, the shortlist was whittled down to three candidates, but Pep still wasn't happy. Then, in October 2016, the perfect solution presented itself. Her name was Sìlvia Tremoleda.

Tremoleda is the wife of Xavier Sala-i-Martín, renowned ultra-liberal economist, fervent supporter of Catalan independence and close friend of Pep Guardiola. He was vice president of finance at Barça during the club's glory days under Pep and also served as president for a brief period in July and August 2006.

Sala-i-Martín was already established in New York when the Guardiola family moved there for their sabbatical year. The two couples became firm friends and Xavier and Silvia regularly babysat the Guardiola children. Before the move, Sala-i-Martín spent time with Maria, the eldest of the Guardiola girls, telling her about life in New York and also helped the family find their apartment and schools for the kids. Pep also attended many of his friend's economics classes at Columbia University.

Two years on, under Tremoleda's direction, City's football academy canteen has become, according to several players, the best restaurant in Manchester. Some of them ask for takeaway bags at the end of their working days.

Tremoleda was initially unimpressed by what she found at City. "I spent that first week observing and quickly realised that it just wasn't good enough. They were eating the same kind of food every day and it looked to me just like the stuff you get in a university refectory. I knew we'd have to start from scratch."

She began to offer a more interesting range of dishes, with nutritional content aimed at improving athletic performance and aiding recovery.

It's obligatory for all players to have breakfast and lunch at the CFA on training days and they'll also have dinner there on matchdays.

Soon after her arrival, Tremoleda realised that there was another area of the players' lives that urgently required her attention: their downtime eating habits. Both Kevin De Bruyne and İlkay Gündoğan were immediately on board and asked her to draw up personal menu plans, and soon she was sharing menus and recipes with more and more players.

Tremoleda knows that she has to be vigilant. These are young lads, after all. "I get it. You want to pig out on pizza when you're 22. Of course you do! So, occasionally I'll let them have pizza after a game. Just not every day."

Here's the kind of thing on offer on any given day:

Bread: white, wholemeal, multigrain, gluten-free or bagel
Soup: mixed vegetable; kale and asparagus
Cold selection: avocado, celery and cherry tomato salad; tomato and crab-stuffed avocado
Proteins: brill; grilled scallops; oven-baked chicken thighs; turkey meatballs
Super-healthy choice: noodles with chicken and vegetables marinated in coconut milk
Carbohydrates: rice; gluten-free pasta
On the hot plate: lentils with vegetables; bulgur wheat with vegetables
Vegetables: courgettes and carrots; spinach; oven-baked sweet potato and squash

The four chefs – Jean Luc, Mirco Sardo, David Vickers and Jorge Gutierrez, who worked at Barça during Luis Enrique's time in charge – follow Tremoleda's menu plans to the letter.

Tremoleda was born in Madrid in 1974 but moved to Barcelona a year later. She was a talented and successful youth-level tennis player, but at 18 she decided against pursuing a professional career in the sport and opted for a degree in nutrition. She graduated aged 22 and set off to do a masters degree in New York.

As a triathlete and Catalan champion at *padel*, exercise has always been an important part of Tremoleda's life, and she has successfully completed several ironman competitions. Ironman is the most challenging form of triathlon, consisting of a 3.86km swim, followed by a 180km bike ride and a 42.2km marathon, to be completed within a time limit of 17 hours.

"When you're regularly doing 10 series of 1,000m runs, you learn to appreciate the benefits of a healthy diet. My background helps me a lot in my job because these guys are elite athletes and it's important that they see that I know what I'm talking about."

Nowadays, Tremoleda's daily exercise regime is less intense. Just an hour and a half every day. At 7.30am she's working out in the CFA gym, followed by a run or a cycle. Then she starts her long, busy day.

First off, she checks the results of the players' blood tests. Monitoring blood parameters plays a key role in preparing the optimum nutritional plan for each individual.

"I'll look at the results and decide what each player should be eating. Then, when they come in for lunch, I might say to one of them – today you should have some fish."

Everything served in the canteen has been carefully checked and sourced. Certain algae, for example, have to be analysed with the anti-doping tests in mind. All meat and chicken is organic and halal, the fish carefully sourced from a reputable fishmonger in Chorlton and the fruit and vegetables from a local, hand-picked supplier. The *pan de coca* (a flat cake popular in Catalonia) is, of course, specially shipped in from Barcelona.

Perhaps the trickiest and most important part of Tremoleda's work is persuading the players to eat something after a match. They are drained after 90 minutes on the pitch and have no interest in eating, so the food has to be especially appetising – which is straightforward if it's a home game. If not, food preparation has to be done at the hotel before they leave for the stadium, or even on the bus.

"They're not hungry so we have to get it just right. It's a vital part of their recuperation," Tremoleda explains.

As soon as the game finishes each player is given his personal choice of fruit juice, plus a fruit-flavoured energy gel. These are designed to kick-start the recuperation process and are a key part of injury prevention.

The dinner menu that day will also have been meticulously planned to tempt even the most reluctant eaters.

This was the players' menu at home after the Stoke City game on March 8, 2017:

Pan de cristal (a Catalan bread similar to ciabatta)
Iberian ham
Olives
Courgettes with tomato and low-fat mozzarella
Spanish tortilla
A range of pasta dishes: gluten-free spaghetti bolognese or pesto pasta with chicken
White rice
Sandwiches with Iberian ham, cheese or truffle
Pinchos (mini bruschetta) of tomato, courgette and salmon marinated in lime, soy sauce or Japanese *ponzu* sauce
Hamburgers with caramelised onions
Chicken burgers with avocado and mango sauce
Dessert: pear tart or apple pie

Tremoleda considers the players' preferences in her planning. Curry is a big favourite amongst the English players and now makes a regular appearance on the menu. There are also special dietary requirements to deal with. Gaël Clichy, for example, is vegetarian and a great deal of work went into providing him with a varied choice every day. Only soya milk is offered in the canteen because cow's milk is considered too hard to digest. And there's also a wide range of juices, made to order from a range of fresh fruit: apple, ginger, lime, pear, strawberry.

All players must have a milkshake made with soya milk, yoghurt and oatmeal immediately after a training session or a game. The drink provides them with the right mix of proteins and complex carbohydrates. Tremoleda adds: "We have to watch players' weight carefully because not everyone burns calories at the same rate. Ederson won't be given the same number of calories as, say, Bernardo Silva."

For Tremoleda, nutrient-packed snacks are a key component to the players' diet. "I couldn't believe it when I was told they weren't given snacks," she says. "Having a background in marathon running myself, I couldn't get my head round it. How can they work so hard for 90 minutes without an energy boost? In marathon running you'd never make it to the end without refuelling."

Tremoleda can sometimes be seen literally chasing the players during half-time, trying to ensure that everyone gets a snack of some sort. And she knows her work has paid off: analysis statistics reveal improved performance in the final stages of games.

Of course, pre-match meals are just as much of a priority. Here's what was on offer for the same March 2017 fixture against Stoke:

Bread: white, wholemeal, multigrain, gluten-free or a bagel

Sweet potato soup
Cold selection: sweetcorn, avocado, tuna, lean ham, smoked salmon and boiled eggs
Tuna, tomato and onion salad
Proteins: chicken fillet or steamed sole
Silvia's banana bread (a great favourite) with a mango, orange and banana shake
Vegetable: mashed sweet potato
Carbs: gluten-free pasta in a tomato sauce
On the hot plate: basmati rice, quinoa, porridge in soya milk, banana and cinnamon puree or rice pudding
Dessert: banana with honey

Since coming to Manchester, Tremoleda has been a huge support to Pep. On their return from a defeat (and the end of their championship challenge) at Stamford Bridge in his first season, Tremoleda treated Pep to a night at the theatre where they watched *Birdie*, performed by the famous Catalan theatre company, Agrupación Señor Serrano (Mr Serrano's Ensemble). She had even managed to arrange a couple of backstage passes and the pair raised a few glasses with their new-found friends after the show. Tremoleda's glass contained nothing stronger than a sparkling water or a fruit juice.

City's nutritionist doesn't drink. She thoroughly disapproves of *anyone* drinking. She's banned alcohol from the football academy. Which explains her fury and frustration on the night City became champions in 2018. While the entire squad and staff celebrated, Tremoleda was fuming, in the knowledge that most of them would be marking the achievement with alcohol. And that was that: no more boozy celebrations at City.

ELEVEN

FROM SAGNA TO ZINCHENKO: THE FULL-BACK SOLUTION

Pep Guardiola's first season in England, 2016-17, had ended without a trophy. During the two transfer windows, City had racked up a net spend of around £150m, yet in the end they had needed a run of four straight wins at the conclusion of the league season just to finish third, behind Chelsea and Spurs and with Liverpool and Arsenal snapping at their heels. They had been knocked out of the League Cup by Manchester United; an Alexis Sánchez goal in extra-time had ended their FA Cup run at the semi-final stage; in the Champions League, Monaco had eliminated them – spectacularly – in the round of 16.

At their peak, Pep's team had produced some of the best football the Premier League had seen, but he ended the season deeply frustrated and determined to step up the construction of a squad capable of executing his gameplan.

City spent more than £200m in the summer of 2017. That included the recruitment of key players such as Ederson, Bernardo Silva and Aymeric Laporte, but there was one key strategic problem that was Guardiola's focus as the window opened: the full-back positions. The exodus of players who could play those positions in Pep's team left no doubt about where their priorities lay.

City were either saying goodbye to, or clearing out, Gaël Clichy, Aleksandar Kolarov, Bacary Sagna, Pablo Zabaleta and

Jesús Navas (who Pep, desperate for solutions, had dragged back from the right wing to become an auxiliary wing-back).

Guardiola's strategy during his first season in England had been adjusted to account for the gap between the kind of full-backs he needed to best execute his gameplan and the ones he had. The difference in the productivity of his wide attackers – typically Raheem Sterling and Leroy Sané – between the first season and the next two, can be explained in part at least by the way their roles were influenced by the personnel playing immediately behind them. Pep assessed that he did not have full-backs capable of providing attacking width, and so his attackers were told to play closer to the touchline-hugging tradition of the winger. After spending over £120m on three elite full-backs, City's forwards were unshackled and their numbers in terms of goals, assists and chances created skyrocketed.

As soon as Guardiola began to search for solutions to this problem, his gaze turned to Tottenham Hotspur. From almost the instant he landed in the Premier League, Pep had been praising Mauricio Pochettino's team – particularly his full-backs. "[Kyle] Walker and [Danny] Rose are unstoppable – easily amongst the best in the league in their positions. England should be delighted to have them," was his verdict after Spurs held City to a 2-2 draw in that first season.

Rose and Walker were both high on the list of potential recruits when City began to work out how to solve their full-back dilemma. However, the agents representing both players were in absolute agreement on one issue: there was no way Spurs would sell both of their England international full-backs. City would have to choose.

Txiki Begiristain explains the decision-making process: "Walker was the key decision because the market gave us other attainable options for left-back. We already had Benjamin Mendy on our radar. In terms of someone who could give us defence and attack down the right touchline, we didn't think there was anyone better than Kyle."

That same week in July 2017, City were on the point of closing a deal for Dani Alves. The club's press and communications department even had the announcement written and prepared for issue – just waiting on the go-ahead from the board. A schedule of media interviews with Alves, which would theoretically take place during the preseason tour in the US, was being put together. Then Alves changed his mind, and the deal fell apart.

The Alves affair was a brutal lesson. Alves and Guardiola, who had experienced historic success together at Barça, had a conversation on Friday, July 7. Alves was getting married the next day, to the model Joana Sanz, whom he had met while playing for Barça, and this was Pep's chance to congratulate the player with whom he was soon to be reunited. The marriage was taking place on Formantera. It was agreed in principle that on the Monday the Brazilian would complete his signing for City.

That same Friday, the French sports-paper *L'Équipe* reported an agreement between Paris Saint-Germain's (PSG) Nasser Al-Khelaïfi and Alves that would take the player to Paris. Alves' representatives claimed that the first they knew of it all was on the Sunday – the day after Alves' wedding – and that they were stunned by the reports in the press.

City's principal objective had always been Walker and the collapse of one transfer only made them more determined to sign the younger player. Domènec Torrent, assistant manager to Pep in the first two seasons, said: "Kyle brought us so much – huge intensity. In winning the title in 2018, I think he was the world's best in his position. He's a beast, astonishing physical ability, a force of nature, so fast, so strong."

Beyond his ability on the pitch, Walker has changed the dressing room at City. "Kyle is a cornerstone of the team spirit," added Torrent. "It's something we possibly missed in Pep's first season, when the quality was high, but the characters were all very similar."

At the Christmas party Walker turned up dressed as Mrs Doubtfire, and he chose a lie detector test broadcast on YouTube as the moment to admit that he pees in the dressing-room showers. "But I'm not the only one – you just use a bit of shower gel and it goes down the drain, right?"

Walker is close to his England teammates, Raheem Sterling and, in particular, John Stones. They often arrive together for training and Walker's signing coincided with the former Everton centre-back coming out of his shell.

Walker is an R&B and hip-hop man: Chris Brown, Travis Scott, Kendrick Lamar. During his pre-match massage, he'll listen to Ghetts or Kano and he has ambitions to open his own recording studio once he stops playing. Music is in his blood. Both of Walker's parents were northern soul dance-hall fanatics, and when young Kyle began to feel the isolation that comes with a youth dedicated to sport, his mother, Tracey, had to remind him of the stakes.

Walker was 15 when he said to his mum: "I've had it. My mates are all out having fun and here's me, back home and heading for bed at 9pm because I've got a game the next day."

Tracey had seen the work her son had already put in and replied: "You can't chuck it now – you've come too far already."

And he had. Paul Archer, one of Sheffield United's scouts, spotted six-year-old Kyle mucking about with a ball in the park one Sunday morning.

He moved through the age groups at United and was loaned out to Northampton, but United recalled him and threw their 18-year-old rookie into the starting lineup for an FA Cup tie against Leyton Orient. "That day there was a big crash on the motorway down to London and my parents were caught up in the huge traffic jam, halfway between home and the match," he recalls.

The game was postponed, played the next day, and Walker's parents were able to see their boy's debut for the club where he'd spent the formative years of his life. Nine years later they were also present in London to see him lift the first trophy of his senior career, as he played in City's 3-0 win over Arsenal in the League Cup final of February 2018.

"That day she warned me not to quit, not to throw it away, she was spot on and I'll always owe her for that," he says.

As he progressed through the youth teams at Sheffield United, Walker was developing physically at a slower rate than his contemporaries. As United played a robust brand of football, their young prospect's physique was seen as a problem. His coach had a remedy: a bowl of cornflakes every night before bed. "I followed his instructions, every single day," says Walker.

It's hard to imagine Walker once having been either frail or under-sized now. In his first season at City, the opposite seemed to be true.

Walker was experiencing calf pain in training. The club's medics did all the tests but found nothing to help them identify or treat the problem. It was a mystery. Until Ally Marland, senior kit man, spotted that the full-back was so muscular in the calves that his socks were simply too constrictive.

Kyle Walker: "Pure intuition from Ally – one day he just took the socks, cut a little slit in them down the back and the problems disappeared right away."

Walker locked down the right-back spot to such an extent that there were few more certain starters on Pep's roster by the time the newly-minted treble winners acquired some fresh competition with the recruitment of João Cancelo in the summer of 2019. For a variety of reasons, the left-back position presented Pep with a more complicated dilemma.

Benjamin Mendy was hand-picked to fill that position. He had been one of Monaco's stars as they knocked City out of the Champions League in Pep's first season, prompting James Ducker, of *The Telegraph*, to write: "City need a wing-back who's as complete a footballer as Mendy. His brilliant incursions only underline exactly how much the team lacks in that position. Given how much importance Guardiola's philosophy places on this type of footballer who can do these things, the inability to reinforce that position last summer seems negligent."

Six months later Mendy moved to Manchester as part of City's final business of the transfer window – £52m and a lot of hard work for the dealmakers.

Initially, it seemed like the perfect fit, but Mendy played only five matches before his knee was badly damaged in a tough challenge with Andros Townsend of Crystal Palace. Mendy was able to walk off the pitch unaided, but alarm bells began to ring as soon as the medical team assessed him. Mendy's ankle had swollen like a balloon and he arrived at the CFA the next morning on crutches.

He was sent to Barcelona to be examined by surgeon Ramón Cugat, and the grim confirmation that Mendy's cruciate ligaments were ruptured followed almost immediately.

"Bad news guys – I'll be joining Injury FC on loan for a couple months with ruptured ACL, but will be back soon & stronger, hopefully," he wrote on Twitter. Mendy has a strong social media game.

"Mendy has a special talent, that little spark which can draw a smile out of anyone," reckons Aymeric Laporte, who's known him for years – they are the same age and moved through the France youth teams together.

"He's the maddest guy in the squad – no question about it," admits Brandon Ashton, the kit man who's not short on character himself. "Mendy's the one who unifies all the little groups across the dressing room. There are always little clusters of guys who hang together, but he's the free spirit – doesn't belong to any one group and flits from one to another. You see the Brazilian bunch, Mendy's there. The English, he's with them now. With the Francophones – he's everywhere."

Not even Walker, a grandmaster in the noble art of fooling around, has managed to stem Mendy's mischief. Soon after arriving at City, the Frenchman posted a GIF on Twitter of Walker suffering an absolute beauty of a nutmeg, inflicted by Crystal Palace's Jeffrey Schlupp.

"He's relentless – always up to something new. I've got no real option but to dial it down a little," shrugs Walker.

Mendy is notoriously one of the last to arrive to training and will proceed to confiscate any items his colleagues have failed to secure. For example, Bernardo Silva's football boots were once found hanging from the ceiling. During one rehab session, he arrived at the CFA wearing a crown which he refused to remove all day long. He has sprinkled the dressing room with confetti and arrived to work carrying an inflatable shark.

Mendy became even more vociferous during his rehab, throwing himself into writing a monthly column in *The Times* named *On the Mend*. He gave details of his time out, shared the mood of the squad and showed, publicly, some of the madness which endears him to his fellow squad members.

Adidas, his sponsors, organised a PR event in one of their stores. Naively, they left him alone in charge of one of the tills. Shortly afterwards, they had to revoke his customer service privileges after he spent his entire time offering discounts and giving merchandise away to customers.

That exuberance can also test the boundaries of team discipline. During 2018-19, Mendy's extra-curricular activity included arriving three hours late for treatment the day after he had attended an Anthony Joshua title fight; an Instagram post that claimed he was in Hong Kong and that prompted Pep to swear live on Sky Sports (Mendy was in Paris, as agreed); and finally a 3.30am nightclub appearance that again led to Pep being put on the spot in front of the media. "I am not his father. I would prefer him to go home earlier, but I don't control the players in that situation."

City, however, did not pay Monaco £52m for a social media kingpin, or a dressing-room jester. They bought the full-back who was one of the authors of their downfall in the Champions League and – injuries aside – that's who they got.

"He's a phenomenon, just gobbling the turf up and down that wing. He probably wouldn't have the same impact playing inside, but it's not as if City don't have a host of good options for that," says Torrent, assistant manager during Mendy's first season.

"With Mendy and Walker owning their respective touchlines, you can have Sterling playing from out to in. Sané's qualities mean he's more effective playing wide and he'll give you impact if you bring him on. But you can also have Bernardo Silva or Gabi Jesus there. It all depends on what effect you want to achieve."

In the five matches Mendy completed before his horrible injury, he put more crosses into the opposition penalty area than Kolarov and Clichy combined during the whole of the previous season. So successful was the Frenchman's rehab that he forced his way back into the team before the season ended. By April 13 he was turning out for the under-23s in a derby against United. He managed 45 minutes, watched from the stands by a group of his first-team colleagues, Walker included. The academy kids took advantage of their special guest star – most had a selfie with Mendy before they left the stadium. And that comeback set him up for three more appearances for Guardiola's first-team before the victorious end to the season.

That summer, he became a World Cup winner, making one appearance for France – 40 minutes from the bench in their 0-0 draw with Denmark. And he started the new season, 2018-19, like a champion – with four assists in his first four league games.

The moments of brilliance couldn't disguise the occasional lapses of discipline however, leaving Pep with mixed feelings after watching the ebullient left-back provide two assists in City's 3-0 win at Arsenal in their opener: "Mendy is Mendy. He is what he is. Sometimes you want to kill him. Sometimes you say 'wow, what a player we have'. He gives us this extra energy, with Kyle, helping the attack so consistently. Mendy has a lot of things to improve and hopefully we can convince him to forget a little bit about the social media and improve a few things."

The player's response to his boss's chastening words? A post on social media. "Oops. I promise I'll behave!"

Mendy's second season in England was also derailed by injury. After damaging his foot early in the season, he fought back to fitness only to suffer a serious meniscus injury in November 2018, robbing him of an international call-up for France and sending him straight back to Barcelona and Dr Cugat, who operated on the knee at the Quiron Clinic in Barcelona on November 14. Mendy was back playing within weeks, but made very few appearances for the rest of the season – coming on against Burton Albion in the Carabao Cup and as an emergency solution in the return leg of the Champions League quarter-final against Spurs.

By the end of the season he had played in 15 games. All that Guardiola's team achieved in 2018-19 was largely done without one of the players around whom their strategy was based.

"We signed guys who we know can keep marauding up and down their touchline," explains Mikel Arteta. "Primarily because there are few guys like them anywhere in the world. But also, and this is a personal opinion, there's no comparison between playing in England and playing in Spain or Germany. For City, or any top side, it's obviously great to have players who'll bring you control of the ball, control of matches. But in the Premier League it's vital to have guys who'll offer massive amounts of intensity and athletic aggression in key one-v-one moments. If you don't have that, then, for however much you construct intricate interior play, the big beasts of the Premier League will eventually press you and rob the ball from you.

"It's vital to have versatility – a variety of options. It's not enough to have four full-backs in our squad who bring guarantees in terms of keeping possession. For City there will often be moments when we impose ourselves so much on an opponent that we can have too much control. Perhaps that's when an explosive, anarchic wing-back can offer the breakthrough run – which is why having players with different skillsets who offer different solutions is so vital to us."

Full-backs who bring control, defensively and in terms of possession, are also extremely important. Fortunately for Guardiola, he already had a candidate in his squad on arrival.

In the record-breaking season of 2017-18, Fabian Delph emerged as an important full-back option. "The way things went with our wide defenders in the first season maybe we could have experimented with Delph earlier, but we didn't," admits Guardiola. "That idea didn't become clear until the following campaign."

Torrent adds: "By the end of our first season in charge it gradually began to occur to us that Fabian might be able to do an important job for us – partly because, as a midfielder, he could easily play inside and associate with teammates in the centre of the pitch, rather than just play down the line like a wing-back. I mentioned it to Pep, who agreed that he saw possibilities in Fabian. We immediately tried him out in that position during a training match, which led to something spectacular. We took the risk of changing his position and he rewarded us with several huge performances, especially a spell of about 15 consecutive matches during which he was absolutely magnificent."

Stoke made Delph a good offer in the close season of 2017 but he instead chose to stay and fight for his place. Not a bad decision as it turned out. During season 2017-18 he played 29 times, scored once and gave two assists. A total of 2,324 competitive minutes – four times as much game time as the previous term.

Delph had an important benefactor in Arteta. "I really didn't want Fabi to leave City. I knew him inside out, partly from playing against him, partly from coaching him. He's the type of player who, with very little adjustment, could give us back an enormous amount. Moreover, we didn't have anyone else like him in the squad. Using him offered us options for three at the back, playing two in central midfield or having four inside-creative players."

After a summer spent in Russia with England, Delph was soon City's starting left-back once more, following another injury to Mendy. Between November and December he played eight out of 10 league games and saw Champions League and Carabao Cup action. In November, Guardiola described Delph as "a guarantee".

Then Leicester happened. Delph was at fault for Leicester's first goal in a 2-1 Boxing Day defeat. His error then forced Laporte to concede the corner from which Claude Puel's team scored the winner. Finally, he received a straight red card for a high challenge on Ricardo. Delph would see just 10 minutes more of Premier League action for the remainder of the season (against Huddersfield, but only once the match was won).

Delph had been in the line-up for City's league defeats at the hands of Chelsea and Crystal Palace, and his performance at Leicester was the point at which Pep and his assistants began to lose confidence in him. There would, however, be a chance to redeem himself in one of the biggest games of the season, the away leg of the Champions League quarter-final against Tottenham.

Pep didn't have a lot of options. Oleksandr Zinchenko was injured and, although Mendy had played in the FA Cup semi-final against Brighton days before, it was clear that his knee was bothering him. For the coach it was a straight choice: play Delph or improvise with Laporte at full-back. In the end he trusted Delph, with less than spectacular results.

There were many reasons for City's defeat at the brand-new White Hart Lane that day. And a Delph error was one of them. As Son charged towards a ball which had tempted Ederson to chase out of the six-yard box, Delph simply stood still, arm in the air claiming the ball had gone out. It had not. The Brazilian keeper scampered back to his near post but Heung-Min Son easily cut round Delph before striking a shot which a disoriented Ederson could not prevent from going under him. The winner on the night and, in due course, a key moment in City's expulsion from the Champions League.

Post-match, Guardiola defended the decision to play Delph: "In the last few days I watched Delph closely, and playing here was too much for Mendy after four or five months injured. We had a clear idea for the game and the players always know why we take the decisions we do."

Delph never played for Manchester City again. In 2018-19 he played around half as much first-team football as he had done the previous season, with one assist and no goals. By the summer of 2019 he was made available for transfer. Everton completed a three-year deal for Delph, paying an initial £8.5m rising to £10m with add-ons.

If Delph had been City's first successful improvisation on the left of their defence, he would not be their last. But before they arrived at another imaginative solution, they turned to the transfer market. Danilo, signed from Real Madrid in the summer of 2017 (bringing the total spend on three full-backs in one window to £130m), was acquired as back-up for Walker, but swapped flanks to cope with Mendy's injury.

Begiristain: "We spent a bundle on Mendy and Walker, but we finally chose not to add Ryan Bertrand, who we were also working on, because in the final analysis, without Dani Alves, Danilo [for £26.5m] gave us cover in both wing-back positions."

City had been following Danilo since he was a Porto player. While at Bayern Munich, Pep also had the Brazilian on his list. "Half of Europe wanted him," reckons Torrent.

However, Danilo never became the versatile solution to City's issues on the left when Mendy was missing. As they defended their Premier League title in 2019, he completed the league season with only 11 appearances and switched to Juventus as part of the deal that brought João Cancelo to City. He had swiftly been overtaken by an unexpected rival for the left-back position.

On May 4, 2016, the Manchester City owner Sheikh Mansour was in the luxurious Villa Magna Hotel in Madrid meeting with Txiki Begiristain, Ferran Soriano, Joan Patsy and Brian Marwood, another City executive. Manuel Pellegrini's City were about to take on Real Madrid for a place in the Champions League final, but this meeting was about summer transfer business. The City decision makers wanted to brief the boss about two young players they sought to recruit: Oleksandr Zinchenko and Marlos Moreno. It's the kind of update Mansour insists upon, where he asks the recruiters to explain the moves they are making.

Moreno had just won the Copa Libertadores with Atlético Nacional, having been named man of the match four times in the tournament. The Colombian winger appeared a sure thing to all five men in the room in Madrid, who moved forward with a £4.75m transfer. But that's not the way it turned out. Moreno saw no first-team action for City in the first three years of his five-year contract, with loans to Deportivo and Girona in Spain, then Flamengo in Brazil, then, in 2019, Santos Laguna in Mexico.

He was 19 when he joined City, the same as Zinchenko, the young Ukrainian who arrived as an attacking midfielder. He had been unearthed by City's Eastern European scouts playing for Ufa in Russia. Begiristain was immediately interested, but there was a dearth of information on the player – "barely thirty minutes of video" according to the director of football. It was enough, and in the same summer of 2016 as Moreno signed, Zinchenko moved from Russia to England for £1.8m.

Operations manager Marc Boixasa was responsible for keeping track of an unusual assimilation process – a teenage recruit from Eastern Europe. "He was just a kid. You could barely get a word out of him because he couldn't string four words together in English – although nowadays he chats away in this amazing Mancunian accent."

Pep and his team decided that a season-long loan to PSV Eindhoven would be perfect for their new recruit – PSV and the Dutch league in general were a great fit for his game. He went to Holland as Moreno departed for Spain, but at the end of 2016-17, the Ukrainian's story took a different turn.

PSV asked to bring Zinchenko back for another loan, but Pep decided to retain him. He had no specific plan for the young player, but thought a season training with the first-team would benefit him.

In September 2017, Mendy was injured against Crystal Palace. Pep slotted Delph in as an emergency stopgap, but immediately began to assess other candidates with the skill set for the position: left-footed players capable of playing all the way up and down the line. Zinchenko seemed to fit the bill.

Carles Planchart leads Pep's analysis team: "Coming up with the Zinchenko move was Pep's inspiration. Pure Cruyff. We needed something and had to invent a solution. It wouldn't have occurred to the rest of us because we didn't think he'd be up to it, but Pep knew he could make it work."

Despite rarely figuring in the starting XI during 2017-18, Zinchenko played a vital role in some big games from the bench. He had shown potential for improvement, but how would he fit into the changing plan for the following season?

In their assessment of the existing squad, the coaching staff had Mendy as their No.1 left-back, followed by Delph, who had surprised everyone during the 100-point season. Zinchenko was third choice. There was also growing interest in the Ukrainian from other Premier League clubs and when Wolverhampton Wanderers offered £16m, as well as improved terms and conditions, City agreed to let him go.

"We've got Mendy and Delph. You're hardly going to get a game," he was told.

Zinchenko turned down the transfer. He wanted to fight his way up that list. Another more lucrative offer followed from Fulham. Then a last-minute move by Real Betis. Zinchenko stood his ground.

By February 2019 it looked like Zinchenko had gambled and lost. He had played three times in the league. Then Mendy was sidelined through injury, Delph looked less reliable and, given his chance, Zinchenko made the position his own.

By the end of the season he had played 29 games for a total of 2,339 minutes, scoring one goal and making five assists. His absence from the Champions League quarter-final against Tottenham was seen at the CFA as one of the factors in their elimination. He had gone from a likely sale to a decisive member of the first-team in three months.

Amongst the many factors behind his transformation, many

at the CFA point to his dedication to the personal fitness plan developed for him by Lorenzo Buenaventura's team. The young, skinny boy who arrived from Ufa has become an imposing, elite athlete. When he first broke into the team, analysis showed him flagging after 70 minutes. By the end of 2018-19, he was one of the benchmarks in terms of physical endurance.

Joan Patsy: "At the end of the day, Txiki and I will head down to the gym for a workout on the bikes and Zinchenko will be in the gym, still going strong."

Aymeric Laporte: "He's sent us videos on the squad's group chat or his own social media – him in the gym, bare-chested, pedalling away like a madman. He'll attach a slogan like 'no off days'. None of us really believe him of course."

Nutrition has also been a key part of the change. The team is expected to eat lunch around 1.30pm and then sit down again at 4.30pm for a pre-match meal. It can be difficult to adapt to the routine and players who've had a big lunch usually don't feel hungry enough to eat so soon. Initially, Zinchenko opted to miss the later meal until Silvia Tremoleda and her assistant Tom Parry explained that in England players tend to eat a light lunch to allow for the pre-match top-up. That second meal is vital – the fruit juices and energy bars would have a crucial impact on his performance. Zinchenko listened, saw that the rest of the squad, including the captain, followed the plan, and did what he was told.

This willingness to use the depth of support available to him, allied with a phenomenal work ethic and elite talent, all paid off as Zinchenko's fortunes transformed during the second half of the season. Even when he made a glaring error, the day ended in such a way that it could feed his rampant development.

At Southampton, City were 1-0 up when Zinchenko was caught in possession by Pierre-Emile Højbjerg, who drove the ball high past Ederson to equalise. There was no debate around his culpability for the goal. Eight minutes later, however, he worked a one-two with David Silva and curled in a precision cross for Sergio Agüero to head in the decisive goal in a 3-1 win.

"Oleks was the best player on the pitch because after the mistake he never hid, he never said he didn't want the ball," Pep explained post-match.

"I said to the players at half-time: 'Learn from Zinchenko today, guys.' Everybody can make a mistake but what he did after that, in a game where he could have felt bad or guilty for the team, was absolutely outstanding."

Planchart explains how the adaptation in Zinchenko's position has developed. "He's crucial when we're trying to create superiority in games where we have 80 percent possession. We convinced him that if he could correct a couple of things, then he could play on the wing for the next 10 years and he'd do brilliantly."

Manel Estiarte: "Zinchenko has played some great football but perhaps his greatest gift is his determination to fight for what he wanted from day one. And what he wanted was to succeed at City. That was always his real strength. He wanted to stay here. He was willing to wait for his chance and fight for it."

TWELVE

KHALDOON AL MUBARAK: THE MAN AT THE TOP

August 21, 2017. Man City 1 Everton 1.
An awkward home draw, salvaged by a Raheem Sterling strike with less than 10 minutes left. Pep Guardiola is in a rage, all the frustrations of the previous season resurfacing. How many games like this did he see? Total domination – 19 shots at goal despite playing more than half the game with 10 men – but a failure to penetrate a well-organised defensive opponent.

He retreats to his office, demanding that he not be disturbed. Not by Cristina and the kids, nor by Everton manager Ronald Koeman, his former Dream Team colleague and one of his closest friends. There is a knock at the door. Enter Khaldoon Al Mubarak, the managing director of the City Group.

"You're our man," he tells Pep. "There's no one else. Don't worry, it won't be like last season."

The relationship between Guardiola and Khaldoon was cemented on that August evening, when their record-breaking season started so inauspiciously against Everton.

"That evening was a tense, difficult moment which would spawn thousands of wonderful ones," Khaldoon said. "When you set out to do something so difficult and ambitious, the joy and the stress go hand in hand."

Khaldoon Al Mubarak lives for three things: horses, business and football. He is the man to whom Sheikh Mansour bin Zayed Al Nahyan, the deputy prime minister of the United Arab Emirates, turned after he purchased Manchester City for £250m in 2008, to become chairman of the club.

Khaldoon was born in 1975, and when he was nine his father, the UAE ambassador in Paris, was assassinated by the terrorist group Abu Nidal. He studied economics and finance at Tufts University just outside Boston, the alma mater of Eugene Fama, who won the Nobel Prize for Economics in 2013, and Pierre Omidyar, the founder of eBay. Today he is one of the most trusted advisors to the Abu Dhabi royal family, and the CEO and managing director of the City Football Group. His appointment of Ferran Soriano in 2012 set this story in motion.

Khaldoon attends most City games, arriving in his private jet either the night before or more often on the day of the match. These are also opportunities for face-to-face time with Soriano – the two men talk on the phone every day and have developed a close relationship.

These visits are not ceremonial affairs. Khaldoon will grab something to eat while talking business with Pep and Soriano in the tunnel of the CFA; after a home game, he'll grab a shower at the academy and jump back on his plane.

He typically spends the morning of the match meeting with Soriano and his right-hand man, Omar Barreda, perhaps joined by Txiki Begiristain. Such meetings usually take place in 'Khaldoon's room', a large space Pep once had designs on.

"That room can't be touched!" Begiristain told those who were planning for Guardiola's arrival.

"But Pep wants it," Txiki was told.

"Well, I'll speak to Pep. That's Khaldoon's room. Hands off!"

And so it remains, 20 metres from the offices of City's head coach and director of football.

Khaldoon makes a point of speaking to as many staff as possible, from Manel Estiarte and Lorenzo Buenaventura to the chef who prepares his lunch or the new security guard. He's interested in and respectful of the work of all his staff, but as one of them puts it: "He's very courteous but you're always aware that he answers to the big boss and therefore demands results. He wants you to explain things – it always makes you feel a bit under pressure. Ferran, Txiki, all of them must feel the same way."

Khaldoon doesn't have much to complain about, however. The club has performed brilliantly since the arrival of Soriano and Begiristain, with the team producing some of the best football England has seen.

Ferran Soriano: "He's never once asked us to revise a decision and always respects whatever we choose to do. He just wants an explanation of why we've come to that conclusion.

"I remember when we were selling Álvaro Negredo for £12m and considered signing Radamel Falcao. We'd kept Khaldoon up to date as usual, so he knew all the options. In the end we decided against Falcao, but he kept insisting, 'Why not? It's a good idea financially.'

"We explained that the coaches didn't want him, but we went back and forth a couple of times after that. Then he raised it again on a phone call about something else. I asked him to give me five minutes and got Txiki and Manuel Pellegrini on a video conference call. They gave him their reasons and he said, 'Okay, you're the experts.' And that was it. We didn't sign Falcao."

Guardiola and Khaldoon have an interesting dynamic. The people around them tend to be fascinated by this relationship: the meeting of two driven, high-achieving individuals in their field. Part of that fascination comes from the fact that it developed during Pep's first season in charge, when despite his stellar reputation and a huge spend, instant results were not forthcoming for the new coach.

"I can't quite put my finger on the reason, but I get the sense that his relationship with Pep has developed into a real friendship," says Pere Guardiola. "Pep trusts him totally and has a lot of affection for him. My brother is usually slow to bond with people, he doesn't tend to trust people quickly but the two of them get on very well."

Begiristain saw the bond between Pep and Khaldoon form over three important but contrasting matches during the second season: the troubling, awkward draw at home to Everton in August 2017; the 4-1 thrashing of Spurs in December of that year and the happiest of all: the 5-0 win over Swansea on the day that City could finally celebrate winning the title again, April 22, 2018.

"It was the way Khaldoon talked to him, he really showed how much confidence he had in us," Begiristain says of the 1-1 draw against Everton at the start of the 100-point season, a game that saw all the frustrations of the previous 12 months resurface. "It had been a dreadful day, we'd been the better team but hadn't got the result and everyone was feeling a bit shaken, and Khaldoon was fantastic. I think that was the day Pep finally accepted what Ferran and I had been telling him. Khaldoon told Pep that he knew it wasn't easy, but that he had complete faith in what he was doing and that, in his eyes, there was no other way for the club to proceed. Only his way – the Guardiola way.

"Was that what Pep needed to hear? Of course. But he said it with such conviction that Pep believed him."

The bond between the two men has been a central factor in Pep agreeing to his longest-ever contract extension – three years. Before that was announced, in May 2018, Guardiola had often said he would sign every six months if he could get away with it. His decision to commit to City until 2021 surprised even his wife Cristina, and it's one worth breaking down. It talks of how happy he and his family are in Manchester, and the respect he feels he gets from those he works with – including his employers. Also, Guardiola also knows that he can squeeze a great deal more out of this young, hungry team in the future, and he has one clear objective: to take City to their first Champions League final.

"We've all known each other for a long time, but it's rare for things to be this healthy," said Pep, putting his current situation in context against his other two managerial spells at Barcelona and Bayern. "Txiki is part of my family and everything is organised so that the club is as stable as it can be. I know Khaldoon very well and he knows that I'd step aside if things weren't going to plan. I'll give everything to avoid that happening and make every effort to move things forward, no coasting."

He signed the contract at City's London office, No.10 Brock Street, the day after being named as the Premier League coach of the season. Immediately afterwards, his first call was to Abu Dhabi.

"Pep is tireless, we know he won't become complacent," Khaldoon tells us. "He knows we'll give him all our support, just as we have until now.

"Pep's decision to commit to three further years is a direct result of the atmosphere at the club and the philosophy we want to underpin the whole organisation, starting at the very top, with the owner, Sheik Mansour, who has a great relationship with everyone here. It wasn't really a negotiation, it was just a chat. We looked each other in the eye and agreed we were happy to continue this journey together."

THIRTEEN

MAKING-OF MATCH: BOURNEMOUTH 1 MAN CITY 2 AUGUST 26, 2017

Five days after the Everton game that left Pep Guardiola so pessimistic, he is at the seaside. City are in Bournemouth to play their third match of the season and he is enjoying the sunshine. His mind is in Barcelona, though.

His city is in mourning after the recent terrorist attack and thousands are on the streets today to express grief and outrage.

The blue skies are a welcome change from City's last visit to the seaside town: an evening game back in February. Utterly miserable. It was also a Monday. Pep hates playing on a Monday.

At the Vitality Stadium, Pep has Ederson in goal behind a four-man defence: Danilo, Nicolás Otamendi, Vincent Kompany and Benjamin Mendy, the summer signing from Monaco making his debut at left-back.

Fernandinho anchors midfield, between David Silva and Kevin De Bruyne, while Sterling and Bernardo Silva are on the wings. Gabi Jesus is the central striker.

City's last game wasn't great – 1-1 at home to Everton – and today's match also starts badly. Charlie Daniels puts the home side one up after just 13 minutes, smashing home from a tight angle inside the box.

David Silva needs just eight minutes to produce the response and square things up. A lovely assist to Gabi Jesus, who's clever in losing his marker. In the second half both Otamendi and Bournemouth's Josh King hit the post and it's still 1-1 in the seventh minute of added time.

City have had 70 per cent possession and eight efforts on target from a total of 19. At the death, they find one more. And it counts.

Silva is the cornerstone of the move. With a quick spin and a crisp pass he finds Sterling in the second-striker position. He and De Bruyne exchange passes to win space on the right, and here comes Danilo on the charge. The Brazilian centres on the run, but it's a cut-back rather than a chip to the back post and Sterling, in full Gerd Müller mode, slams on the brakes, drops off his marker in the penalty box and, when he swivels to strike the ball with his right foot, it loops upwards off the lunging Andrew Surman and into the net. It's the 97th minute, the move has taken place in an ultra-crowded penalty area and the arc of the ball seems to follow its gravity-enforced parabola in super-slow motion.

A delighted Sterling sprints over to the away fans, closely followed by the rest of the team. Everyone goes wild. Eventually the stewards have to intervene.

After fighting like warriors for the win and celebrating like brothers-in-arms out on the pitch, the atmosphere in the changing room evaporates. Everyone's staring at their phones, lost in their personal bubbles. Their leader is disbelieving and furious.

"That Bournemouth game was probably the angriest I've ever seen Pep," Kompany will later admit. "We'd won the game at the last minute and he bawled us out because we didn't continue celebrating enough!"

Guardiola doesn't hold back. He tells them that if they're not capable of celebrating today's win, everything they did out there, then they don't deserve to call themselves a team.

His players are stunned, but this will prove to be a turning point. The importance of celebrating their victories on the pitch and in the dressing room has been registered. The next weekend is an international break and their first game back together will see them slaughter Liverpool 5-0.

"For me that was an absolutely critical moment for us," says Pep. "We went on to beat Liverpool in our next game and I could see it meant much more to the team. The previous year we'd struggled against the top teams but that was the day their attitudes changed and it made all the difference."

The Bournemouth game would prove to be the catalyst for City's subsequent run of 18 consecutive wins.

Bournemouth (5-3-2): Begovic; Smith, Cook, Ake, Mings, Daniels; Gosling, Surman, Arter; King, Defoe (Afobe 73, Mousset 94)
Man City (4-3-3): Ederson; Danilo, Kompany, Otamendi, Mendy; De Bruyne, Fernandinho, D Silva (Stones 90+10); B Silva (Agüero 66), Jesus (Sané 82), Sterling
Goals: Daniels 13, Jesus 21, Sterling 90+7
Bookings: Cook, Ake, Smith, Mings, Arter, Kompany, Mendy, Otamendi, D Silva, Sterling
Sent off: Sterling 90 + 9
Referee: Mike Dean
Attendance: 10,419

FOURTEEN

KEVIN DE BRUYNE: THE ORCHESTRA CONDUCTOR

January 30, 2015. Bayern Munich's unbeaten progress through the Bundesliga season comes to a crashing end. Pep Guardiola, their coach, watches from the bench as Kevin De Bruyne scores two and assists on one of Bas Dost's double in a 4-1 win for Wolfsburg.

That same night, Pep is talking about the young Belgian on a call with his old friend Txiki Begiristain. "The guy's a machine," says Pep. From that moment on he was determined to sign De Bruyne.

However, Bayern did not see the recruitment of the midfielder as straightforward. There was the status quo at the German champions to consider: how would the high-profile, expensive capture of a rising star in the Bundesliga affect Arjen Robben, Franck Ribéry and Thomas Müller?

There was no such hesitation at City. In August 2015 – shortly after De Bruyne had orchestrated another defeat for Guardiola's Bayern, this time for the DFL-Supercup, a £55m transfer made him the second most expensive British signing in history and he was the marquee signing of Manuel Pellegrini's final season as coach. De Bruyne was returning to England, less than two years after Chelsea had sold him to Wolfsburg following limited first-team opportunities.

Mikel Arteta knew De Bruyne's armoury of talents inside out. He'd even played against him. He has observed the changes since

Guardiola inherited the player he so coveted in Germany. "Pep's arrival instilled more method in a player of natural ability," said Arteta. "He'd become accustomed to being allowed to find his own space and do marvellous individual things with the ball which were beautiful to see but probably didn't control a game or a result. Now he sets the tempo of a game. He's like the orchestra conductor. The game's mapped out in his head. He can speed the rhythm up or slow it down and he's got the ethic to drop deep and link up play with smart, short passes which get the team to where they need to be. This wasn't his original style. Pep's given him a new way of viewing things, a new way of controlling a match. A few years ago he couldn't have played pivot, because he didn't quite have the capacity to transmit order to those around him. Now he can, he understands the pitch, his team, the demanding, associative football which links parts of the team with passes and movement. Previously he had the ability to accelerate the game. Now he's got a choice of six gears and he'll move smoothly through them at exactly the right time."

In Pep's first season, City's title hopes had all but died at Stamford Bridge, in a 2-1 defeat by Chelsea in April 2017 that left them fourth and put their hosts on course for the title. When Pep, City and De Bruyne returned the following season, on September 30, 2017, they had learned their lesson.

Domènec Torrent: "Pep's pre-match talk was superb. He set it all out so clearly: how to control them, how they played, what we would do to counter that."

City had 61.9 per cent possession and 17 shots on goal, six of which were on target. Antonio Conte's Chelsea managed four shots with two on target. Guardiola's players made 653 passes, their hosts just 395. Having utterly dominated the match the winning goal arrived, spectacularly, in the 67th minute. De

Bruyne worked a one-two with Gabi Jesus and struck a rasping, left-foot shot from the edge of the box which whistled past Thibaut Courtois, the Chelsea goalkeeper.

After the whistle, a party started in the away dressing room at Stamford Bridge. De Bruyne was still outside, receiving his man of the match award. As he entered, bare-chested, the Belgian erupted, dancing into a huddle of his teammates, who burst into a chorus of 'Oh, Kevin De Bruyne' (to the tune of White Stripes' *Seven Nation Army*). The chant was taken up by everybody in the room – even Pep Guardiola, who shared the moment with Benjamin Mendy by holding up a phone, connecting the recovering defender in his hospital bed with his victorious colleagues.

Domènec Torrent: "That Stamford Bridge game was a vital part of what came next. You play away against the champions, who have their own very distinct playing style, five at the back and vertical, one they've been developing for five years. That's a tough ask. But that day we were the better team and we began to really believe in ourselves. When you win like that, the whole team starts to understand that we can go all the way."

Mikel Arteta: "When we played the big sides the previous year, we were definitely the better team and deserved to win. Despite that, however, we just couldn't quite get the results. At Chelsea it was like: '*This* is how it's meant to be!' We dominated the game and we won. You could see the difference in City. We played with such authority."

Guardiola also marks that game down as a crucial turning point: "Beating Chelsea like that was vital. That was where we began to understand how good we were. Of course, we'd had good days before, when the players knew they'd done well, when the self-belief was there, but at Stamford Bridge everything just clicked. And one of the players most positively impacted by the victory was Kevin."

Kevin De Bruyne: "Pep and I are on the same wavelength. We've all had to learn to do things his way and I think it's been exactly what the team needed."

Under Pep, De Bruyne has developed into a new role. In the past he'd been a midfielder capable of playing on the inside or the wing. He's now one of the most formidable playmakers in the world, who creates constant danger in the centre of the pitch: a turbine engine when he's working deeper; one of the very best in England when he plays further forward.

His stats for season 2017-18 speak for themselves: 52 games, more than any other City player; 12 goals, and 21 assists – including a Premier League-best 16; he also scored the most goals from outside the box (5) for City and was joint top with Fernandinho for number of tackles won (62).

Some of the staff at City will point to fatherhood as being a factor in the maturity that De Bruyne now shows. Others mention added responsibility in a footballing sense, handed down by Guardiola.

"I gave him some captaincy roles," says Pep. "It was clear that he understood that players don't just have to go out and play well, they also need to take on a bit of responsibility. He's a strong person, always ready to take on a new challenge, as he's demonstrated again and again."

Those who have watched the Belgian's workrate confirm how closely Pep has mentored the player, at training and in one-to-one feedback sessions.

"If he maintains his self-belief and keeps up the same work rate, then without a doubt he'll be one of the world's great footballers over the next five years," argues Torrent.

Pep is certain. "He'll do it. Look at his consistency, how reliable and solid he is. A great example for our other players."

And the Chelsea game was the catalyst. "He gave a recital," recalls David Silva. "You know you'll find him, that he's looking for you, that he's going to do the smart thing on and off the ball."

People describe De Bruyne variously as 'a serious guy', 'very mature' and 'quite formal'. As a youngster, people have said he was excessively introverted, and he himself has spoken about how others responded to his shyness. "People said I'd never make it because of my personality," he said. "I said to myself, 'Let's just see who has the last word.'"

Beneath the baby face there's plenty of aggression. It's not often on show but it rose up at half-time in a Champions League match with Napoli. "Let me talk!" he screamed at his teammates, who were trying to restrain him from facing up to the referee. Only David Silva had any impact on their runaway Belgian that day. City players still joke about it.

In retrospect, De Bruyne can also see the funny side. "It was nothing. It was all over in a second. It's like the kind of fight I have with my wife. A bit of aggro from time to time can do wonders. It lets everyone know where they stand."

It's not the first time the Belgian has lost it during a game. At Wolfsburg, he once turned on one of his own team's ball boys. "Give me the ball, imbecile!" he screamed at the poor kid, desperate to get the game restarted. Later, De Bruyne made a public apology to the boy and gave him a signed shirt. These explosive incidents shouldn't be taken as representative of his character, however.

In his personal life, he's extremely laid-back. His long-time mates back in Belgium still nickname him the 'dryer' because the text messages he sends them tend to be abrupt and bone-dry. No messing about, on or off the pitch. Like many players, he has a few rituals, one of which is taking a jog round the pitch with kit man Brandon Ashton, before training or a game. He's close to all three kit men. "When he first arrived he used to sit with us after training and if another player came up needing something we'd tell Kevin to go and get it, as a joke. And he'd do it! No bother, as if it was completely normal. Now that Pep's in charge we tease him about being too important to spend time with us every day," Ashton laughs.

In fact, De Bruyne does still spend a lot of time with Ally, Brandon and Mike. He doesn't take a massage before a game, preferring instead to hang out with the three men. "The four of us sit and have a natter. We talk about everything: our families, our kids, just like I do with all my mates. It's become a habit, just a normal part of life," says Ashton.

The medical staff at City are astounded by De Bruyne's shooting ability. He strikes the ball far more powerfully than a player of his strength should do – they think it may be down to the fluidity of his movement. If the game at Stamford Bridge – decided by De Bruyne's weaker left foot – was pivotal in the transfer of power from Chelsea to Man City, by the time the two sides met again, Guardiola's team had opened a chasm between themselves and the team they were about to usurp as champions. On March 4, 2018, the league was already in the bag and both sides were in the middle of Champions League ties that would end with them exiting in the round of 16. A Bernardo Silva goal won the game for City but that does not tell the story of a match in which they dominated the outgoing champions completely. Pep's team achieved 71.3 per cent possession and 976 passes (a Premier League record) with İlkay Gündoğan becoming the player with the most passes in a single game: 167. Conte's men failed to produce a single shot on goal.

At the end of the season, Mohamed Salah's 32 goals led to him being named Footballer of the Year. There was at least one dissenting voice at the news: Guardiola. "When you analyse it over nine or 10 months, there's been no better player than Kevin in terms of consistency, of being at such a level every three days," he told the press when news of the award broke. "Others may have beaten him in numbers, but I'm sorry, no one's been better than him this season."

De Bruyne followed a triumphant season for City with an unforgettable World Cup, as a key part of the Belgium team that finished in third place. That deep run in Russia meant De Bruyne was one of a group of City players instructed by the club's medical staff to report back a bit later than most of their teammates.

However, those precious extra few days of holiday cost him most of preseason training. He missed the Community Shield and was only just approaching peak fitness when he was derailed completely.

On August 14, 2018, the Amazon documentary about City's record-breaking 2017-18 season, *All or Nothing* was celebrated at the Printworks cinema in Manchester. De Bruyne turned up on crutches, wearing a protective brace on his right knee after sustaining ligament damage during morning training.

The medical staff's prognosis was three months out, but the Belgian made it back in a little over two. He was four games into his return when Pep decided he needed to step it up with 90 minutes against Fulham in the Carabao Cup. De Bruyne rewarded his coach with a superb performance and the Spanish teenager Brahim Díaz had City 2-0 up when, in the 86th minute, the Belgian midfielder went down, clutching his other knee.

As the player left the pitch, barely able to hold back the tears, he was informed that his partner, Michelle, had just given birth to their second child, Rome.

Pep called to congratulate the new mum the next day. "Now you've got three kids to look after. Your two children and Kevin," he joked.

This time De Bruyne was out for 43 days. Eleven matches.

Pep did his best to include him in his plans for the last part of the season, but De Bruyne was struggling to get back to full match fitness and also coping with muscular problems.

He battled on until the return leg of the Champions League quarter-final against Spurs when, ironically enough given the final score and City's controversial elimination, he gave his best performance of his season, dominating the centre of the pitch and providing three assists.

Sadly it didn't last. In City's league game with Spurs on April 20, he went down again, this time as a result of the muscle problems that had been hampering him during the second half of the season. In the dressing room, De Bruyne's frustration and fury at his disastrous run of luck was released. He was in a rage, kicking and throwing things all over the room as teammates and staff watched on in silence. Nobody intervened or tried to console him.

"With a bit of luck he'll be back for the FA Cup final," the medics told Pep.

Once again, he defied even their most optimistic prognosis and was back for the last league game, in Brighton, winning the title with his boots on and then playing a pivotal role in the FA Cup final. At Wembley, De Bruyne came on in the 55th minute, and took the game away from Watford. He produced an assist for Gabriel Jesus, plus a goal of his own.

He was awarded man of the match. There were others who played better, or influenced the game for longer, but De Bruyne broke Watford in that spell. He put the game on a plate for City.

He lifted the trophy at the end of a season in which he had missed 29 games through injury. Weeks later he admitted: "It hasn't been easy. I feel sometimes my season was double the length of other players because every time you need to work almost double the hours, you never have a day off because you need to work on your recovery. It's more draining than when you're playing. A lot of the time you're alone, but you have to do it. I did it and I'm happy I'm back."

Alone in the CFA, but not at home, where the silver lining in a dark year professionally was the time he got to spend with his children, baby Rome and Mason, and Michelle, his rock throughout a difficult year.

"She's the most important person in my life. She sacrificed everything to move away with me when she was 19 years old, to help me follow my dream. We've been on this journey together. I look up to her, in a way. She got me to come out of my shell with people a lot, and the way she's handled everything is remarkable," he wrote in the *Players Tribune* in April.

In the same article, the player shared his thoughts about his coach. "Pep and I share a similar mentality. He's even more intense about football than I am. He's so, so stressed – all the time. However much mental stress we are under as players, I think he is under twice as much. Because he is not just interested in winning. He wants perfection. The first meeting I ever had with Pep, he sat me down and he said, 'Kevin, listen. You can be – *easily* – a top five player in the world. Top five. Easily.'

"I was shocked. But when Pep said it with so much belief, it changed my whole mentality. It was kind of genius, I think. Because I felt like I had to prove him *right*.

"Most of the time, football is about negativity and fear. But with Pep, it's about extreme positivity. He sets goals that are so high that they're almost impossible to reach. He is a tactical master, yes. There's no doubt about this. But what people on the outside don't see is the pressure he puts on himself to try to achieve perfection."

FIFTEEN

PEAKY BLINDERS

"It was our first day at training and we were all thinking, 'What the fuck are they doing? They're nuts,'" laughs Domènec Torrent.

The nuts in question were City's kit men, a trio he now refers to as the Peaky Blinders – Ally Marland, Brandon Ashton and Mike Clitheroe.

Ashton is the most mischievous of the three. Small and shaven-headed with a luxuriant ginger beard, his thick Manchester accent is incomprehensible to outsiders on first acquaintance. He's 25 and has been working for City for a decade. "I first set foot in the stadium in 2004 and immediately got the idea in my head that I'd like to work here one day."

Sure enough, he landed his first job with the club before he'd even left school, through his dad's friendship with Les Chapman, known to everyone at City as Chappy.

Between 1966 and 1987 Chappy played midfield for half a dozen teams in the north-west of England, though not City. He ended up as player-coach of Stockport, and continued to coach until 1997, when he moved to City to take on the role of kit man. Over the next 17 years he became an institution at the club, a huge personality, much-loved by staff and players. Now semi-retired, he still works in the media department, where he helps produce content for club videos. In fact, it was Chappy who was driving Pep's taxi in the viral promotional video shot on the day Guardiola arrived at City.

So it was that a teenage Ashton began his career as the great man's apprentice, starting out with a short internship and, after much pleading, landing a summer job which included travelling to Germany with the squad for preseason training. As the new season began, he was given a year's contract on the strict understanding that he'd stay for that season and then go to university. Ten years on he's still there, telling anyone who will listen that he has learned everything he needs to know at the University of Life: the streets and pubs of Rochdale, his neighbourhood, Smithy Bridge, and the dressing rooms of the Premier League.

His fellow Peaky Blinders came to City much later. Ally Marland arrived in 2012, just after City won the title with Agüero's big moment. The club had just lost a kit man and Marland came highly recommended from Bolton Wanderers.

When Chappy transferred to the media department, Marland was promoted to kit manager and Mike Clitheroe arrived as his assistant. The two men were already on good terms: they'd been in Burnley's youth team together.

City's kit men have a non-stop schedule: they have to collect the dirty laundry, wash it, prepare the players' training kits, organise the equipment and clothes needed for the weekend, ensure each player's boots are in the right place, keep the balls properly inflated – everything needs to be perfect, every single day, whether it's training or a game.

"I don't think the kit men at Bayern Munich bother going out to the training pitch every day. But we like to do that and have done since Roberto Mancini was in charge," Ashton explains.

"I remember at the start most of us were a bit star-struck over Pep and I was running about like a mad thing, chasing lost balls or whatever else needed doing. On the second day, the boss came up to me, slapped me on the back and said: 'I love this intensity! Brilliant!'

"And would you believe it? I started running around even harder than before!" he laughs.

Marland, as kit manager, is in charge of the in-house software which allows him to manage the players' kits: what kit each man has, their sizes, what they will need and when, their favourite bits of gear. They run a tight ship.

The players' boots are given special care and those which require it are steamed before training sessions and matches.

The kit men are also quite happy to break-in new boots by wearing them for the player for a few days, and place no restrictions on shoe size. "Agüero has enormous feet but he'll always get me to do it," Ashton smiles.

Vincent Kompany has known the kit men longer than any of his teammates. "They're the glue that holds everyone together. If our performance ever dipped, even just 10 per cent, they'd push and prod us until we sorted it."

Torrent remembers one particular evening in Swansea during the first season. City were playing the Welsh side twice in four days and were booked into a hotel for the whole period. The kit men decided that a barbecue was just the thing. "They put on this show, performing Michael Jackson songs. We were all in pieces, it was hysterical. You've no idea how important that kind of thing is to team unity."

In February of that season City had travelled to Bournemouth for a league game on a freezing winter's day, with a windchill factor of minus three. During a pre-match stroll along the beach, some of the players began to tease Ashton, daring him to take a dip in the icy water. "You don't have the balls to go in."

He resisted for a while, but when the coaching staff joined in, it was too much. Stripping down to his pants, he sprinted towards the water, straight into a battle with a bad-tempered dog which had previously staked out the beach as his personal territory. Shaking off the furious canine as best he could, he made it to the water and dived into the freezing sea, closely followed by the dog.

Guardiola has asked the kit man to lift the trophies on behalf of all the backroom staff, first at Wembley after City hammered Arsenal in the final of the League Cup in 2018. "We were at the post-match party and Pep told me: 'Brandon, lift the trophy.'

"So I did. What a feeling! We all went mad. But that wasn't enough for the gaffer. On the flight home that weekend he came over to me to say: 'When we win the league you can lift it again.'"

After the Huddersfield game on May 6, 2018, once the players had lifted the trophy in front of the fans, the technical staff gathered in the middle of the pitch. Dozens of them. Then, a gleaming bald head and a brilliant smile emerged from the crowd. Ashton, surrounded by his delighted colleagues, raised the Premier League trophy proudly in the air. "I'll remember that moment for the rest of my life."

SIXTEEN

MAKING-OF MATCH: MAN CITY 7 STOKE CITY 2 OCTOBER 14, 2017

Matchday 10 in the 2017-18 Premier League season. The two Manchester clubs are level on points at the top of the table. Today, City take on Stoke and United go to Anfield, where the Kenny Dalglish Stand is being unveiled. A few hours prior to the match, King Kenny declares: "Klopp is doing a fantastic job but I don't think anyone can stop City in the league."

At Pep's pre-match press conference, the burning issue of the day was Mauricio Pochettino. A few days earlier, the Spurs manager had accused Guardiola of being disrespectful. In attempting to compliment Spurs' star striker, he had called Tottenham 'Harry Kane's team'.

"Guardiola showed a lack of respect. Every single member of this team deserves credit. And he's annoyed a lot of people by saying what he did. When I was coaching Espanyol and he was at Barça I never called them 'Leo Messi's team'."

Pep's response is terse. "Pochettino's got it wrong. I've never been disrespectful to any of my peers."

For Guardiola, the whole thing is a tiresome misunderstanding. The episode at least provides the City manager the chance to add to his repertoire of English idioms: a storm in a teacup.

Sergio Agüero is back for today's game but will remain on the bench throughout. Gabriel Jesus plays down the middle, with Raheem Sterling on the right and Leroy Sané on the left wing.

The game is an absolute spectacle. City are on fire. Jesus scores the opener, 17 minutes in. City recapture possession in the same time it takes Stoke to restart from the centre circle and lump the ball down the inside-right channel. After scoring a goal, City are without the ball for 10 seconds. What follows is pure Pep.

Nico Otamendi imposes himself between his opponent and the ball, wins possession and back-heels to Fabian Delph, waiting on the touchline. Delph calmly strokes it back to the keeper and the ball is then passed up the pitch, from Fernandinho, to John Stones, Kevin De Bruyne and then Kyle Walker. De Bruyne takes it back and finds David Silva, who sends it back to Otamendi. Now Delph's in possession and he feeds Silva, who has seen Sané's run, hugging the touchline like he's supposed to. The German winger powers towards the line, stops and takes Tom Edwards, Stoke's 18-year-old full-back, for a little dance around the edge of his own penalty box. Then Sané erupts. He cuts the ball back to De Bruyne, and stays just on side as Edwards switches off. De Bruyne shapes to shoot but disguises a lovely reverse pass to Sané, who's now free to lay the ball into the path of Sterling, who has dropped off Erik Pieters, leaving himself an open goal to fill. Sterling slams it straight into the back of the net. A goal of transcendental beauty.

Jesus is the only City player not to have touched the ball during the possession that led to the goal. It has taken City 43 seconds and 16 passes to produce a textbook example of the kind of football upon which their coach insists.

Pep Guardiola: "We run to recover the ball. We don't run for the sake of running. We don't press without a purpose. We always understand that if we rob the ball high up the pitch, then we're closer to scoring. But even if we don't get it back high up, we must always still be focusing on scoring. And that means we have to look for a pass. When we don't have the ball, I want everyone running. When we're in possession, we play the ball around and let our opponents do the running, so that, at the right moment, we can attack and score. That's why we have to link up, keep passing the ball patiently, waiting for the chance to score. Timing the moment to go for their weakness is vital."

Henry Winter, chief football writer at *The Times*, is blown away by the quality of the goal. "It was the most sparkling and fascinating football seen on an English pitch in the last 50 years," he writes.

Pep Guardiola: "The most difficult thing is to make football that simple! This was our best performance since I arrived."

City achieve 80 per cent possession and have 20 shots on goal. De Bruyne scores one and also produces one of the assists of the season, a razor-sharp diagonal pass, rasping across the surface from one side of the pitch to the other, straight into the path of Sané's sprint. "It was so cool. I'd just screamed like, 'Hey! I'm here!' and then suddenly the ball's at my feet," marvels the German, who converts the pass for City's sixth goal.

De Bruyne is named man of the match and even the defeated manager, Mark Hughes – a Barcelona player when Pep was in the academy and doubling up as a ball boy on matchdays – is impressed. "He was sensational. He's significantly better than any other player in the Premier League."

After the game Pep says: "I'm here to win. I'm not here to entertain. I'm not a magician. But this is the way we want to play."

Today's game is a statement of intent. This is the Manchester City we'll see for the rest of season, dominating the ball and slamming goals past their opponents.

At Anfield, the game between Liverpool and Manchester United ends 0-0. City are now two points clear and will continue to widen the gap as the season continues.

King Kenny. Right again.

Man City (4-3-3): Ederson; Walker, Stones, Otamendi, Delph; De Bruyne (Gündoğan 66), Fernandinho (Touré 73), D Silva; Sterling, Jesus (B Silva 63), Sané
Stoke (4-4-1-1): Butland; Edwards (Sobhi 53), Zouma, Wimmer (Martins Indi 45), Pieters; Diouf, Fletcher, Cameron, Choupo-Moting; Shaqiri; Jese (Afellay 45)
Goals: Jesus 17, 55, Sterling 19, D Silva 27, Fernandinho 60, Sané 62, B Silva 79; Diouf 44, Walker 47 (og)
Bookings: Afellay
Referee: Craig Pawson
Attendance: 54,128

SEVENTEEN

MANEL ESTIARTE: THE MINDER

The covered training pitch at the City Football Academy is deserted apart from three international footballers and a film crew. Kun Agüero, Nicolás Otamendi and Danilo are shooting a commercial for Cambodia Beer, one of their employers' official partners, but things are not going smoothly. The over-zealous director is working the players hard to get everything he needs. But Agüero has been having problems with his ankle and is visibly concerned that this extra-curricular activity could make things worse.

From the sidelines, a tough, athletic figure strides toward the camera crew: "That's enough. You're putting them under too much strain. You'll have to do something else."

The crew try to oblige, but they have work to do; the commercial requires some action from the players. They push on with their demands; Agüero's anxieties increase.

The enforcer re-enters the scene, taking Kun by the arm, and starting to lead him back to the dressing room, only to find his path blocked by one exasperated crew member, who curtly demands that the player stay put.

"He's staying. We still have more to film and we need him here."

"Okay," snarls Agüero's self-appointed minder. "You won't let me take him away? In that case, don't you worry, all three are coming with me."

A stand-off ensues. City's marketing department intervene, the film crew apologise and City's superstars complete their obligations with minimal physical exertion.

Manel Estiarte 1 Film Crew 0.

Estiarte has been at Pep Guardiola's right hand at Barcelona, Bayern and now in Manchester, but his role has evolved at each stop. At City, he works in an executive role as head of player support.

If there's a problem brewing in the squad, Estiarte is the first port of call for first-team delegate Marc Boixasa. "I could tell Pep things, but if Manel's around, it's better to speak to him so that he can then explain it to Pep."

The extension of Estiarte's remit beyond Guardiola and into first-team affairs has led to Boixasa's department being amalgamated under Estiarte's control.

Sometimes his role is that of a gatekeeper, or perhaps a shop steward, defending the boundary around the team and its manager from the bombardment of requests and demands that come from the communications and marketing departments. Often, that creates a stand-off between Estiarte and Ferran Soriano, City's chief executive: on one side, the sanctity of the dressing room; on the other, the corporate responsibilities of a gigantic organisation.

"We're both working for the same end – the success of Manchester City," adds Soriano. "We need the players to participate in our campaigns and promotional work, but obviously they're very busy. And Manel often puts his foot down. He's pretty inflexible."

He can also be hot-tempered. Referees, coaches, opposing players, sponsors – they've all been on the receiving end of an Estiarte tongue-lashing down the years.

Manel Estiarte was the Leo Messi of water polo. Almost 20 years after his retirement from the sport, he is still regarded as the best there has ever been. He was the first water polo player to compete at six Olympic Games and was voted the world's best for seven straight years from 1986 to 1992.

Water polo is a tough sport. Players have to both employ and repel the dark arts used to gain advantage. In his day, Estiarte faced some of the dirtiest players in the sport, and he was no shrinking violet himself. They punched and kicked to goad him into retaliation and to get him sent off. He recalls a certain Florentine opponent who used to kick and scratch him underwater before the match had even begun. And there was abuse out of the pool, too, for the proud Catalan who competed under the Spanish flag.

Estiarte doesn't get involved in the football, but his experience as an elite international sportsman gives him a powerful insight into group dynamics and dressing-room life.

Pep Guardiola: "That's where his expertise lies. That relationship with the squad. He'll come to me and say, 'Everything's great. They're on board. They'll do anything for you.' Or another time, 'Watch out, something's up. We need to nip it in the bud.'

"He has this sixth sense. He knows exactly how everyone's feeling and can tell immediately if they're committed or not. That's crucial to me because nothing works if the squad's not united behind me. He was a superstar athlete in his own day and has been in hundreds of dressing rooms. If there's one thing Manel knows about, it's how that vital area of a squad's wellbeing functions."

Estiarte is also unafraid of offering the boss constructive criticism. He might reel Guardiola in if he thinks he is overloading the players with information before a game. Or divert the boss's strategy in an altogether different direction. On one occasion Pep discovered that City had an unexpected break coming up (six consecutive days without a game – a rarity in professional football). His first thought was to use the time on an away trip to Barcelona. For extra training.

Estiarte had a more practical suggestion. "I think they'd be happier getting two days off, rather than going all the way to Spain to train." That's what they did.

Estiarte and Guardiola grew up 10km apart and were already both established as elite sportsmen when they met, in 1992. Johan Cruyff's Barcelona, with Pep in his breakout season, had just clinched the title. It had been a tough campaign and Barcelona had gone into the final matchday trailing leaders Real Madrid by a single point. In a thrilling finale, Tenerife beat Madrid 2-0, gifting Barcelona the league.

Estiarte, himself a devoted Barça fan, had heard all about the young, talented midfielder, Pep Guardiola, from his friend Joan Patsy and insisted on meeting him. Ricard Maxenchs, director of communications at the club, introduced the two in the Camp Nou dressing room soon after that victory and they clicked immediately.

Each was about to compete in the 1992 Olympics and as Pep headed down to Valencia for the football tournament, Manel joined the rest of the Spanish water polo team in Barcelona. Their paths crossed only twice during the games: once at the inauguration ceremony in the Montjuïc Olympic Stadium and once at the football tournament final in the Vila Olympica, where Pep and his Spain teammates beat Poland to win gold.

Listening to the raucous celebrations of his fellow athletes that night, Manel lay awake till the small hours of the morning, praying: "I hope that's me tomorrow."

The next day was the final day of the games and Spain's water polo team would face the mighty Italians in the gold-medal match. The Italians scored in the final seconds of the game and Estiarte left the Olympics with a silver medal round his neck and a bitter taste in his mouth.

Patsy was a television journalist during the Barcelona Olympics, and he would often bump into Estiarte in the athletes' village. Sixteen years later, they were in the same city but entirely different places in their lives. Estiarte was retired and Patsy was now advising the board at Barcelona on, amongst other things, a new hire in the PR department. "Manel is great with the media," he told them. "They really respect him – he'd be brilliant."

In the summer of 2008 Estiarte was on holiday in Pescara when he was contacted by Ferran Soriano, vice-president of finance at the Camp Nou, asking him to come to Barcelona. Soriano was looking for someone to head up external communications and to act as liaison between the board and the players. The two met at the Casa Fuster Hotel in Barcelona and talked about the future of the club, about Pep, about their common vision.

Estiarte then had a follow-up meeting with Joan Laporta. The president, known for his laid-back approach, spent most of the meeting eulogising Estiarte and ended up offering him the job on the spot.

Later that day, Estiarte called Pep, who had been in the dark about the whole idea and was taken aback by the news. "He said something like: 'What on earth do they want from you?'" Estiarte remembers.

After the initial surprise, Pep was delighted with the appointment – and the new regime at Barcelona had its second Olympic hero.

These were tough times at Barça – the board was fighting a vote of no confidence. They would emerge victorious, but only at the expense of Soriano, who chose to resign.

Estiarte travelled with Pep and the team to St Andrews in Scotland for preseason training. It was a pivotal camp, and

July 8, 2016: Pep Guardiola is unveiled as the new manager of Manchester City. *Barrington Coombs/Getty Images*

Manchester City chief executive Ferran Soriano, Pep Guardiola, chairman Khaldoon Al Mubarak and City director of football Txiki Begiristain at the Etihad in August 2016. *Getty Images*

The Brains Trust: Pep Guardiola with Domènec Torrent (right), his assistant manager for the first two seasons at City, and Mikel Arteta who replaced Torrent after his move to New York City FC. *Getty Images*

Pep and assistant Manel Estiarte wear yellow ribbons in support of jailed Catalan politicians during the Carabao Cup final between Arsenal and City at Wembley Stadium. *Getty Images*

Brandon Ashton, the popular kit man, celebrates with the FA Community Shield during the club's celebration parade after season 2018-19, when they completed a domestic clean sweep. *Getty Images*

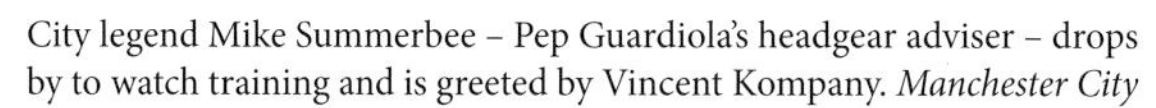

City legend Mike Summerbee – Pep Guardiola's headgear adviser – drops by to watch training and is greeted by Vincent Kompany. *Manchester City*

Pep issues instructions to John Stones as City's defensive frailties are exposed during the 2017 Champions League loss to Monaco at Stade Louis II. *Getty Images*

Bernardo Silva of Monaco gives his audition for Pep in that same match, here easing his way past Fernandinho and Sergio Agüero. *Getty Images*

Claudio Bravo (left) was Pep Guardiola's first attempt to solve the goalkeeping position, following the departure of Joe Hart. However it wasn't until Ederson's (right) arrival in the summer of 2017 that the club found their undisputed No.1. *Getty Images*

£120m worth of full-backs: Danilo, Benjamin Mendy and Kyle Walker. *Getty Images*

David Silva with his son Mateo, born prematurely in December 2017. *Getty Images*

And scoring in the 2018 Carabao Cup final, Pep's first trophy. *Getty Images*

İlkay Gündoğan clashes with Watford's Nordin Amrabat in December 2016, a challenge which ripped his cruciate ligaments and sidelined him for 32 matches. *Getty Images*

Noel Gallagher, Oasis frontman and celebrity City fan, celebrates the 2018-19 title alongside talismanic midfielder Fernandinho. *Manchester City*

Pep Guardiola's early relationship with star striker Sergio Agüero proved challenging after the arrival of Gabriel Jesus together with the Catalan's insistence that the City legend contribute more to the team's overall play. *Getty Images*

However, Agüero adapted his game and, together with Jesus, spearheaded City's domestic dominance in Pep's second and third seasons. *Getty Images*

Vincent Kompany celebrates on his day off after hearing the unexpected news of City's title win in April 2018. Manchester United's surprise loss to West Brom had handed them the league. *Getty Images*

And Kompany lifts the trophy on May 6, 2018, against Huddersfield. *Getty Images*

Kevin De Bruyne comes up against Bastian Schweinsteiger as he impresses Pep for Wolfsburg v Bayern in the Bundesliga on January 30, 2015. *Getty Images*

And becomes City's most important player during the 100-point 2017-18 league season. *Getty Images*

Signed as a midfielder, loaned out and then set for a transfer, Oleksandr Zinchenko transformed into City's starting left-back. He sends teammates selfies of after-hours gym work. *Getty Images*

Aymeric Laporte, signed during the winter window in 2017-18 after a lengthy pursuit, became Guardiola's first-choice at centre-back. *Getty Images*

The rivalry between Jurgen Klopp and Pep Guardiola was exported from Germany to the Premier League and has produced new standards in English football. *Getty Images*

John Stones clears the ball off his line against Liverpool in January 2019. Goalline technology showed the ball was 11.7mm away from crossing the line. Sergio Agüero and Leroy Sané would later score to give City the win and inflict Liverpool's only defeat of the whole campaign. *Manchester CIty*

After the crushing Champions League defeat by Spurs, Phil Foden's energy at training convinced Guardiola to start the teenager in the Premier League rematch. He was rewarded with the game's only goal, a diving header. *Getty Images*

After thrashing Watford 6-0 at Wembley, the City players celebrate their 2019 FA Cup success. *Getty Images*

'Don't shoot, Vinny!' Vincent Kompany's spectacular strike beats the despairing dive of Leicester goalkeeper Kasper Schmeichel to decide the key fixture in the 2018-19 title run-in. *Getty Images*

Raheem Sterling lifts the 2018-19 Premier League trophy. *Manchester City*

The City players and staff celebrate winning the 2018-19 Premier League title in the dressing room at Brighton. *Victoria Haydn/Manchester City FC via Getty Images*

Manchester is blue: the players celebrate historic trophy haul in front of their fans at the Etihad on May 12, 2019. *Manchester City FC/ Getty Images*

The authors interviewing Aymeric Laporte (above) and Bernardo Silva (below).

Estiarte integrated immediately with the technical team. When they returned to the Camp Nou, Pep told him: "We need you working with us, with the team and the coaches. You're wasted doing anything else."

The request was made to Laporta, Guardiola got his way and Estiarte joined the technical team. For the next four glorious but brutal years, Estiarte was Pep's constant companion. His influence now permeated the club – he was still consulting with the board on certain issues, but he was now focused primarily on his work with the new head coach.

From the start, Estiarte was ferociously protective of Pep. He'd happily take on some of the more onerous tasks of the boss's job while still juggling his external relations and press liaison duties.

Then, on April 24, 2012, everything changed. Barcelona 2 Chelsea 2 – a result that sent Chelsea to the Champions League final and denied Guardiola's team the chance for a third crown in four years.

For months before that game, the same question had followed Pep: would he extend his contract and remain at Barcelona beyond the summer?

"He hadn't said anything to me until then," says Estiarte. "Pep was always talking about 'next year' so I went along with the idea of staying on, but I could also see he was running on empty and I wasn't sure it was the right decision. It was a tough call to make. There were so many reasons to stay. And just as many to move on."

In the minutes after that heartbreaking Chelsea result, Pep took Estiarte to one side and told him he had made the decision to leave at the end of that season. Estiarte was the first to know. No new contract – the end of an era.

Estiarte remembers being struck by his phrase. "He said, 'There's still so much I could give to these players, but I can't give them *everything* I've got.'"

The following morning Estiarte called Sandro Rosell, who had replaced Laporta as president, to tell him that he, too, would be leaving the club.

At Bayern, Pep wanted things to work a little differently. During his time at Barça, Estiarte had been employed by the club, and his duties extended far beyond his work with Pep. Now Estiarte's time and energy would be dedicated solely to Guardiola and the first-team, but he wouldn't have an official job title.

Estiarte continued to act as a bulwark for Pep, heading off potential internal conflicts as they arose and even on occasion stepping in to "save Pep from himself", as a mutual friend wryly puts it.

After Germany, the move to Manchester did not come as much of a surprise to Estiarte. "It was this gradual process. After we'd been at Bayern for a while, Txiki and Joan Patsy started to turn up out of the blue. 'We're here to see Gündoğan,' they'd say. Or, 'We've just popped over to talk to Sané.' I knew they were up to something."

The closest person to Pep Guardiola on the City staff is also the one most likely to notice how he has changed over the years, from Barcelona, to Munich and Manchester, and how he has not.

Manel Estiarte: "The fundamentals haven't changed. He does tend to make the same kind of mistakes he used to, but now he spots it and sorts it out much more quickly. He really throws himself into every job and puts a lot of pressure on himself. He's paid a price for that over the years but I think it's a bit easier these days. He still works with that same intensity, still applies those same exacting standards, but he's definitely learned to focus his energy better."

EIGHTEEN

MAKING-OF MATCH: MANCHESTER UNITED 1 MANCHESTER CITY 2 DECEMBER 10, 2017

City and United have played 15 league games and Pep Guardiola's team are 12 points ahead of José Mourinho's. However, it is impossible to overstate the gulf in their respective playing styles.

Despite the fact that the two men's homes are about seven minutes apart, they have never bumped into each other in the 18 months since Guardiola arrived in England. They have been spotted at two of Manchester's finest eateries – Tapeo & Wine, and Wings – on the same days, just not at the same time. The paparazzi still chase the next chapter of the Pep and Jose Show, whether it's tea-for-two or full-on fisticuffs.

The Special One appears to be beneath a permanent thunder cloud. He is criticised on all sides, while Liverpool, Spurs and, above all, City are lauded for their attacking football. United have been dreadful for some time, but there is always someone else to blame: a player who failed to follow orders; a recruitment team who failed to sign the correct player; a referee who failed to make the right call.

City are on epic form, in the middle of a magnificent run of 18 straight victories. They set off for Old Trafford having walloped Liverpool and Arsenal at home and reigning champions Chelsea away.

City score from two set pieces – goals from David Silva and Nico Otamendi, either side of a Marcus Rashford strike. There are great saves from both goalkeepers, but City dominate the game and afterwards United are hurting. Post-match, the drama has an unexpected third act. Unsurprisingly, Mourinho is centre stage.

The City players have returned to the away dressing room. They put on their music and they are celebrating.

Mourinho goes to the City dressing room. He is unhappy with the noise levels. His words to Ederson light the spark. "Show a bit of respect, you've not won anything yet." The goalkeeper is a product of the harsh streets of São Paulo and not one to back down from confrontation. Edu Álvarez, the physio, drags the keeper away from trouble. In the middle of all this, Benjamin Mendy impishly increases the volume of the music.

Meanwhile, back-up has arrived for the United manager, with a delegation headed by Romelu Lukaku now filling the tight space between the corridor and the doorway into the away dressing room. Also caught in the crush are a couple of police officers who had been stationed, as is routine, in the tunnel.

The confrontation escalates suddenly. A bottle is thrown at Ederson, completely missing him. It bounces off Mikel Arteta, cutting his eyebrow, and then hits Álvarez in the face. All of it – furious shouts, bad-tempered shoving, spraying energy drinks and flying bottles – is over in a matter of seconds.

One United player recalled Mourinho's criticism of those who had missed the action. "When I went out, it was all over. It happened really fast. Then the boss started slagging us off, saying that only Lukaku and a couple of other players had had the guts to defend us. He told us we had to behave more like a real team. But there just hadn't been any time."

And where was Pep Guardiola in all of this? In the showers, the whole time. He emerges to tales of the bust-up, and his response is decisive. He tells his players: "You have every right to celebrate how you played and what you have achieved." Mendy produces confetti from somewhere. The celebrations continue.

Man United (4-2-3-1): de Gea; Valencia, Smalling, Rojo (Lindelöf 45), Young; Herrera (Mata 82), Matić; Martial, Lingard (Ibrahimović 76), Rashford; Lukaku
Man City (4-3-3): Ederson; Walker, Kompany (Gündoğan 45), Otamendi, Delph; De Bruyne, Fernandinho, D Silva; Sterling, Jesus (Mangala 59), Sané (B Silva 88)
Goals: Rashford 45+2; D Silva 43, Otamendi 54
Bookings: Rojo, Young, Rashford, Herrera, Walker, D Silva
Referee: Michael Oliver
Attendance: 74,847

NINETEEN

LEROY SANÉ: CHANGING GEARS

Looking back, Leroy Sané may remember 3pm on January 1, 2017, as the moment his life changed forever. As he walked out of Pep Guardiola's office that afternoon, one thing was clear: he was in deep shit.

Sané had joined the club the previous summer, a £37m signing from Schalke, a German international with the world at his feet. Yet by the turn of the year the 20-year-old winger had lived up to neither his price tag nor his reputation.

Sané had managed just 12 games so far, most as a substitute, and had missed out on almost all of City's big matches. He was not selected for the Champions League clash against Barcelona, he'd only been given 30 minutes against United and just three against Tottenham.

As the new year began, nobody would have predicted that 18 months later he would be voted the 2018 PFA Young Player of the Year, least of all Sané. He was under no illusion. He'd fucked up.

On New Year's Eve 2016, City lost 1-0 at Anfield, a contest that looked crucial to their title hopes in Pep's debut Premier League season. Two weeks previously, Sané had scored his first goal (against Arsenal) and hopes were high that his performance on the pitch might begin to match the brilliance he showed in training. Then, with brutal timing, he developed some minor muscle pain and was out for the game against Liverpool. The result and performance at Anfield made for a miserable end to the year for City's players.

The foreign players were bemoaning the lack of the winter break granted by other leagues around Europe. City would be playing Burnley at home on January 2 – no time to party.

Everyone was on their best behaviour. Except Sané. In a moment of youthful folly, he chose to spend New Year's Eve with his friends. He partied all night and showed up late for training the next day. Sané's showdown with Pep is still remembered in the corridors of the CFA, both for its brutality and for its transformative effect.

Afterwards, Guardiola would describe the young German as a "different guy" and talk about him as if he'd been a new purchase in the January market. That was precisely how the staff at City felt: the player they thought they had signed in the summer had finally arrived in Manchester.

Sané went on to play 24 times in the second half of that season, producing nine goals and eight assists over the whole campaign (he'd managed 12 games, one goal and two assists in the first half).

Guardiola had first spotted the young German's potential back when he was managing Bayern. Sané recalls: "I was playing at Schalke and my dad told me that Guardiola had expressed an interest. Then Pep himself called me up a few days later and we talked about his plans. He told me that he was going to City and that he had one intention – to make history. Obviously, when someone like him tells you that, you sit up and take notice. I knew he was a great coach and I already admired his work at Bayern and Barcelona."

It wasn't a difficult decision for the talented winger. The time was right to try something new.

"I like a challenge. I like the idea of discovering new things – playing for a different club. I was really excited. It was such an honour that the best coach in the world had called me up and said: 'I want you in my team.'"

In his enthusiasm the youngster may have been underestimating the difficulties involved in moving to a new club, in a different country, at such a young age.

Initially, he struggled. "Every country has its own culture and practices. At the beginning everything about the lifestyle here was difficult to get used to. I struggled with the language and didn't think I was ever going to feel at home in Manchester.

"I was nervous at the start but I'm not the kind to give up and I don't scare easily. I respected my new teammates, but I wasn't intimidated by them. You come here and you have to prove yourself in front of these great players, in front of the coach and the entire world. You need to show everyone that you've got what it takes and you deserve to be here, in this championship, in this club."

He arrived at City carrying an injury, missed much of preseason and didn't debut in Guardiola's squad until City's fourth league match. That was the derby, at Old Trafford. With City ahead and half an hour left he took over from Raheem Sterling. He found a lot of space behind the United defence and spearheaded several counter-attacks, but nothing came off. In the end City fans would have been left with the impression that they had signed a talented kid. One to keep an eye on.

"It's such an enormous stage," he remembers. "I'd never played at that level before and was a bit thrown by it."

Sané had taken the world by storm in a spectacular Champions League debut for Robbie Di Matteo's Schalke as the Bundesliga side went toe-to-toe with Madrid, winning 4-3 in the Santiago Bernabéu in 2015. This, however, was an altogether different experience.

"Back then I was still living with my parents," he recalls. "Schalke was like my second home and I had known my teammates for a long time. I felt totally secure, well within my comfort zone – even against Real Madrid at the Bernabéu. Then I came on at Old Trafford. It was my first game with City and I'd only been training for about two weeks. It was totally different! I mean . . . *Old Trafford*!" Sané had never lived away from home before and opted to buy a flat in the same building as Gündoğan, Silva and Guardiola, making do with the city centre Radisson Blu Hotel whilst the construction work was done.

It was a new situation in more ways than one. At Schalke, Sané had been the star. In Manchester, he was just another player. "My teammates didn't know me when I first arrived, but they'd probably heard a few stories and I worried they'd be thinking: 'Why the hell did we pay big bucks for this guy?'

"People expected me to perform immediately and it felt like huge pressure. I was grateful because Pep, his team and the rest of the club had my back. They were always very encouraging and he kept saying, 'Don't worry about it. Relax and just play your game.'"

Leroy Sané was born on July 11, 1996, in Essen, a city of 590,000 inhabitants in the Ruhr Valley, the industrial centre of Germany. Football was in his genes. His father, Suleimán, had emigrated from his native Senegal and ended up in Germany playing for FC Wattenscheid 09. He was a talented footballer: good enough to play for Senegal in three different African Cup of Nations tournaments.

Sané's mother, Regina Weber, is one of the best-ever German gymnasts, winning 32 medals during her career, including a bronze from the Los Angeles Olympics in 1984. Regina was a popular sports celebrity in 1980s Germany, known for her no-

nonsense personality, as her middle son can confirm. "If you ask me who's tougher, Pep or my mum, I'd have to say my mum. She's ferocious.

"My parents never pressured me about my football. They always said that the most important thing was to enjoy playing. They wanted me to follow my passions and luckily football's always been the thing that matters most to me."

All three Sané boys followed their father into football and his little brother Sidi is a nifty centre-forward currently playing for Schalke's under-16 team.

Leroy started out at Wattenscheid before signing for Schalke, aged nine, in 2005. After a stint at Bayern Leverkusen between 2008 and 2011, he eventually returned to the Schalke academy, where his career really took off. He played for Germany at every youth level before progressing into the national team. He made his debut in November 2015 in Paris, a game that took place as suicide bombers and gunmen struck outside the stadium and elsewhere in the city.

He had yet to play a full season as a regular for Schalke, but already clubs across Europe were positioning themselves in pursuit of the young winger. Near the front of the pack was a fellow German, who had witnessed Sané's emergence in the Bundesliga and was now working in England.

Jürgen Klopp, now Liverpool manager, spoke to Sané on several occasions, but in the end, the player went with Pep and City, a decision he's never regretted.

"When you start out you have no idea how far you can go, but from our very first day I felt that Guardiola made me a better player. He's shown me how I should play, how to move with or without the ball, how to make use of space. He told me that I had complete freedom on the pitch, like Messi. Well, not exactly like him because obviously that's impossible [he laughs]. He told me to enjoy my football, to just do what a forward does best."

Under Pep's guidance, Sané has found his place both on the pitch and in the dressing room. He is very close to three of his English teammates: John Stones, Raheem Sterling and Kyle Walker, and regularly competes with Sterling and Walker to see who is the fastest. When he registered a speed of 35.48 km/hour, Sané became the fastest player ever clocked in the Premier League.

He also comes out top in another category. "Leroy Sané has the best physique in the team," says one of the medics. "The smallest percentage of body fat in the squad, about 6.5 per cent, which is less than Michael Jordan in his prime. He's just fibre and muscle, it's incredible. He's an athlete and could easily make it as an 800-metre runner."

Sané also gets on well with his fellow German, İlkay Gündoğan. It's not long ago that the fierce Ruhr derby made them rivals, if not quite enemies. They played on either side of that historic rivalry, Gündoğan for Thomas Tuchel's Dortmund and Sané for the Gelsenkirchen club Schalke 04. Each of them will still nip back to see their respective *alma mater* clubs in the Bundesliga when they can. At which point the rivalry resumes.

Unlike many of his peers, Sané has no particular match rituals and doesn't consider himself superstitious. He does, however, have a penchant for body art and attaches great significance to his eight tattoos. "They all relate to my family, my friends or my childhood." One of them covers his whole back and is an image of the player himself, arms outstretched in his goal celebration.

He credits much of his technical development at City to the many hours he has spent with Mikel Arteta. "People always ask me about training under Pep, but the things I've learnt from Mikel Arteta! When I was being used more as a wing-back than an attacker or winger, I remember Mikel saying to me one day: 'I know that you hate that position, but you have to be smart about this. You're young and you can use this to learn.'

"We get on brilliantly, he's a lovely guy and a great coach. And he's always right. He'll watch me at training and then afterwards he'll tell me what he thinks. He doesn't just suggest something and leave me to get on with it. He'll repeat it again and again and watch me trying it out, so that I don't forget. That way I've always got his instructions in my head. We talk a lot about my movements, how to move into space, what to do with the ball, when I need to use my speed. He'll also tell me to have more patience, to hold back so that I can open up the field, even if I'm not getting a lot of time on the ball."

Arteta breaks down the way Guardiola's wide attackers are coached to use their explosive pace only when they can cause maximum damage to an opponent.

Mikel Arteta: "Our strikers have to learn to control their sprints, to hold back and wait before erupting. To go through the gears. The natural thing is to try to hit sixth gear, top speed, because they're so fast these guys. But it's important to mess with the defender's head – to vary your pace and trick him. Sané's really improved in that sense. We've told him when he cuts inside, he needs to immediately slow down, thereby forcing his marker to decelerate, then when he speeds up again, he'll lose the guy. Messi produces all these nuances at a hundred miles an hour because he's technically brilliant. These lads aren't quite at that level yet, so if they exaggerate the changes of pace, it works better.

"Leroy was a bit disoriented when he first arrived and required a period of adaptation. We totally expected that. A player like him needs time to build his confidence, consolidate his position and earn the respect and trust of his teammates. He also had to learn to take control of phases of games – things could pass him by initially. But then something just clicked and he made a huge leap forward.

"Even the way we train was completely new for him. We do everything in tight spaces with everyone moving very fast with no room to run into. It was very tough for him."

Sané agrees. "I found the training at City much harder physically – a mirror image of the Premier League itself. But the most difficult thing for me was the speed the ball moved at, particularly in training. One-touch, one-touch, one-touch. It's crucial you know what you're going to do well before you receive the ball."

Arteta was the ideal man to show him how to play the City way. "I tried to boost his confidence," remembers the coach. "I think he was maybe a bit thrown and that can create a lot of insecurity in a player, particularly one so young. When he wasn't on the ball he lost focus and dozed off. We used videos to show him where he should look for space, what his options were. We talked him through the mistakes he was making and taught him to show much greater intensity."

By his second year at City, Sané had realised all the potential shown in the second half of his first season. In the fourth league game, against Liverpool, he shone, scoring twice and leaving Klopp's team in tatters with a breathtaking second-half performance. He was taking over games against top-six contenders and backs-to-the-wall relegation battlers alike. He gave one such memorable performance on a freezing night at the Emirates, on March 1. Stuart Brennan from the *Manchester Evening News* scored Sané 10/10 in the man-by-man ratings, that rarest of accolades from any football writer. He scored and gave two more assists all in the space of the first 33 minutes. "Sa-né! Oh Leroy Sané runs down the wing for me!" they chant in the terraces and the bars around the stadium, to the tune of Buddy Holly's *Heartbeat*.

Sané finished the second season with 14 goals and 19 assists across all competitions. In the Premier League he was behind only Kevin De Bruyne in assists and had played a part, one way or another, in 25 goals. It was, by every measure, his best season yet.

Sané was named PFA Young Player of the Year in the summer of 2018 and appeared a certain selection for Joachim Löw, the manager of the Germany team heading for Russia to defend their World Cup. However, Löw left the winger behind – reports suggested that the coach predicted problems with the player if he was not a regular starter. From that moment on, Sané seemed to be under a cloud.

Despite being one of the few City players to have the summer off, he began the first three league games on the bench and for the fourth, against Newcastle on September 1, he was omitted completely from the squad.

Both Guardiola and, separately, Sergio Agüero and City's other captains felt the need to talk to Sané about his behaviour at training and within the team. They were concerned about what they perceived as a change in attitude and focus, and they wondered if it was related to changes in his personal life: Sané had just become a father to a baby girl and had recently lost some of his close confidantes.

Manel Estiarte: "The reality is that it's very common for sportsmen to go through that kind of thing and people often pass judgement without having the slightest idea of what's happening in the person's personal life. Leroy's very young. Barely 23 years old and he's still learning. It's a process. Totally normal. We can be far too demanding of players at times. It's important to try to understand what they're going through."

However, 2018-19 wasn't a total washout for the young German. He played 1,000 fewer first-team minutes than he had during the previous season, yet he still marked up 16 goals and 18 assists (ranking 10th and 11th respectively in the Premier League). Not too shabby.

This paradox was illustrated perfectly in a match that carried huge personal significance for Sané. Back at Schalke, his boyhood club, in the Champions League, Sané remained on the bench until the 78th minute, when City were 2-1 down and reduced to 10 men after a red card for Nico Otamendi. Sané levelled the score with an incredible free kick and provided the perfect spark for a City revival completed by Raheem Sterling's late goal. In the starting XI for the return leg, Sané produced another goal plus three assists in a 7-0 win. He also scored the decisive goal against Liverpool on January 3 in a win that would have a huge influence on the title race. He scored the crucial second goal in the final Manchester derby of the season, one of the games City simply had to win if they were going to beat Liverpool to the title.

Despite turning to Sané less frequently, Pep and City rebuffed a move by Bayern Munich for the player in the summer of 2019 which included public comments by some of the German club's superstars praising the 23-year-old.

Then, 12 minutes into the Community Shield, the first game of the new season, Sané damaged his anterior cruciate ligament and his participation in the entire campaign was placed in doubt. Bayern diverted to other targets.

Interviewed for this book shortly before that injury, Guardiola spoke about a young player for whom he is prepared to wait, but he also hinted at the complicated curve of Sané's career at City.

"Sané struggled a bit when he first arrived, he was very shy, but once he hit his stride, he went on to have two incredible years. Last season was maybe a bit tougher for him, but he had moments of sheer brilliance. It's up to him to continue to progress because he's got everything it takes.

"An athlete's career doesn't always follow a progressive line and you'll always have less successful years. It happens to all athletes, apart from one [he's referring to Leo Messi].

"It's about his mental attitude. If he wants to keep improving, if he wants everyone to see how much he's progressed, then first he has to accept that there's room for improvement and apply himself. Then he'll be a better player. Because he's got the talent.

"But there are some things a coach can't give you. You're the only one that can make it happen. I'm sure he's more than capable of it. He's got the intelligence, the hunger and the talent. He has an impressive physique and is still very, very young. He's still got everything in front of him."

TWENTY

TORRENT, KIDD, ARTETA, PLANCHART AND BORRELL: THE BRAINS TRUST

Pep Guardiola's attitudes about the coaches in his team crystallised one night after he watched a documentary about the All Blacks. "I don't want followers around me, I want leaders; people who are willing to take full responsibility, who take ownership of their decisions and can think for themselves."

Txiki Begiristain: "The best thing about Pep's team is that they'll never go along with what he says just to keep him happy, they always speak their minds. They question, pick ideas apart, help him develop new concepts. The final decision is up to Pep and he'll do what he thinks best, but not before it's been debated back and forward. It's how he makes decisions."

Domènec Torrent has been Pep's assistant since Guardiola left Barcelona. A talented, athletic winger in his youth, capable of explosive bursts of speed, he was scouted by Barcelona as a teenager and offered a contract. The young Torrent met with the club's representatives in a local bar in his home village of Santa Coloma de Farners, signed the contract and was all set to move to the big city when word came through: Barcelona had realised that he fell just outside of the age bracket for the intended age group.

Torrent signed instead for Zaragoza. His first game for the *Blanquillos* was a friendly against Atlético Calatayud. He was stretchered off with a shattered knee, his dreams of elite football in pieces. Torrent took a job with the tax authority and began to coach the kids in his village. His reputation grew and he moved swiftly through the coaching levels. In Spain's lower leagues, he coached Palafrugell, Palamós, and then Girona, before he joined Guardiola during his time with Barcelona B. The two men remained in tandem until Torrent agreed to become head coach of New York City in the summer of 2018.

Pep was sad to lose Torrent, but understood his friend's need to take up the challenge in America.

"Domè deserves it. I've never wanted yes-men around me, and he's never been that. He's happy to try new things and take risks, so don't think for a minute that he's ever held me back. At times it's been me saying, 'Come on man, you've gone too far this time.' I just hope he gets the same kind of luck that I've had. Nothing would have turned out the same for me without him."

The backstories of Torrent and Carles Planchart, Manchester City's head of analysis, are intertwined. Their mothers were friends, and so the two boys were close as they grew up. When Torrent first met his wife, Gemma, he discovered that her father had completed military service with Planchart's dad. They have spent a lifetime talking football.

Planchart hails from Arbúcies, a village near Girona, where he started playing for the local club at the age of 16. A tough, powerful central defender, he quickly earned the captain's armband and became something of a celebrity on Spain's amateur football circuit. "It wasn't that I was a thug, I was just … let's say, quite an aggressive player," he laughs.

"Aggressive?" Torrent teases. "I've never seen anything like it. He was like Otamendi and Puyol and any three more like them, all rolled into one."

Planchart never expected to make it in professional football and after studying law (which he loathed) went to work for the family business in Mollet, near Barcelona. He continued to play at the weekend, striking fear into unsuspecting strikers and always wearing his lucky (if somewhat shabby) vest under his strip. Until one Saturday game in the town of Artes.

It was the weekend of the local *fiesta mayor* (an annual street party) and the Saturday match got out of hand. Planchart's lucky undershirt was torn beyond repair. There was a Sunday game too and, forced to play without his vital vest, he tore all the ligaments in his knee. He tried to return to the game he loves, but after six matches Planchart had to admit defeat and stop playing for good.

However, the misfortune provided the two old friends with the chance to work together as Torrent progressed on his coaching journey.

Today Planchart's job is to study the opposition's game as well as their own. At City he coordinates the work of three analysts. Planchart can give you a detailed, second-by-second analysis of the game's key moments as they happen.

He learned his trade in the Spanish third division, when the games he watched were played by amateurs on muddy pitches and the idea of opposition analysis was in its infancy.

"Initially we'd send Gordillo, one of our former players, to video games with one of those cameras you use to record baptisms and communions. He'd give us the film on Monday and we'd connect up two VHS recorders to cut it, leaving us with six minutes of film to show the players on Thursday. You should have seen it! It was rough and ready, but it did the job."

Whilst working in the lower divisions, Planchart and Torrent got to know Alexanko, then youth system coordinator at the Camp Nou. He offered them jobs as scouts for Barça B, who were about to be coached by Guardiola. They'd spend their weekends watching up to seven games each whilst Planchart's niece's boyfriend would film the opponent they were most interested in. The rest of the week would then be spent preparing reports for Pep.

To begin with, they made do with the equipment already available: Nacsport (video analysis software previously used by Pep's assistant, Tito Vilanova) and the Digital Video Sports programme used by Barça's handball division.

That same year, Barça B were promoted and Joan Laporta, the club president, appointed Pep as first-team coach. Guardiola got on the phone with a simple message: Meet me in The Cave. Guardiola was referring to the coach's office at Barça, hidden away deep in the bowels of the Camp Nou, using the shorthand of a man who had spent the majority of his life at Barça.

"We didn't even know where the first-team's dressing room was, never mind the coach's office, so we kept getting lost," remembers Planchart.

When they finally arrived, they were faced by the power triumvirate of Laporta, Begiristain and Pep.

"I can't coach the first-team without these two," Guardiola told Laporta.

The president turned to the two analysts. "Okay. How much would you expect to earn?"

Recalls Planchart: "We were completely out of our depth. We said: 'Oh, whatever you think is fair Joan, we don't really know how all this works.'"

It was July 14, 2008. Torrent's birthday.

Almost as soon as they graduated to the first-team, they switched to a specially designed software package nicknamed 'Eric' which they continued to use throughout four trophy-laden years with Pep at Barcelona.

When Pep took them with him to Munich, they switched to Sportscode, the most widely used football analysis software in the world. The efficiency of the Bundesliga was a revelation. "It was heaven," Planchart says. "The stadia facilities were all top-notch. We could work in real time, go down to the dressing room at half-time – the Bundesliga made our job so much easier."

At City, Planchart and his assistants work with state-of-the-art software and their biggest challenge is the drastic time pressures caused by England's incessant flood of matches.

"I'm not necessarily the best analyst in the world but I do have one big advantage: I know exactly what Pep needs and that allows me to respond to his questions very quickly," says Planchart. "He'll say something like, 'Do you remember how we built that defence against Schalke?' and I'll know exactly what he's talking about. It makes a huge difference when you're preparing five matches in 10 days."

Like Pep, Brian Kidd won the European Cup at Wembley as a player. On his 19th birthday, in 1968, he scored the decisive third goal for Manchester United against Benfica. Today, the former Busby Babe is the voice of experience on the City staff.

Kidd was born in Collyhurst, north Manchester, and still lives close by. He played for both Manchester clubs with distinction and has coached both through glorious eras: as assistant to Alex Ferguson as he turned United into a winning machine, and then with Roberto Mancini, Manuel Pellegrini and now Guardiola at City.

When Pep arrived, Txiki Begiristain made the call to include Kidd in the new coach's young and predominantly Spanish technical team.

"Brian has done so much for us. I knew nothing about him when Txiki first put his name forward but boy, was he the right choice," said Pep. "I didn't come to Manchester with a 20-strong entourage. I came with four people and it's only worked because everyone at City has been so welcoming and accommodating, Brian even more than most. He has put his heart and soul into this project and I'll be eternally grateful. He's not only the most courteous person I know, he understands the parameters of his role here and respects them. If I ask Brian something, I know I'm going to get a clear, carefully judged answer."

Fitness coach Lorenzo Buenaventura: "I work with him a lot. We organise the outdoor training sessions together. I always try to grab a coffee with him after lunch. He's got so much to teach us and has been a huge help to me personally."

Brian Kidd: "I felt so honoured when they contacted me to say they wanted me on board. I'd followed the boss's career and I was assistant to Ferguson when he played against us for Barcelona, so I knew what a naturally gifted player he was. He's also very sharp, but in many ways he's not what I was expecting at all. This is a man who's famous all over the world, who achieved so much at Barça and Bayern and yet what strikes you immediately is his humility. He reminds me of the great Matt Busby, my first coach. It's something about his mannerisms, the way he speaks to the team.

"He's created such good team spirit here and it's not only the sense of unity and brotherhood you see out on the pitch. That sense of shared purpose goes right to the top. It's something we all feel, at every level of the club."

Guardiola and Kidd play golf in Abu Dhabi when the team is there. It's Pep's chance to pepper his assistant coach with questions: "What was Sir Bobby Charlton like to play with? Tell me about Summerbee as a footballer. What about George Best?"

Pep Guardiola: "It's like sitting in the front row watching your favourite movie."

Kidd is guided by a strong faith and told Pep on day one that he would attend mass on Sunday mornings, regardless of the fixture list. For away trips, Marc Boixasa's support team finds him a church close to the team hotel.

"It's important to me," explains Kidd. "I never miss. It's not about feeling obliged to attend. It's the opposite of that – a personal decision I've made because my faith gives me serenity and certainty. I never pray for anything football related. I pray for more personal things."

The vastly experienced, 70-year-old Kidd sits on Pep's technical team alongside a colleague at the start of his coaching career – one who is still close enough to his elite playing days to join in the most demanding small-sided sessions running at the CFA.

Mikel Arteta was born in San Sebastián, where he grew up playing on Concha Beach. Barça signed him when he was 14. Arteta was a No.10, but his new club quickly saw his potential as an organising midfielder – a position then held in the first-team by one Pep Guardiola. Aged 16 he was promoted into the first-team's pre-season camp, but within a year he'd been loaned to PSG.

Mikel Arteta: "Pep was 29 and captain. Then there was Xavi queuing up behind him. Imagine! I knew that if I wanted to get any game time, I'd be better off developing my career elsewhere."

His decision paid off. In France, Arteta flourished, influenced by his talented new teammate Mauricio Pochettino, and the two became very close. "He's like a big brother to me."

Even then, this was a star-studded PSG. He played alongside Ronaldinho, Gabriel Heinze, Juan Pablo Sorín, and Nicolas Anelka. Arteta shone. At the end of a season and a half, PSG wanted to make the move permanent, but Rangers moved in with a better offer and he was off to Scotland, where he won a domestic treble in the first of two seasons.

A brief, unsuccessful return to Spain with Real Sociedad followed in 2004, before he returned to Britain by signing for Everton in January 2005. He stayed at Goodison for eight years until becoming captain of Arsenal.

Arteta and Guardiola always kept in touch, and Arteta lived in the same neighbourhood as Pep's brother, Pere, when he was based in London. When Barça drew Chelsea in the Champions League (in 2012), Pep picked up the phone to pick his old friend's brain about their upcoming opponent. Impressed by Arteta's critical analysis, Pep made a mental note to seek his advice more often.

In season 2015-16, Pep's Bayern Munich played Arsenal in the Champions League and Arteta got a chance to talk to Pep in the players' zone after the game.

"We had a good chat and at the end he told me that he wanted to work with me if he ever moved to England. So when I retired I called him and said: 'Is that job still available?'"

There was just one problem: Arteta had already agreed with his wife, an actress, that, if she took care of the domestic side of things during his playing years, he would free her up to pursue her own career when he retired. She's now doing just that and lives in Los Angeles, with the couple's children. The situation is not perfect, but Arteta has learned to make the best of it.

At City, Arteta works closely with the players, often on a one-to-one basis, helping them understand key concepts or giving them the guidance they need to improve their performance. "It's vital that management is in touch with the players and Pep just doesn't have the time to spend time with all 24 of them every day," explains Arteta. "It's crucial that they feel able to tell us what they think they need to improve."

His tiny office has three glass walls, through which he can often be seen huddled round the meeting table next to a player or gesticulating at the touchscreen whiteboard as he explains tactics or set pieces with a group. Most of City's stars have spent time with him there over the last three years.

Arteta has been on a sharp learning curve since joining City's coaching team in July 2016, immediately after retiring as a player. "From the start I was absolutely fascinated by Pep's work ethic, by his ability to transmit his ideas to the players and convince them that they're going to work. It's incredible to see how he simplifies even the most complicated things so that they appear straightforward and easy. It's very difficult to reach footballers like that.

"The very first day Pep took training, he got the whole squad out on the pitch and told them: 'Manchester City does *this* when we have the ball and we do *that* when we don't have it.' And all of them understood exactly how we were going to play. It was non-negotiable. That talk lasted just 15 minutes, but in those 15 minutes City was born. Everyone knew what would be asked of them from then on.

"He explained that sometimes we would adapt our game – 'There'll be alterations here and there depending on how our opponents attack and defend but basically our football will be exactly as I've just said.'

"We'd all watched his Barça and Bayern play and Pep insisted that this philosophy would continue. He showed them footage and kept talking the players through his ideas. It was clear that there was no going back. We knew how Pep's Manchester City was going to be. And all it took was 15 minutes."

Although he's worked closely with a lot of players, he has had a particular influence on Leroy Sané. "He was just a kid and here he was, at a different club, where everything felt strange and new. I had a similar experience when I went to PSG, so I had some idea of what he was experiencing. You just have to push through it, but it's not easy and you need to know that the coaching staff are behind you. Everything's different: training methods, having to play in much tighter spaces, a much faster game with no space to run into – and he struggled initially.

"My priority was to reassure him how much faith myself and the rest of the technical team had in him. I thought he'd be feeling a bit lost and that always makes you insecure, particularly at that age. We wanted to boost his confidence. We showed him a lot of videos so we could point out where the spaces were, what options he had, the mistakes he was making, how he could increase his intensity. That's really my role here: to look for what's missing in a player's game. If I spot something, there's no point in waiting for the guy to tell me about it. He might take three months to get round to it. Opening up like that to a coach, pointing out your own weaknesses, that's not easy. What we do is create a safe place so that the players feel comfortable about sharing with us. That way we can then give them the tools to make the improvements they need."

Pep showed Arteta that same level of trust when he arrived at City. The Spaniard had joined a technical team that was already a functioning unit, but immediately felt like a trusted lieutenant. Pep called him into his office one day in his first season, prior to a home match against Arsenal.

"You're in charge for this game," the coach told him. "You're more than capable of taking the team through the game. So, it's up to you. Do what you think is best."

Pep remembers the game well. "He knew the team much better than I did, he'd only stopped playing with them two months before. He knew what to expect from Wenger and I really had no doubts about entrusting the game to him. So I spoke to the players and told them, 'Mikel's in charge this week.' I think they were maybe a bit taken aback initially but it was the logical thing to do, given Mikel's experience with our opponents."

Mikel Arteta: "I'm not an idiot, so I'd already done a bit of preparatory work. I assumed he'd ask my opinion. So I told him how I saw it going – 'This is what they'll do, so I'd plan to play like this.'

"He liked my ideas and we went with my plan." The result? A 2-1 win, with the decisive goal from Raheem Sterling.

Arteta still likes to participate actively in training, but now the competitive spirit takes a back seat to his analytical mind. "It's also a brilliant way to judge how effective we are, because you're seeing it from the inside. I can see immediately if a certain position doesn't give me enough time to close down a space, or if I'm arriving too late, or ending up on my own as we press – 'No, this won't work. They'll outnumber us in this zone.'

"As a player you follow orders, you do what you're told. But your perspective changes when you coach. You can observe how the tactics you've planned actually work, from the inside. And then you see things you wouldn't have spotted otherwise."

Rodolfo Borrell is the fourth pillar of the technical team. Borrell first came to England in 2009 to join Rafa Benítez's Liverpool after 10 years working in Barça's youth system. At Liverpool he started out managing the under-18s and then took over the academy where Sterling, amongst others, learned their trade. Begiristain initially brought him to City to develop the training methodology in City's own youth academy and, when Pep arrived, Borrell took on the role of player liaison.

Borrell also helps the technical staff identify those youngsters who are ready for first-team action, without, in the first instance, thinking about what position they'll fill. He has a forensic knowledge of academy players throughout English football.

These five men – Torrent, Planchart, Arteta, Kidd and Borrell – formed the team without which, according to Pep himself, he'd never have come this far. However, in the summer of 2018, Torrent departed for the big job in New York.

He had been the architect of City's set-piece game that played a huge role in their record-breaking 100-point season. In 2017-18, they scored 17 goals from set pieces (eight from corners, one direct free-kick, three indirect free-kicks and five penalties). That's 16 per cent of all the goals they scored on the way to the title. They conceded just three goals from set pieces – 9 percent of the total in the 'against' column.

Planchart: "You have to put a lot of work into that kind of strategic planning and it never feels like there are enough hours in the day, but we've made the most of the work we have done. For a team like us, who defend zonally, we've been extremely efficient."

Torrent's great sadness is that his mother, Carme, passed away before seeing him win the Premier League in 2018. "I was at the hospital with her on the day of the Feyenoord game [in 2017] and we watched it together [the only game Torrent missed that season]. She was very ill, but she loved her football and that day she said to me, 'You're playing brilliantly. You're going to win everything this year.' She was a visionary, my mum."

TWENTY-ONE

DAVID SILVA: THE MAGICIAN

It is December 13, 2017, and City's players are in the Marriott Hotel, Swansea, when David Silva gets a call. It's his girlfriend, Yessica Suarez, and she has dreadful news: 24 weeks into her pregnancy, she is losing blood. Silva is desperately worried and tells his long-term friend and club physio, Edu Álvarez, what's happening. Even before they leave the hotel for the Liberty Stadium, plans are being made to fly them to Valencia from Manchester the following day. There, Yessica will be treated at the Casa de Salud hospital.

But there's still a game to be played and Álvarez is on the point of telling Pep not to let Silva play. The player is literally shaking at the thought of losing the baby and Álvarez doesn't believe it is feasible for him to clear his mind. Not only does Silva start, but he's the best player on the pitch, scoring two goals and just missing out on a hat-trick.

The following day he and Yessica take a private plane to Valencia, a trip he'll make back and forth frequently over the next few months: from the CFA to the hospital in Valencia, which is where he'll be when he celebrates City winning the title.

"I'll be grateful to Pep for the rest of my life. What he did for us was absolutely incredible," said City's No.21.

What did Pep do? When Silva's boss realised what was happening, he called the player into his office. Manel Estiarte was also there.

Pep said: "You must go to Valencia when you need to and come back when you can. Just tell me when you can play and don't worry about a thing. Just let me know when you think you'll be able to play."

Guardiola looks back on this as an automatic decision. "Anyone in my position would have done the same. David played whenever he could. What was happening in his personal life was much more important."

Silva was absent for the Tottenham game (the first he'd missed so far) but made it back to play Bournemouth on December 23, where he was spectacular. Four days later, City were in Newcastle celebrating another win while Silva was in Valencia, welcoming his son into the world.

Baby Mateo had been born prematurely and his parents were worried, particularly because male premature babies often struggle more than females. Pep's official line in public was that Silva had taken some leave for personal reasons, but after wild rumours began to circulate, the player issued a statement: "I want to thank all of you for the love and good wishes received in the past few weeks. Special thanks to my teammates and all at the club for understanding my situation. Also I want to share with you the birth of my son Mateo, who was born extremely pre-term and is fighting day by day with the help of the medical team."

Silva values his privacy – his friends say that in a perfect world he'd be pixelated when he plays, so that nobody would know what he looks like, allowing him to be completely anonymous during his downtime. The added public attention his absences attracted made an already painful situation far worse.

Silva broke down just once during this period – the day his son was born. The doctors told him the news and the tears came. "I saw how hard Mateo was fighting to survive and I said to myself: 'If he can keep fighting like that, I'm certainly not going to let this beat me.'"

Silva limited his absences as much as possible – a policy that wasn't helped when some dodgy shellfish in Valencia gave him food poisoning. When he did manage to play, he was superb.

The first time City played without Silva, after news had reached the squad that Mateo had a problem with his lungs, Pep didn't give a traditional pre-match team talk. He simply told his men to play for Silva, to win the match for his newborn son.

City thrashed Tottenham 4-1 that day. After scoring, Kevin De Bruyne ran to the corner to celebrate in front of the cameras. Lifting two fingers of his right hand and his left index finger, he formed the number 21.

During this time, a photo of a private zone of the CFA (where no phones are allowed) was doing the rounds on social media. Pep was furious and banned all mobiles for three days – all except that of Silva.

Silva played 3,198 minutes across 40 games in season 2017-18. Only seven players played more. He scored 10 goals and made 14 assists. The top four players in the Premier League assists table were all City: Leroy Sané, Kevin De Bruyne and then Silva, tied for third with Raheem Sterling.

Kevin De Bruyne: "David's the player of the year. He does what he wants, when he wants."

Mikel Arteta: "David's mental strength has been amazing. I always said that he's the Premier League player I found hardest to mark. He controls the space behind you brilliantly. I was a defensive midfielder and he'd roam all over the pitch. It used to drive me nuts. Whenever I'm asked which of our players has the most unique qualities, it's the same answer: David. For me, of all the greats who have come to the English game, he's the best. People don't always get how rare it is for a midfielder to create space like that. It's enormously difficult to achieve what he does. He's also very consistent, always at the top of his game. You never see him go down a gear. No one should underestimate how tough it is to maintain that level of performance."

Silva isn't comfortable with this kind of individual praise, but he's had to suck it up, not least from Guardiola. "I knew he was good, but he's blown me away," says the manager. "When Silva played for Valencia, Unai Emery told me to sign him, but for some reason he slipped through our fingers. Just think what he could have done playing in that Barça side! Getting the chance to work with him was one of the reasons I came to City."

When faced with such tributes, it is toward Pep that Silva most readily redirects the conversation. "He's done tremendous work for this team and deserves huge recognition for it. It hasn't been easy. We play attractive football and it's also a very participative game – if not unique, then identifiable to us. Fun to watch, fun to play. Pep makes very smart decisions. For example, he's changed my position. I used to play more on the wing but now I'm closer to the middle of the pitch and have much more freedom to roam. It suits me down to the ground, because I get much more time on the ball."

Mancunian Brian Kidd sees strong comparisons with one of England's all-time greats. "Bobby Charlton was exactly the same in attitude. Whether or not he personally was having the best game, it didn't matter: he always wanted the ball. Always showed, never hid. David's spectacular, one of the best we've seen in this country. When you have that kind of player who always wants to be on the ball, bossing things, who never looks pressurised – that's a great sign."

After nine years in England, Silva is at last getting the recognition he deserves. Take, for example, the words of Thierry Henry: "He's the best creative midfielder I've ever seen in the Premier League."

Or Jamie Carragher: "David Silva is the best player in the history of Manchester City."

At City he's enjoyed the level of recognition he deserves from the very first day. The story goes that Danilo was so bowled over by his performances at training that he sought Pep out to ask: "is David Silva always that good?"

"David Silva is one of the best I've seen in my life," says Mike Summerbee, the former City winger, now international ambassador for the club. "He has an excellent football brain, interprets matches perfectly and does everything with such style. His name will go down in the history books as one of City's greats."

Summerbee recently took a holiday with his partner in Gran Canaria, where Silva was born. They stayed in a hotel recommended by the player ("they let us have the most spectacular suite you've ever seen") and, even in absence, somehow Silva once again came up with a solution to a particularly tight spot. When the holidaymakers went to the player's hometown of Arguineguín, they visited a famous restaurant there, only to discover queues snaking out of the building. Summerbee went for the Hail Mary, walking to the front of the line and explaining that he was a friend of the town's favourite son. "We were immediately led inside."

Before each game, the Peaky Blinders on the kit staff heat up his boots, by special request of *El Mago*, using a steamer acquired for the job. For away games, a hairdryer must suffice. The tricks of the magician's trade.

In June 2019, David Silva arranged a press conference in Gran Canaria. He wanted to confirm a plan that had been long discussed: he would leave City at the end of season 2019-20, completing 10 years at the club as one of the greatest and most influential overseas players to have graced the Premier League. "I can never see myself playing against City for another team," he said. A curtain call at Las Palmas, in his native Gran Canaria, is hardly ruled out by that statement.

TWENTY-TWO

BERNARDO SILVA: THE MAGICIAN'S APPRENTICE

"He's been the best. Not just in our team, but I don't vote in those awards. He can do everything."

Pep Guardiola was speaking about Bernardo Silva on the eve of the final league match of the 2018-19 season, a game at Brighton where a City win would claim the second of three domestic trophies. The PFA had named the Liverpool centre-back Virgil Van Dijk – a player City had tried to recruit – as the player of the year. The coach of the champions saw it differently.

David Silva and Bernardo Silva have the kind of talent that can be lost in the forest of numbers that has grown around the Premier League. Statistics do not quantify the use of space on the pitch, the construction of passing lines, the orchestration of the geometric strategy that Guardiola's team is designed upon.

"Bernardo approaches football like a mathematician. He applies the rules of logic to everything he does," confides Bernardo Silva's dad, Paulo. He watched young Bernardo start kicking a ball aged two. A year later, his son was sitting on that football ("it was as big as he was") in front of the television, watching the Barcelona team managed by Bobby Robson: Guardiola, Luis Enrique, Vitor Baia, Fernando Couto.

Cast your eye over the technical team's end-of-season player reports, press your ear to the dressing-room door, or grab a pint with the City faithful in Mary D's or the City Arms on matchday and the assessments will be identical: Manchester City in season 2018-19 was Bernardo Silva plus 10 others.

At the end-of-season party, Vincent Kompany, the outgoing captain, insisted that Bernardo was the first to step up and lift the unprecedented array of trophies accumulated by the team.

A versatile and intelligent playmaker, Silva brings cohesion and control to City's game – a pivotal factor in a historic tally of 198 points over two title-winning years. He is the embodiment of his manager's central football philosophy.

Mikel Arteta, the coach who, for season 2018-19 became assistant manager, uses Bernardo as an example to younger players of the work ethic required to make it at City. "I wish all our players were like Bernardo," he sighs.

Bernardo Silva was City's first signing in the summer of 2017, shortly after he had orchestrated their downfall in the Champions League of the previous season, as a Monaco player. They must have been cursing their hesitancy. Scouts from City had reported on Silva as he progressed through the youth system at Benfica. Reports had been filed, data analysed. None of them were sufficiently convinced to take a gamble on Bernardo.

His name kept cropping up though, particularly during Txiki Begiristain's meetings with the agent Jorge Mendes. Mendes was evangelical about the midfielder and would repeatedly warn City's director of football: "You need to realise that Bernardo's going to become the best in the world."

Bernardo's progress in the Benfica B team peaked in 2013, at the age of 19, when he was the second-string's stand-out player and began to be introduced to the first-team squad. However, it was made clear to him that his promotion would come with an incredible condition: he would be playing as a full-back. He would play only 31 minutes for Benfica before, on the advice of Mendes, leaving on loan to Monaco in the summer of 2014.

In Monaco, he was given plenty of playing time and the French club was so impressed that in January 2015 they exercised a clause in the loan agreement to buy Silva for £11.25m.

Then, in 2017, he was part of the team that knocked City out of the Champions League in the round of 16, after which he briefly met Guardiola as they waited to participate in post-match interviews. When Monaco defeated Borussia Dortmund to progress to the semi-final, Begiristain was present, alongside Mendes. The agent introduced the Manchester City shot-caller to Bernardo and his father, who were having dinner with some other Monaco players after the game.

"Txiki and I had a chat that night and we clicked immediately," recalls Paulo Silva, Bernardo's father. "He didn't offer us anything and gave me no indication that he was interested in signing Bernardo. There was absolutely no negotiating, but I came away with a very positive impression. Jorge had always told me that Bernardo should work with Pep. I could see that the environment and ideas at City were tailor-made for how Bernardo plays and thinks. So, when we did sit down to negotiate a couple of months later, it was all pretty straightforward."

In a neat twist of fate the club's lead negotiator, Ferran Soriano, already knew Bernardo's father. Soriano explains: "It was such a coincidence. Years ago, I had a business in Barcelona called 'Cluster' and one of our clients was a Portuguese company that Bernardo's father ran. When we were introduced this time around, I immediately said to myself: I know that face. We worked out what the connection was. Everything was plain sailing from then."

Negotiations with Monaco went without a hitch and City bought the young midfielder for £43.5m. Two years on, the football department assess that his market value has more than doubled since he arrived in England. The performances behind that spike were also reflected in his own contract. On

March 13, 2019, Silva's salary was doubled and he extended until 2025.

"Bernardo's really special and I'm not just talking about how he plays," says David Silva, usually rather more restrained with his praise.

"He's had a spectacular season," agrees Laporte. "This year he's led the field in Europe. The amount of running he does! Still, he's still the butt of everyone's jokes. But it never ever bothers him and sometimes I get the impression that he's the one laughing at us."

Bernardo is always the target. He arrives to training to find his clothes have been hidden, or his football boots are dangling from the ceiling. He is perhaps the worst-dressed player on the roster and tolerates with a smile the barbs of his designer-clad teammates ("why have you come to training in your pyjamas?").

Manel Estiarte, the individual most observant of the special alchemy that binds a squad together, believes Bernardo plays a special role in maintaining the unity within the champions – by his cheery acceptance of his role as punchbag, but not only that. Fluent in English (he attended an English school in Lisbon), French, Portuguese and Spanish, the midfielder moves around the various tribes within the dressing room constantly.

"There are a lot of great lads in the team and I value every single one of them," says Estiarte. "But he's special. Not better or worse, just special."

"I played with Spanish speakers like Di María, Aimar, Garay, Cardozo and Gaitán for years at Benfica and then I went to France and had to learn the language," explains Bernardo.

He'll sit talking with the French speakers and then have a game of pool with the Brazilians. He's particularly close to Gabriel Jesus, one of his principal tormentors in the dressing room.

"I prefer not to stick with just one person in the dressing room. I usually have breakfast with the Brazilians – we all speak

Portuguese – but I also enjoy spending time with John Stones and the other English players over dinner. I'm very close to Mendy and we hang out a lot – he's dangerous to be around but a great lad all the same. And then there's Laporte and Mahrez, with whom I talk French. Put it like this, I never get bored because I get to hang out with all these different groups."

Team manager Marc Boixasa: "He was a bit shy when he first arrived but that's normal and he's very different now that he's been here a while. He wears ordinary clothes, lives in an ordinary apartment and drives an ordinary car and is perfectly happy to shop at his local supermarket. It's just that when he pulls on his football boots something magical happens."

Pep Guardiola: "I've never once seen him in a bad mood, even when he's not playing much. I can't tell you how important it is to have players like him in the dressing room. Bernardo's that kind of guy, who always seems to be in the right frame of mind. In that sense he's quite unusual. He's going to be around for a long time to come and, as long as I'm in charge, Bernardo's going nowhere."

This ability to connect was not just a social skill. In his first season, Bernardo was the all-action conduit for the team whether starting five games in a row or coming on in the closing minutes. Arteta began to see him not just as an asset, but a role model. "For his teammates, veterans and newcomers, Bernardo quickly became the guy to watch and emulate. He turned our plans upside down because, although he's not your typical winger, we found that he could do amazing things if we played him out wide. We never expected him to perform as well as that there. He basically showed us that we aren't as smart as perhaps we think we are."

Bernardo Silva: "I think I've improved over the two seasons and, with time and experience, my confidence has certainly grown. Pep told me that it's not about how you perform on any given day, it's about maintaining a consistent level day in, day out. So that's what I've done. I run as hard as I can, push myself as much as I can, every single day. Everything you do matters. If you have the right work ethic, then everything else follows automatically.

"You have to watch your teammates – everyone has his own particular skill set. It's like when I was a kid and I used to watch my idols playing. I noticed David Silva straight away – his game is very like my own. He's not as physically strong as Kevin or Fernandinho and he's also left-footed, like me. It's just my luck that we both ended up at City."

Bernardo has played in six different positions at City: left and right attacking midfield, both wings in a front three, false nine and even wing-back. Pep hasn't had an offensive player as versatile as this since Andrés Iniesta. At Bayern Munich, Philipp Lahm had a similar ability to adapt to several positions, but in a more defensive role.

Bernardo Silva: "I'm most comfortable on the right wing cutting in on to my left. As far as I'm concerned my right leg's just for walking. I'm useless with it on the pitch. I also don't think I'm particularly fast, so it suits me to play on the right.

"I got as much advice as I could to help me understand what was expected of me. And Mikel Arteta was one of the people who helped me the most. He's got tremendous expertise and is a great support to all of us. Him and Pep think exactly the same way.

"It just takes a bit of time to get your head round it. They're not difficult concepts and everything's explained very clearly. I just needed a bit of space to memorise it all, although it turned out to be easier than it looks – honest!"

Bernardo is 5ft 8ins – in the City squad Raheem Sterling, David Silva and Phil Foden are shorter still. But Guardiola's Barcelona was founded around players of similar stature: Messi, Xavi, Iniesta, Alves and Pedro are all shorter than the Portuguese.

"I've always been one of the smallest, even back when I was a kid," he says. "I learned early that you have to find other qualities to compensate. If you run faster than everyone else or tackle harder, it doesn't matter what height you are."

Silva averaged 52 minutes per game played in his first season in Manchester. In his second, 2018-19, which ended in a domestic treble, that rose to 80 minutes. He became not only a reliable goalscorer and provider (13 goals and 12 assists) but his pivotal role in the team's attacks was a cornerstone of that success.

"He has a geometrical brain and sees the pitch in terms of sines, cosines and tangents," explains his dad. "I think that's how he sees football, like an architect. He thinks faster than his opponent, which is how he's managed to cope with the Premier League.

"Pep instinctively understands Bernardo and, for my son, Guardiola is God. He's his teacher and guide, the one who has found the essence of Bernardo's game. It's like my son's an orange and Pep's the machine that's squeezing every last drop of juice out of him. That's why he does everything Pep tells him to."

TWENTY-THREE

MAKING-OF MATCH: MANCHESTER CITY 2 MANCHESTER UNITED 3 APRIL 7, 2018

City are 90 minutes away from the Premier League title. They face Jose Mourinho's Manchester United at home. The stage is set for a historic derby occasion, but the pre-match build-up has been focused on the fallout from City's Champions League quarter-final first-leg defeat to Liverpool, three days earlier.

Jürgen Klopp's side thrashed Pep's men 3-0 with all the goals – scored by Mo Salah, Alex Oxlade-Chamberlain and Sadio Mané – coming in a whirlwind 19-minute period during the first half. It has put an entirely different complexion on the visit of United to the Etihad.

At the pre-match press conference, Guardiola is hit by a barrage of questions on the cataclysmic defeat at Anfield. He deals with the questions as best he can before acknowledging the huge significance of the United game to the club's supporters.

"I completely understand, it would be the same for Barça fans if they had the chance to win the league by beating Madrid."

However, Pep has been reminding everyone that if they don't win this one, they'll still have six more shots at the title. He's fooling no one.

For fans who have endured a generation and more of United domination under Sir Alex Ferguson this is City's day – they'll play like champions and claim their crown.

For 45 minutes, they do. At half-time, Pep's men are 2-0 ahead and it's the least their superiority merits. They score when Vincent Kompany powers home a header from a Leroy Sané corner; then again after Ílkay Gündoğan works a delicious one-two with Raheem Sterling to slide a low shot past David de Gea.

However, in the second half, United mount a comeback. Ten minutes after the restart they are level through two goals from Paul Pogba: the first after he runs on to a chest-pass from Ander Herrera, the second a dominant header from Alexis Sánchez's cross. Then, metre by metre, tackle by tackle, decision by decision, they overwhelm City. Chris Smalling heads home the winner from a Sánchez free-kick and United win a game which looked beyond their retrieval.

Henry Winter of *The Times* slams Pep's tactics. "Pep underestimated the derby by resting [Kevin] De Bruyne, [Kyle] Walker, [Sergio] Agüero and Gabriel Jesus because he had his sights on the return leg of the Champions League against Liverpool. If he had played with a real No.9 the game would have been over at half-time."

Guardiola and his staff know, however, that Agüero wasn't in shape to play. Sterling, the improvised centre-forward, danced rings round United's defenders, and manufactured three one-on-ones with de Gea. Daniel Taylor writing in *The Guardian* observes: "The derby would have been a comprehensive victory for City if Raheem Sterling hadn't confused the dimensions of United's goal with those of an enormous cathedral."

Pep is devastated. The following day, after training and the debriefing session in which he tries to unpick the reasons for the defeat, he heads home, still mortified by the loss. And the clock is ticking down to the second leg of the Champions League quarter-final.

As he stops at a red light, another car pulls alongside his Mercedes and the driver leans on the horn. It is two United fans and they've recognised him. "Fuck off! We're United and Manchester's still red. We beat you, you bastard!"

Pep mutters "Okay, let's all calm down," hits the accelerator on the green light and, with a swift glance over his shoulder, speeds off into the night.

Three days after the United setback, there is a special atmosphere throughout the first half of the return leg of the Champions League quarter-final against Liverpool. The fans inside the Etihad have seen enough this season to believe that their team can perform sporting miracles. At times it seems possible, but Liverpool run out 2-1 winners in Manchester, for a thumping 5-1 aggregate win.

That scoreline does not tell the balance of the tie for most of the 180 minutes. In the first leg, two marginal decisions went against City. The first goal of the first leg, which handed Liverpool an advantage they never surrender, came when James Milner's pass found Mo Salah on the halfway line, and the striker looked to have strayed offside. City's chance at redemption appeared to have arrived in the second half when Gabi Jesus converted from Sané's shot, but the German winger was ruled to be fractionally offside.

Then, with half-time approaching in the second leg, Sané's goal is wrongly disallowed for offside when Spanish referee Antonio Mateu Lahoz fails to spot that Loris Karius, the Liverpool goalkeeper, punches the ball off Milner and into the German's path. That call comes with City 1-0 up on the night (3-1 behind on aggregate) and a minute after Bernardo Silva has struck a shot off the post. Eleven minutes after the break, Salah scores for Liverpool to make it 4-1 on aggregate and the night's drama is punctured, as is the fight of the home team, by the time Roberto Firmino rolls in the final goal of an epic tie. City had lost three big games inside a week, but with so much still to play, Guardiola needed to re-set the mindset of his wounded players.

"When things go badly like that, it's important to reassure them. I'll say, 'Lads you're fucking superstars.' That's what I kept telling them that week."

Two weeks later, City win the Premier League.

Man United (4-3-3): de Gea; Valencia, Bailly, Smalling, Young; Herrera (Lindelöf 90 +4), Matic, Pogba; Sánchez (Rashford 82), Lukaku, Lingard (McTominay 85)
Man City (4-3-3): Ederson; Danilo, Kompany, Otamendi, Delph; Gündoğan (Agüero 76), Fernandinho, D Silva (De Bruyne 72); B Silva (Jesus 72), Sterling, Sané
Goals: Kompany 25, Gündoğan 30, Pogba 53, 55, Smalling 69
Bookings: Danilo, Kompany, Fernandinho, Sterling, Jesus, Agüero, Pogba, Herrera, Lukaku
Referee: Martin Atkinson
Attendance: 54,249

TWENTY-FOUR

MANCHESTER IS BLUE

It is April 14, 2018. Spurs v City at Wembley. Pep's men have just suffered three straight defeats, but that doesn't come close to telling the story of the past 10 days. They blew a once-in-a-lifetime opportunity to win the league by beating their biggest rival. And they were overwhelmed by Liverpool across two legs in the Champions League.

The silver lining? Redemption is rarely possible so swiftly. Should City defeat Tottenham, and United fail to win against West Brom 24 hours later, the title is theirs. Not very likely though. The Baggies are in last place and will end the season 69 points behind the champions. Nobody in the CFA is counting on winning the league this weekend.

In fact, post-Liverpool, Pep's anxiety levels are rising. Suddenly the 13 points between them and second-placed United seem like nothing, compared to the 18 still up for grabs. The stress is showing.

On Friday morning, Pere Guardiola pops in to see his brother. He's at the CFA for a meeting with Begiristain but has an inkling that Pep is struggling. "I'd spoken to him on the phone on Thursday and I could tell there was something up," he recalls.

When he gets there, Pep opens up.

"Pere, what if we lose tomorrow in London and miss another chance to win the title? What if we don't win again this season?"

Pere Guardiola: "I was about to confirm his calculations. Yes, no more wins would probably mean we'd miss out on the title. But in the end, I thought it would be better to reassure him. We were definitely going to win at Wembley, no worries. And I fully believed it."

After the visit from his brother, Guardiola appeared calmer by the hour. Spurs away is a fixture for which Pep places extra demands on his team. He wants every morsel of information. Spurs, led by Mauricio Pochettino, are the team who are most adept at multiple changes of system during a game. This results in a kind of pressure that Guardiola was familiar with while coaching in Spain or Germany, but remains less common in England. And it is a challenge he relishes.

"Football, like any sport, requires tactics, otherwise it makes no sense. I became a coach because I love the tactical side of things, but I know that eventually I'll start to focus less on systems and more on the human aspect. Now I can spend two hours watching a game and one day I'll stop that and spend those two hours talking to one of my players, or the chef, or the physio."

In truth, this is a change that is already underway. Guardiola's messaging to his players has pivoted from detailed tactical instruction to more motivational communication across his time in Manchester. This balance has occurred as his players have mastered his system, but there is another reason, too.

As coach of Barcelona and then Bayern, Pep often needed to remind his players that their opponents carried a threat. ("We'd be playing, say, Getafe or Cologne and it was easy to fall into the trap of believing they were going to be a pushover.") They did this by focusing on detailed strategies aimed at exploiting a particular weakness.

However, in Manchester Pep and his technical team soon realised that this approach wasn't working. In fact, they were convinced it was making the players nervous. Pep realised a new approach was called for. "I realised in the summer [of 2017] that we were actually lacking a bit of self-confidence. I have total faith in them and now I tell them that as often as possible, because they're very, very good."

It is a bright, sunny day in London as City arrive at Wembley. Pep doesn't even mention tactics today. He tells his players that a truly great team picks themselves up after a fall. He tells them that they have done this before, a thousand times, and they can do it today. He tells them that they are better than they think. He tells them to show today that they want to be champions of England.

It works. City rip Spurs to shreds. They win 3-1, with goals from Gabriel Jesus and Raheem Sterling either side of a Ílkay Gündoğan penalty.

After the game, Pochettino cannot contain his admiration for Pep's team: "They were the better team today. They made mincemeat out of us in the first 20 minutes. But they've been the best team all year anyway. That's why they're going to win the league."

As City's players return to the dressing room, having delivered their 14th away win of the Premier League season, Pep leaps up and goes into Wembley's tunnel. He is rounding up the stragglers. He finds Kyle Walker chatting to his ex-teammate Danny Rose at the end of the tunnel and tells him to get back to the dressing room.

Leroy Sané and Kevin De Bruyne are being interviewed by Sky. De Bruyne has been voted man of the match and Sané has been asked by the rights-holders to join in the presentation. After that there are more TV stations queuing for interviews. Pep puts his foot down and insists that the two players have shared enough.

The three of them sprint back down to the dressing room, closely followed by an official who needs Sané for an anti-doping test.

In the dressing room, Pep tells his team that the title is in their grasp. The players should report for their usual post-match training in the morning and then take a three-day holiday.

"You can start thinking about the Swansea game on Wednesday," says the coach. "You have achieved something amazing and you can be proud of yourselves."

Pep's final request is to ask his players to keep their celebrations to a minimum out of respect for their opponents. That can wait for Manchester, and the City fans.

The following day West Brom beat United at Old Trafford. So unexpected is this result that nobody from City is paying attention when Jay Rodríguez slams the ball into the net.

The CFA is deserted and Pep is on the golf course with Màrius. He is playing Tommy Fleetwood, the European Tour golfer and Ryder Cup hero. After the game, they have a beer together ("the best part of golf" according to Pep) with Tommy's wife, Clare, who is a big City fan (Fleetwood supports Everton).

On the way home the skies open and they're stuck in a traffic jam. Màrius looks at his phone. West Brom have just scored.

"We've won the Premier League!" gasps Màrius.

"And that's where I found out that we were champions: sitting in a traffic jam on the motorway in the pouring rain. Not exactly how I imagined it," smiles Pep.

Pep had switched his phone off for his day out with Màrius, but he turns it on at home as he and Cristina uncork the champagne. He calls Khaldoon, Ferran Soriano, Txiki Begiristain and the rest of his assistants.

"I congratulated Khaldoon and thanked him for all he'd done the previous season, even when things looked bad, there was never a single word of reproach. I had nothing but messages of support and encouragement from him. Always. And at the time I needed it most," remembers Guardiola.

Messages of congratulation pour in including some kind words from Xavier Sala-i-Martín and Domènec Torrent, who is out taking his customary Sunday stroll.

Torrent is caught in the sudden downpour and takes refuge under the canopy of the old Great Northern Railway Company, now a shopping centre with stores, a casino, a bowling alley and several restaurants.

"I got drenched in the rain and took shelter in front of the Revolución de Cuba. I couldn't stop laughing. We'd just been crowned champions and there was no one there. I said to myself: 'What the hell are you doing here? You've just won the Premier League.'"

Lorenzo Buenaventura, at home in Cádiz, has been out for a stroll with his wife, forcing himself not to keep checking his phone.

Which explains his momentary shock when he bumps into his friend and former English tutor, Patrick (a big Southampton fan). "He walked up to me and said: 'Congratulations, you're Premier League champions.'

"I checked my phone and, sure enough, West Brom had won. I gave my wife a huge kiss and we went off for a cup of tea to celebrate. When Pep called me he said, 'We are going to throw the biggest party ever'."

Mikel Arteta is spending his three-day break in Mallorca and is in the air when the game finishes. "There were about 20 minutes left when the plane took off in Manchester, but when we landed in Palma, I immediately knew that something big had happened. I had 150 messages and 60 missed calls!"

Captain Vincent Kompany watches the whole game at his in-laws' house in Hale with friends and family gathered for the occasion, including one United fan, who has to be consoled as the rest of the household celebrate.

This is Kompany's third Premier League title, as it is for Sergio Agüero, recuperating in Barcelona, and for David Silva, who is in Valencia taking a nap when the ball hits the back of the net. "I'd just got my head down when my dad woke me up to give me the good news. I leapt up and went straight to the hospital. I wanted to share that special moment with my girl and my son."

Kevin De Bruyne is also away on holiday and manages a brief FaceTime with Kompany, his in-laws and friends (minus one unhappy United fan) celebrating in the background.

Then Kompany sets off for the Railway pub in Hale to celebrate with Kyle Walker, John Stones, Bernardo Silva and Fabian Delph, plus kit man Brandon Ashton. Walker's been too nervous to watch the game so he spends the afternoon with his son, putting stickers in his World Cup album until his wife bursts in. "United have lost! You've won the Premier League!" Walker hugs his family, calls Stones and tells his wife: "Sorry, but I'm going to the pub."

Bernardo Silva is still in his pyjamas when he hears the news and he grabs a lift to the pub with Stones.

Delph arrives at the pub just in time to bump into several United fans coming out of another bar chanting: "United! United! United!" He responds with an exultant, "Manchester is blue, lads!"

Team manager Marc Boixasa is also enjoying a Sunday nap when he's shaken awake. The celebrations start at home and then he heads out to pick up the physio Edu Álvarez, who's in the middle of a game of *Fortnite* with his daughter Carla, while his wife Eva watches *Peppa Pig* with their baby Alejandra. The pair check the team's WhatsApp group and head out to Australasia, one of Manchester's finest restaurants, to meet up with the rest of the gang: Gabriel Jesus, Carles Planchart, Xabi Mancisidor and his right-hand man Richard Wright, the other physios (Steve and Carlo) and Sam and Barry, the fitness coaches. They proceed to drink Manchester dry.

When the dust settles, Pep invites everyone – players and staff at every level – to the cinema to see *La La Land*. The players enjoyed the film, although probably as much for Agüero's entertaining commentary as anything else.

Soon after his arrival at City, Pep insisted on everyone based in the first-team building – from the receptionists, to the laundry workers and kitchen staff – being included in club dinners.

One of the favourite venues is Tapeo & Wine (owned by Juan Mata, whose father, Juan Sr, is often around), which offers delicious Spanish food plus enough space for an evening of karaoke. Pep celebrated his birthday here, two years in a row. There were three parties here during the second season, all before a single trophy had been lifted. In this way, Guardiola seeks to transmit the sense of unity that he has built amongst his coaching team and players through the entire organisation.

At each gathering, it was common to see him working the room.

"Hey, thanks for everything you do."

"Are you okay, do you have enough to eat?"

"Are you going to do some karaoke later?"

To the last question, even the shiest members of staff will answer 'yes'. Pep usually goes for *Wonderwall* by Oasis.

The official ceremony takes place on May 6, after a tenacious Huddersfield manage to hold the newly-crowned champions to a draw. Among around 1,000 guests are Oasis's Noel Gallagher and the Smiths' guitarist, Johnny Marr and Richard Scudamore, the executive president of the Premier League, who presents everyone who has played more than five games in the competition (the whole squad except Brahim Díaz, Phil Foden, Lukas Nmecha and Arijanet Murić) with a medal. Shauna Miller, the coach of City in the Community, then presents them with the trophy.

Later, more than a thousand people gather to celebrate in a hangar in the south of the city. It's a spectacular party and Ferran Soriano has prepared a surprise.

A huge image of an English city is projected on to the big screen. Soriano asks into his microphone: "Anybody know where this is?"

The chief executive invites Kyle Walker on to the stage and asks him to push a button. An image appears on the huge screen of the England full-back in the Landsdowne Estate in Sheffield's Sharrow neighbourhood, where young Kyle first learned to kick a ball. The words read: *Congratulations Kyle, Premier League Champion 2017-18.*

Then he does it all again with De Bruyne. This time it's Drogen, the club that organises an annual Kevin De Bruyne Cup in his honour.

"Tonight we're going to see where each of you champions started out!" announces Soriano.

For Pep, it's Santpedor town hall. For Phil Foden, Stockport's viaduct. Yaya Touré gets ASEC Mimosas, a club in Ivory Coast. Oleksandr Zinchenko, Radomishl Castle in Ukraine. And so it goes on.

The team then parades through the centre of the city, on Monday May 14, cheered on by 100,000 fans lining the streets. Agüero is missing – he's en route to Argentina to join the national team in preparation for the World Cup. David Silva is in Valencia, he's chosen to miss today's celebration to be with his wife and baby Mateo (now well enough to be at home). But the veteran midfielder has sent an emotional message to the team and their supporters.

Guardiola addresses the crowd: "There was no way I ever expected to end up with 100 points this season, but that's exactly what we've done. Now it's time to celebrate what we've achieved, nothing more.

"It's nearly time for the World Cup so we should all grab a beer or a glass of wine, sit back on the sofa and enjoy it. And then we'll come back, stronger than ever."

TWENTY-FIVE

CHRISTMAS IS CANCELLED

In December 2018 Pep was looking forward to the club's Christmas party and a chance to celebrate with staff. Everyone was invited, from the workers in the CFA to the star players of the first team. It is a tradition the Catalan introduced in his first-year in Manchester – a night to remember. This year, for all the wrong reasons.

A Christmas feast was laid on in Manchester's Great Northern Warehouse for the 400 guests who gathered to celebrate what had been a glorious year.

The previous summer, City had celebrated an unprecedented achievement in the Premier League: 100 points, 106 goals, a style of football that had never been seen in England.

Compared to Pep's first two summers at the club, City had been quiet during the close-season transfer window: Riyad Mahrez, a £60m capture from Leicester City, was the only heavyweight signing, and none of those leaving the club had been key figures in the record-breaking league campaign.

The new season had started with a 2-0 win over Chelsea to claim the Community Shield, a double from Sergio Agüero making sure the first trophy of the season wore sky blue ribbons.

And as Christmas approached, they were lining up challenges in all four remaining competitions. Despite a fright in their first Champions League game – Lyon left the Etihad with a 2-1 win

– they qualified with something to spare, dropping points only in the return fixture in France, which they drew.

In the Premier League, they had dropped seven points in 17 games – two draws and a solitary defeat, at Chelsea. The title race was already distilling to a duel between City and Liverpool.

The week before preparations for the party began, City had progressed to the semi-final of the Carabao Cup via a penalty shoot-out against Leicester.

All in all, it looked like being a very happy Christmas.

Pep led the celebrations, delighted to spend time with the whole City 'family' as they ate, drank and danced the night away. It was all over too soon and, as the lights went up at the end of the evening, City's players were keen to party on. In the full knowledge of some of the management team, they headed over to Chinawhite, one of Manchester's most fashionable nightclubs. Hours later, as dawn broke over a sleeping city, they were still there. Not the wisest of moves with training the next morning in preparation for the weekend's game against Crystal Palace. However, the majority arrived at the CFA bright and early Thursday morning, looking refreshed and ready to work. No harm done. One or two, however, had clearly overdone it on the Christmas spirit – and Pep wasn't impressed.

City were the clear favourites but Pep had a bad feeling about the game. It started well for the home side with Íllkay Gündoğan putting City ahead in the first half. Then, before half-time, things began to unravel. Jeffrey Schlupp scored from a Palace counter-attack and then Andros Townsend produced the goal of his life. His long-distance volley set off like a missile then descended perfectly to fit between the post and bar of Ederson's top-right corner. The Premier League goal of the season – a work of art.

Losing 2-1, City reappeared after the break and played disastrously. Kyle Walker conceded a stupid penalty and Luka

Milivojevic converted it. A Kevin De Bruyne consolation could not prevent City falling to a home defeat – their only one of the season.

Pep was furious. Three weeks later he sat down with his assistants and suggested that from now on a Christmas party curfew might be a good idea.

The players – some of them, at least – didn't appreciate this results-based analysis of the situation. They suggested that had they roared out of the blocks and scored three times in the first 20 minutes against Palace, by the end of it everyone would have agreed that celebrations like that only strengthen team unity. And anyway, they were unlucky against Palace. They should have won.

In fact, this was City's second defeat in two weeks and Pep's party mood was a distant memory. The 2-0 defeat at Stamford Bridge still hurt – it was the first time he'd faced Maurizio Sarri as City coach and his first defeat by the Italian. It was also the day that Liverpool went top of the table, pushing City into second place.

With two defeats behind them and trailing Liverpool by four points, it was a subdued City who arrived at the King Power Stadium on Boxing Day. Pep's previous two Christmas fixtures had gone well: City beat Hull in 2016 and Newcastle in 2017. The health of their title defence depended on the upkeep of this tradition.

Things started well in Leicester. Bernardo Silva opened the scoring in the early stages, but then Fabian Delph had the game that would effectively end his City career. His fingerprints were on both Leicester goals and then he was sent off for a high tackle on Ricardo. He would be usurped by Oleksandr Zinchenko at left-back and play only once more that season, as a last resort in the quarter-final of the Champions League.

An increasingly miserable December also cost Kyle Walker his place in Pep's starting XI. Danilo took his place for all of January's big games after Walker's form crashed. In the grim depths of this winter funk, the atmosphere at the CFA was transformed.

Marc Boixasa, first team operations manager: "Those games against Palace and Leicester were a real blow, you could tell how much pain the whole squad was in. Even those who hadn't played. It was a very tough period psychologically and emotionally."

December has always been a grim month for Guardiola at City. In the seven matches played over the three seasons, City lost six and drew one. City's sports science department has an explanation for this trend. Teams who compete in the group stage of the Champions League have already played at least six extra matches before mid-January. If the same teams are also competing in the FA and EFL Cups they can end up playing 25 official games over 92 days as one year ends and the new one begins. This intense pressure vastly increases risk of injury.

It also means that key players can't be rested as much as you'd like. Playing a match almost every four days takes an enormous toll in terms of muscular stress and physical exertion. Lorenzo Buenaventura runs the training programme at City: "We've had to reduce the seven-day cycle of training. There just isn't time to train. Some days we might have just 14 players available, usually because of muscle fatigue, but joint problems too. People don't realise how tough players have to be – football is a contact sport which definitely requires a lot of recuperation time. And 70 per cent of our guys play every game." Buenaventura has been on a voyage of discovery in England. He's had to reinvent some of his most fundamental concepts in order to adapt to the Premier League.

"We've had to put a lot of thought into it. We vary the level of intensity required for different exercises in the same session. You have to adapt to each player's individual needs. Every moment of every day of the year. It's totally different from Germany, where the Christmas break is 25 days, which gives them time to recover from injury. Pep used to have the whole squad fully fit at the end of January when we were at Bayern."

The demands of the Premier League mean that City's technical team prioritise recuperation over everything else. The trade-off, according to Buenaventura, is a drop in sharpness.

Perhaps that contributed to City finishing 2018 in second place, seven points behind leaders Liverpool, who they would host on January 3. Anything other a win would be unthinkable in the defence of their title.

TWENTY-SIX

KLOPP'S RED MACHINE

"I've never socialised [with Jürgen Klopp], here or in Germany. We're rivals and all coaches want to beat their rivals and that usually means that we don't get too close. He's a nice guy though and I know how good a coach he is because of the work he does. He's very talented. You just have to look at how his teams play: the way he wants them to play."

Pep Guardiola

When Liverpool came to the Etihad on January 3, 2019, the score was 0-0 when Sadio Mané slipped a shot under Ederson which rebounded off the post. John Stones was first to the loose ball, but as he spun around, his attempted clearance smacked off his own goalkeeper and looped into the air, toward the goal. Stones reacted brilliantly, spinning round once more, recovering his position and connecting with the ball as it crossed the goal line. About 10 per cent of the diameter of the ball – 11.7mm – remained in play.

Had Stones' intervention occurred a fraction of a second later, Liverpool would have taken the lead. A win for Jürgen Klopp's team would have given them a 10-point advantage. Instead, Sergio Agüero and Roberto Firmino exchanged strikes either side of half-time before Leroy Sané scored a brilliant goal with 18 minutes left to give City the win and close the gap to four points.

The rivalry between these two great coaches began in Germany. Klopp's Dortmund were seen as the people's champions; Bayern, under Guardiola, the established power. Pep won all three of the Bundesliga titles he competed for in Germany, surpassing Dortmund by 19 and 33 points in the years when he faced off with Klopp. Klopp claimed both Supercups contested by Bayern and Dortmund, before leaving at the end of season 2014-15.

The coaches resumed their rivalry on New Year's Eve 2016, when Liverpool beat City 1-0 at Anfield, a defeat that left Pep's team trailing leaders Chelsea by 10 points going into 2017. By the time of the rematch at the Etihad, a madcap 1-1 draw, the two teams were even further behind the pace and would end the season fighting for third.

The following season, 2017-18, there were glimpses of the huge progress both teams had made. First, in September 2017, a crushing 5-0 win for City – with Liverpool going down to 10 men after Mané's 37th-minute red card for a high challenge on Ederson, which left the goalkeeper with facial injuries. Then, an epic 4-3 win for Liverpool on January 14, 2018, when they became the first team to defeat City in the Premier League that season, despite having to withstand a late onslaught after having been 4-1 up with 22 minutes left.

However, that was merely the appetiser. Klopp's team then knocked City out of the Champions League in April 2018, winning 5-1 on aggregate in a tie that was far more finely balanced than the eventual scoreline suggested.

By the first meeting of the 2018-19 season, it was clear to Pep and his team that Liverpool were a special rival, and their preparations for the October 7 fixture reflected that, as did Pep's words to the media beforehand.

"They are the best team in the world when the game is open and loose. If it's an open game at Anfield, you don't even have a one per cent chance to win."

Carles Planchart, head of analysis: "Whenever we play at Anfield they always cause us a lot of problems, even if they have little domination of the ball or the match. Obviously we have to try to adapt our own tactics to deal with it and make corrections to our game if necessary. I remember that we defended much further back that day."

City recorded 50.6 per cent possession at Anfield, significantly lower than in any other game under Guardiola to that point. Minimal risks were taken in bringing the ball out from the back, or in midfield. City had not maintained a clean sheet at Anfield for 32 years and that appeared to be the day's primary objective.

In the 86th minute, Virgil Van Dijk fouled Sané inside the box. Sergio Agüero had been substituted and the decision on the penalty taker rested with Pep. Riyad Mahrez, the previous summer's marquee signing and a surprise starter, got the nod. The manager believed his new recruit could do with a confidence boost, but the Algerian's recent record showed three misses from his previous five penalties. He stepped up and, without appearing to look at Alisson's goal, launched the ball wildly over the bar and into the stands, as the match ended goalless.

Later, Pep apologised to Gabriel Jesus, who had asked to take the penalty. The game was a thorn in City's side for the remainder of the season. Those who had been with Pep in Spain and Germany thought back to Leo Messi's penalty smashing off the bar in a Champions League semi-final against Chelsea in 2012; and of Thomas Müller having his spot-kick saved by Jan Oblak of Atlético at the same stage in 2016. Missed penalties that cost trophies.

City recovered to top the league until December when things began to unravel. Their first defeat of the season (against Chelsea) was swiftly followed by two disastrous results against Crystal Palace and Leicester, while an unbeaten Liverpool surged to a seven-point lead.

The two sides met again in that first game of 2019, on January 3 at the Etihad. No team had reached this stage of the season undefeated and failed to win the title since Sheffield United. In 1900.

Pre-match, Pep was positive. "Liverpool are, in the moment, the best team in Europe, in their consistency, the way they control the details in their game. Everyone is talking about [what happens] if we lose, but what happens if we win? It's an incredible pleasure to be involved in these games. I'm a manager to play these kinds of games, to see what we can do on the big stage."

Klopp responded in kind: "The opponent is still the best team in the world. Nothing changed."

Guardiola improvises in defence: Danilo, Kompany, Stones, and Laporte as an emergency full-back. Fernandinho, Bernardo and David Silva in midfield; Sterling, Agüero and Sané are up front.

Klopp's selection is: Alisson; Alexander-Arnold, Lovren, Van Dijk, Robertson; Henderson, Wijnaldum, Milner; Salah, Firmino and Mané.

The home crowd know it's do or die. "I've never seen this place like this before. It's the best I've ever seen the atmosphere here," says Gary Neville.

The teams are evenly matched, with 50 per cent possession each. After 18 minutes, Mané looks to have scored before Stones' just-in-time intervention on the line. The scoreline is tied until the 40th minute. Bernardo Silva picks the ball up in midfield and sends it to Agüero in the six-yard box. The Argentine, who has his back to goal, dances past a sleepy Dejan Lovren and sends the ball crashing into Alisson's net. He has scored in all of the seven games he's played against Liverpool at home, although never at Anfield.

Klopp and his men are unhappy with Vincent Kompany's hard tackle on Salah in the centre of the field. They demand a red card, the ref gives a yellow.

Liverpool's perseverance pays off in the 64th minute, thanks to full-backs Trent Alexander-Arnold and Andy Robertson. Alexander-Arnold sends a deep cross to the far post, Robertson picks it up and passes to Firmino, who's right in front of goal to head home.

Then City move up a gear. Sterling picks up the ball in midfield and, exploiting a rare moment of inattention in the opposition ranks, drives forward, Agüero and Sané on his heels. He plays the ball to Sané as the German arrives in the box to slide a pinpoint angular drive past Alisson and in off the post.

City are clinging on as the match heads into added time and Liverpool throw everyone forward, with Van Dijk an emergency centre-forward, but Pep's men hang on.

"A lesser side than City could conceivably have wilted under the pressure. Not this team, though. As the song goes, City fight to the end and it was not just their competitive courage to conjure up a decisive goal, courtesy of Leroy Sané, that delivered a message. It was the spirit of togetherness displayed by Guardiola's players in that nerve-shredding finale when Liverpool started pumping balls into the penalty area," wrote Daniel Taylor in *The Guardian*. "It was the night Manchester City made it clear they have no intentions of relinquishing their grip, finger by finger, on the Premier League trophy."

TWENTY-SEVEN

THEATRE OF DREAMS

Manel Estiarte: "That night, after losing to Newcastle, we flew back to Manchester and you could feel it. Everyone in that plane was convinced we'd just tossed the league title away. 'We've fucked it all up,' Pep kept saying. 'We've fucking blown it big time.'"

By the end of the evening of Wednesday, January 29, 2019, City had lost 2-1 at Newcastle and trailed leaders Liverpool by four points. The pessimism in the camp was down to the next step in the dance: should Klopp's red machine roll over Leicester at Anfield 24 hours later, Liverpool would impose a seven-point lead with just 14 matches to go. A bridge too far.

It had started so brightly at Newcastle. Sergio Agüero scored after 24 seconds, but goals from Salomón Rondón and Matt Ritchie, the second a penalty awarded on 77 minutes, floored the champions and left St James' Park in delirium.

"There was total silence on the flight home," recalls Marc Boixasa, first-team operations manager. "It was our lowest point of the season."

Aymeric Laporte: "Everyone was saying that we'd thrown the league away and it really got to us."

Bernardo Silva: "It felt like we'd just lost the Premier League. We were all completely miserable."

Slumped in his seat on the plane, unable to communicate with his teammates, was Fernandinho, who had conceded the late penalty from which Ritchie had completed a come-from-behind 2-1 win for Newcastle.

Pep was faring no better. "I didn't recognise them out there," was his scathing assessment.

Manel Estiarte: "I think Newcastle had a worse impact on him than losing to Crystal Palace. At the end of any match when we haven't produced the level of football we're capable of, it really affects him. From the start of that Newcastle defeat, even when we were leading, I could see how tense he was. Five minutes in and he was already out on the touchline demanding more from the players. And we were winning! Maybe he immediately knew that it was going wrong, that things weren't working."

Estiarte was watching the game from the stands, immediately behind the City CEO, Ferran Soriano. As Newcastle's second goal hit the back of the net, Estiarte threw up his hands in horror, cursing and, inexplicably, giving Soriano a massive shove, forcing him to cling on to his seat to avoid tumbling down three flights. "I just lost it. It was one of those things that should never happen." Ferran Soriano: "I found out that day what it feels like to be a Yugoslavian water polo player."

As the City plane landed in Manchester and the hangdog superstars climbed down the steps, there was only one note of optimism. As Carles Planchart, the lead analyst, made his way to the tarmac, thinking only of how likely a Liverpool win against Leicester was, he felt a hand on his shoulder. Agüero was right behind him, and the striker leaned forward and whispered conspiratorially into Planchart's ear.

"Don't worry. We're going to win this league. I promise."

Agüero's optimism was not shared by his manager. The following morning Pep woke to freezing temperatures and grey skies, perfectly reflecting his mood as he brooded on City's disastrous performance. It was not yet February and the title seemed to have slipped through their fingers. "I just remember thinking that leagues are usually won or lost in the last two or three matches – and we were only in *January*."

Pep's kids were just as miserable about the result, but as they trooped home from school, through the bleak winter's day, his wife Cristina was planning a family outing. Three months previously, she had bought tickets for the musical *Jersey Boys*, the story of Frankie Valli's band from the 1960s and 70s, The Four Seasons.

As her gloomy family arrived home that evening, she announced: "We've got these tickets for the Palace. So, come if you want, don't if you don't."

Going to the show would deny Pep and the kids the chance to watch Liverpool's game live. The Kop would roar out *You'll Never Walk Alone* at precisely the moment the first high notes of Valli's hits filled the theatre. Pep's daughter Valentina was on board almost immediately and then, one by one, her siblings Maria, Màrius, and finally Pep agreed to go to the show. Things were out of his hands anyway. Maybe it was time to *Walk Like a Man*.

Pep Guardiola: "Normally in that situation I'd just want to stay home, but we had the tickets and we love musicals. I usually watch other teams' matches but I just couldn't face it that night and there was nothing I could do anyway. I remember going into the theatre thinking: 'There's no way Liverpool will mess this up.' They hadn't won the league for 29 years and there was no hint that they were fallible."

Sadio Mané put Liverpool ahead two minutes in and things were looking good for the Reds until Harry Maguire equalised for Leicester just before half-time. At the theatre, Pep, Maria and Màrius were on the edge of their seats for reasons that had nothing to do with Frankie Valli. They spent the second half of the show constantly checking their mobiles.

The show's rousing finale coincided with the referee's final whistle 34 miles to the west. As the cast lined up to take their bows, Pep Guardiola leapt to his feet, clapping furiously.

"People must have thought I was going wild about the show and it was definitely a great performance with brilliant singing. They deserved that standing ovation. But if I'm honest, we were also applauding the fact that Liverpool had only managed to draw."

As the family stepped out of the Palace Theatre into Oxford Road, the world suddenly looked a much brighter place – Liverpool's lead was now five points instead of seven. "I left the theatre that night much happier," he said. "Suddenly it felt like all was not lost."

A text message arrived from Joan Patsy, right-hand man of Txiki Begiristain, Manchester City's director of football. "That's the second time we've dodged a bullet. First Liverpool [referring to the game between the two clubs on January 3, when Liverpool could have gone 10 points clear, but a City win reduced the gap to four] and now today's result. I was totally miserable yesterday and now I'm as high as a kite." Pep's response was short and to the point. "From now on we can't afford a single misstep, not even a draw."

TWENTY-EIGHT

MATCHDAY BLUES

On matchdays, Pep Guardiola gets to the CFA early, whether it is a lunchtime or late kick-off. His erratic record as a driver means that he usually relies on Manel Estiarte to ferry him around.

At the CFA, he has a cup of tea and a small breakfast. He won't eat anything else until after the game, even if he has to wait till midnight. It's a lifelong habit and he still winces at the memory of having to force food down on matchdays as a player. These days he sticks to herbal tea and lots and lots of water. But the loss of appetite is not, he insists, down to nerves.

"These days I'm much less nervous than when I first started out," he says. "And I didn't hide it well back then. So maybe it's just I control it more now."

Manel Estiarte: "I wouldn't say he gets nervous, it's just that he's completely focused and absorbed in what he's doing."

Marc Boixasa: "I'd say he gets a bit tense on matchday. He prefers to spend most of the day alone and we hardly see him unless he needs something. He's totally absorbed in his own thoughts, it's like he's in a world of his own."

Pep Guardiola: "I do like to spend that time alone, but I'm not doing nothing. I'm going over everything in my head, thinking about the game, thinking through what I'm going to say to the players. I'll pace up and down visualising the game, working out what to say to them at half-time, depending how the first half has gone. I go over and over it."

This eccentric behaviour can be a source of great amusement for the players.

Sergio Agüero: "I piss myself laughing when I see him pacing up and down the corridors like that, usually barefoot and talking away to himself. It's like he has no idea where he is. He'll come out of his office, walk straight past Txiki [Begiristain] without a word, come into the canteen and walk about, still saying nothing. He'll stop and stare at us all and then off he goes again, back to his office."

Pep Guardiola: "They must all think I've lost my mind at times, particularly since by that stage all the planning and preparation is done. We don't tend to improvise or leave things to the last minute, so it would be very unusual for me to improvise at that point."

Txiki Begiristain: "I'll be sitting in my office talking to Manel and he'll come in. I never seek him out. We'll then have this weird conversation.

"He'll say, 'So how are you both? Feeling calm?'

"And I always reply, 'It's you who needs to be calm. If you're feeling okay about today, then I'll feel okay.'

"And he'll mutter, 'Yeah, yeah. No worries. We're going to win.'

"And I'll say, 'Okay, great. I'm feeling okay then. We're going to win.' And then he's off again."

Pep never eats with the team, preferring to spend lunchtime in his office, on the phone to Cristina. He won't have much contact with the players on the day of the game, limiting himself to one team talk the day before and another on matchday. Mikel Arteta will do another, focusing on set pieces.

Pep's attention to detail extends to his matchday attire. Through season 2018-19, his regular choice of a €1,500 cashmere-and-goose feather jacket became an instant hit. Serra & Claret,

Cristina Guardiola's clothes shop in Barcelona, was inundated with enquiries, but fashionistas were left frustrated when told that it was one of only three available to buy. The jacket ended the season in less than pristine condition, having taken regular matchday abuse from Guardiola as he vented his frustration with one of his players or the referee, but was nonetheless successfully auctioned off for charity.

Pep Guardiola: "Me? A trendsetter? Maybe, but only because we won. If we'd ended up 10 points behind the leader, with nothing to show for all our hard work, I'm not so sure people would be so keen."

After briefing his men for the last time, Pep shuts himself up in his dressing room and doesn't leave until Estiarte comes to tell him that the team is out. Unlike a lot of coaches, he prefers not to watch the warm-up when City are at home, but on away visits he'll often be the first out.

"I like to go out and just sit quietly on the bench. I try to relax, look at the colour of the grass and watch as people arrive. It distracts me and time seems to pass more quickly. When you're away, the dressing rooms are usually very small, it's just too many people and I get stressed. In any case, I don't want to disrupt their own preparations for the game. They need to be left to play their music, psych themselves up, focus on what they need to do to prepare."

Wherever the game's being played, Pep won't spend time with the other team's coach before the match, unless it's someone he knows very well. Usually it's a quick handshake just as the game's about to start.

He has only one pre-game superstition. Just as the players are in the tunnel, he takes out his phone and calls his wife, Cristina. Then he hugs Estiarte, who heads off to his seat in the stand, and goes to the dugout. Game on.

Post-match, the real torture begins. Media interviews. It's the part of the day that Pep will normally enjoy the least. He's still processing the tension from the game and has to face journalists' questions immediately. "Sometimes you want to talk to the players but a few of them are elsewhere, talking to television reporters. Having to do interviews means I can't even speak to my players when I want to. I have to wait until they've all come back from the mixed zone [where reporters have free, rolling access to players]. At times there's something I need to tell them urgently before they start to relax and switch off. I might be pointing out a mistake or something they've done well, or I've spotted something we can improve on, and I can't. I have to stand there until the interviews are done. It's a disaster."

Manel Estiarte: "Pep's a perfectionist and unfortunately that means that one of his weaknesses is seeing negatives that don't really exist. Mikel [Arteta] has noticed it too. We might have won the game 3-0 and he'll be uptight about some detail or other. It's often something trivial and a bit silly but for him, in that moment, it's super important. The next day he'll be much less bothered about it and, to be fair, it happens less and less these days. But it still happens, which is a shame. It's just not necessary, but he can't help himself."

It's impossible to shrug off the stress and tension of the game before facing the cameras, but Pep is contractually obliged to speak to either Sky or BT, whichever has broadcast that match live, plus the Premier League's official broadcaster and City TV, the club's own media channel. Then it's the press conference with print and online journalists and finally he speaks to all the radio stations. He might choose to do an extra interview with a TV channel which has accreditation.

Champions League matches mean even more obligatory interviews. He'll spend 15 minutes behind a microphone and 20 in the press room. More than 30 minutes before he can make his escape.

Pep Guardiola: "It's a fiasco. I absolutely hate it. You're totally stressed out and have to do not just one but several interviews. Sometimes as many as six. Then there's the press conference. Some days it just drags on and on."

The media work also means that Pep often doesn't have time to have a glass of wine with the opposition coach post-match, a tradition that goes way back in English football.

"It also depends on who the coach is, what time the game is, if we're at the Etihad or not. It's easier if we're at home and I don't have to rush away to catch a flight. It's a nice tradition, but obviously the losing coach doesn't necessarily want to spend time with me, and I get that. It's also a bit awkward if you've won. What do you say to the guy? And if the ref has mistakenly given us a penalty that we didn't deserve? It's happened to me and it really pisses you off. How do you look someone in the eye when you know exactly what they're thinking? Although of course there are some really decent guys who handle it brilliantly."

In any case, there's always a drink and some food available in Pep's office: some good wine, Jabugo ham, mini hamburgers and some sushi and sashimi. The fridge is stocked with juice, water and beer, just in case the opposition coach pops by. If he doesn't join Pep post-match, which is more often the case, the two men will have a chat as they wait for their media interviews.

Pep Guardiola: "I remember spending time with Roy Hodgson for ages after Palace beat us at the Etihad. A disastrous result! But we had a great chat and then, before he left, he said, 'Don't worry, you're going to win the league.' I pointed out how well Liverpool were playing, that game had left us four points behind them, so things didn't look great for us. But he was adamant – 'You're going to win and in May I'm going to sit down and write you a letter reminding you of this moment and I'll post it to you.'

"Come to think of it, I've had my most interesting and enjoyable chats with English coaches, particularly the guys who have been around for a while. Before the game I'll invite them to a post-match drink and I'm always delighted if they come. Tony Pulis is always keen to come. He's a lovely guy, always very friendly. He invites us when we play there, so we like to return the favour, as we do with anyone who shows us hospitality. Not everyone wants to, which is fair enough."

The Cardiff City coach Neil Warnock is another firm favourite. "Great guy. He came for a drink after our last match in the Etihad and he loved the wine we were serving. He's a bit of a connoisseur and said to me, 'If we beat Liverpool and help you win the league, you owe me some of that wine.' So I said, 'I'll give you a whole crate if you beat them.' Then Khaldoon joined in – 'If you get a draw I'll buy you the vineyard and if you win, you can have the whole winery!'"

Cardiff 0 Liverpool 2. Pep's not bitter and has a bottle ready to gift Warnock when they next meet.

The high point of matchday is the moment when, with media work and hospitality done, he can join Cristina and the kids for dinner. And then it's home for a well-earned rest. He usually sleeps well on these nights ("unless something disastrous has happened"). Then the cycle begins again.

"I'll delegate a lot of my work at training the day after a game and my assistants do a lot more with the players, particularly those who played the day before. It's the right thing to do. I can't be hands-on every second of every day. It would kill me. Mikel [Arteta] and Loren [Buenaventura] are usually in charge that day."

Pep is still on duty though, and he'll use post-match training to work with those players who were substitutes the previous day. "I think I owe them that at least," he says.

This is the only day Pep allows visitors to come to the CFA and watch training. He's there to greet them, the captain of the ship.

The game is already history and the next one is just around the corner.

TWENTY-NINE

MAKING-OF MATCH: MAN CITY 6 CHELSEA 0 FEBRUARY 10, 2019

Txiki Begiristain is driving home to Deansgate, talking on the phone to his old friend Albert Perrín. He was on the board at Barcelona during Begiristain's stint as technical director under President Joan Laporta. Both men are wearing the identical watches they gifted each other whilst at Barcelona – much-loved mementos of the glory days of Pep Guardiola's Barça. Perrín, who was also a close friend of the legendary Johan Cruyff, has been in poor health of late but he still gets to Manchester as often as possible and loves talking the night away with Pep and Txiki over dinner at Tast. This evening he is at home recovering from an operation when Begiristain makes the call.

"Did you see it Albert? Did you see the way we played? We were just like Pep's Barça. It's like watching the same team. Albert, he's done it again!"

Two weeks earlier, City lost at Newcastle. It left them five points behind Liverpool and facing a gruelling run of matches against three difficult opponents: Arsenal at home, Everton away and, today, Chelsea at the Etihad. A sequence capable of derailing their title challenge.

Liverpool's draw with Leicester at Anfield the day after the Newcastle defeat took some of the pressure off, but lose to Chelsea and City would be three points behind Liverpool having played a game more. And Pep was up against a coach he has huge respect for: few teams in England take on City with the kind of daring, audacious football Maurizio Sarri employs.

The opposition analysis, led as always by Carles Planchart, produced a preparation plan built on the assumption that Sarri would not relent. Away to the champions, he would still go full throttle.

"Sarri came to the Etihad and immediately went on the attack. He had his team playing aggressive, super-high-pressing football from the outset. They tried to get us by the throat in tactical terms – it was a risky strategy. But we knew he'd do that. We knew that they're the kind of team that puts on the pressure from the start. They make it difficult to bring the ball out," explains Planchart.

"So, what did we do to prepare? Well, we practised bringing the ball out from the back, even more than usual. We knew they'd be trying to get it off us and that they'd be attacking hard. Chelsea back up the front line of the press with both attacking midfielders and sometimes even ask the pivot, Jorginho, to support the press really high up, too. It's the three in the middle that can really make life difficult. We have the kind of keeper who helps us generate superiority – not all goalies have those kind of skills. So that's what we did – created superiority at the back from the start. So, with the keeper, our four defenders plus the three midfielders, we've effectively got eight men up against their six-man press."

City also benefited from Sarri's choice of forwards.

"Once you've established that the maximum number of players they can push high towards you when you're playing out is six, you then take into account a key factor, which is that they played Higuain and Hazard, neither of whom will press you as aggressively or consistently as, say, Pedro will.

"So, while you're circulating the ball the objective is to draw them to one specific place in numbers, beat the press and look for a pass in behind Jorginho if he's pushed up to support their press. If you do that, find space and score the first time you beat their high press, then it's massive. That day pretty much every single time we drew them in and punched through their press, we scored."

City's strategy's worked to perfection. They played the game of their lives. Chelsea suffered their heaviest defeat of the Premier League era.

1-0 Kevin De Bruyne plays a quick free-kick through the Chelsea line to Bernardo, cutting in from the right. His low cross falls to Raheem Sterling, arriving late at the back, who scores. Four minutes are on the clock.

2-0 Moments earlier, Sergio Agüero has missed with a tap-in from two yards after sensational work from Bernardo in the box, one of the biggest misses of his life. This time, surrounded by Chelsea defenders and 25 yards out, he nudges the ball to his right then bends in an unstoppable shot.

3-0 Ross Barkley is short with a headed back-pass from outside his area and has forgotten that Agüero is in the way. No mistake this time.

4-0 Antonio Rüdiger blocks an Agüero dribble but the ball rolls to İlkay Gündoğan. His first-time finish zips low into the bottom-right corner. We've played 25 minutes.

5-0 Sterling wins a penalty, darting past César Azpilicueta, who brings him down. From the spot, Agüero waits for Kepa to move and rolls the ball the other way for his hat-trick.

6-0 A visionary inside pass from David Silva to Oleksandr Zinchenko and his low cross is tucked away by Sterling to complete the rout.

Agüero is ecstatic. Two hat-tricks in seven days against two giants of English football: Arsenal and Chelsea. This is his 11th Premier

League hat-trick (tieing Alan Shearer's record) and his 15th for City. His total goal tally in his last 16 games at the Etihad is an astonishing 25.

Today, after the final whistle, Madness's *One Step Beyond* booms out from the Etihad speakers. It's the anthem played at Stamford Bridge after every home win and City end up apologising for their bit of trolling. While it plays, Rüdiger runs over to Chelsea's travelling support to offer his own heartfelt apology.

"If Liverpool can beat this team to the Premier League title, it will rank as the most exceptional performance of any of the championship-winning sides from Anfield through the years," *The Guardian*'s Daniel Taylor writes.

Out on the pitch Bernardo Silva can hardly contain himself. We speak to him later in the season and he tells us: "When you play a team like Chelsea, you don't expect to be 4-0 up after 25 minutes. It was one of the best games we've played all season. We had a bit of luck as well – they all went in.

"That victory gave us a huge boost. We were back on top after that match, having gone into it thinking we might lose points.

"We went out knowing that we'd hold on to the ball and control the game. When you start a match confident about what's going to happen it makes everything so much easier. You get days when things still go wrong, sure, but that day against Chelsea, everything was perfect."

Begiristain leaves the stadium through the VIP exit in the Colin Bell stand, insisting that it feels like he's just seen Pep's Barça in action. As always he's watched the game alongside Manchester City's ideologue, the biggest football hard drive in the world: Ferran Soriano. City's CEO is justifiably proud of what they've achieved.

"When I'm talking to potential sponsors for the club I show them a web page that gives them the information they need. The last seven seasons? City's won the most league titles. The team with the most points? City. The most goals? Us. Again. The best goal difference? Ditto. The team with the fewest defeats? City again.

"We handed Pep a solid team when he arrived and he's taken it to the next level. Will we win the league every year? No. But, our base, what we call the underline, that's super solid. It doesn't depend on whether we win or lose a game. We may get knocked out of the Champions League, but one thing's for sure, we know we'll be back next year."

To a large extent, this is Guardiola's great achievement. His team's collective talent has hugely decreased the impact that chance has on the outcome.

Man City (4-3-3): Ederson; Walker, Stones, Laporte, Zinchenko; De Bruyne (Mahrez 68), Fernandinho (D Silva 75), Gündoğan; B Silva, Agüero (Jesus 65), Sterling
Chelsea (4-3-3): Arrizabalaga; Azpilicueta, Rüdiger, Luiz, Alonso (Emerson 73); Kanté, Jorginho, Barkley (Kovačić 52); Pedro (Loftus-Cheek 65), Higuaín, Hazard
Goals: Sterling 4, 80, Agüero 13, 19, 56 (pen), Gündoğan 25
Bookings: Gündoğan, Alonso, Jorginho
Referee: Mike Dean
Attendance: 54,453

THIRTY

THE YELLOW RIBBON

When Pep Guardiola lifted his first trophy as manager of Manchester City, he was the subject of an investigation by the FA. He had been under surveillance for some time. The charge against him was that he had pinned a yellow ribbon to his shirt. And the evidence was clear: you can see it peeking out from behind his jacket in pictures taken immediately after the 2018 Carabao Cup final, when he is celebrating his team's 3-0 win over Arsenal at Wembley. And this was by no means his first offence.

Guardiola wore the yellow ribbon for the first time on October 28, 2017, in a league game against West Bromwich Albion. He had worn it at 28 matches before the final.

But it was on the eve of the final that Pep learned he was in trouble with the FA. But there's trouble and then there is trouble. That's the point Pep was trying to make to begin with.

The ribbon represents the ongoing protest against the imprisonment of some of the leaders of the independence movement in Catalonia, the autonomous region in the north-west of Spain, including Barcelona, of which Guardiola is a native.

On October 1, 2017, the Catalan parliament held a referendum on independence, despite the Spanish government declaring such a vote illegal. The Guardia Civil – Spain's national police force – raided several polling stations, using violence against many of those waiting to vote. Guardiola talked about watching those scenes unfold "with great sadness".

In December 2017, he answered a question about the ribbon pinned to his jersey.

"I wear this ribbon because two people are sitting in a Spanish jail for the crime of defending the right to vote, something that those in power don't seem to support. This is not justice and until they are free, this ribbon stays with me at all times."

He was referring to Jordi Sánchez, president of the ANC (National Assembly of Catalonia) and Jordi Cuixart, president of Òmnium Cultural, an association which promotes Catalan culture and language and supports Catalan self-determination and of which Guardiola is a member. The two men were jailed on October 16, 2017, by judge Carmen Lámela, who ordered that they be held on remand without bail.

Several days later the Catalan president Carles Puigdemont, fearing a similar fate, fled to Belgium. Nine members of the independence movement were imprisoned: former vice-president Oriol Junqueras, former president of the Catalan parliament Carme Forcadell, plus Joaquim Forn, Dolors Bassa, Raül Romeva, Jordi Turull and Josep Rull, all former ministers. Seven Catalan politicians fled Spain: Antoni Comín, Lluís Puig, Meritxell Serret, Clara Ponsatí, Anna Gabriel, Marta Rovira and President Puigdemont.

In November 2017, after a Champions League game against Feyenoord, Guardiola again went on the record about the political situation in his homeland: "Everyone knows why I wear this yellow ribbon. I genuinely hope not to be wearing it for much longer because that would mean that the people jailed for having demanded the right to vote are free. I hope the Jordis and the rest of those imprisoned are freed soon so that they can return to their families and get on with living the life they deserve."

He then dedicated City's next Champions League win, against Napoli, to Jordi Sánchez and Jordi Cuixart. "The freedom to share ideas is the greatest expression of civil society," he said. "Both the ANC and Òmnium have fulfilled their duties to civil society by expressing our needs and wants. I sincerely hope that they will be freed soon. For many of us, as long as they are imprisoned, it feels as if we too, to some extent, have lost our liberty."

By February 2018, the week before the Carabao Cup final, Pep was being investigated by the FA for breaching rules prohibiting political gestures. However, he did not know it when he faced reporters for the pre-match press conference, sullen faced and issuing terse, one-word answers. There was another reason for his ill temper.

Later that day, Ràdio Cataluña reported that, in Barcelona, the Guardia Civil had boarded and searched the private plane carrying several of Pep's family members, including his wife and two of his kids. Apparently the police believed Carles Puigdemont might be on board.

"My wife told me what happened. I suppose that the Guardia Civil have the right to stop us and inspect our vehicle. They boarded the plane, saw it was my family and then left," said Guardiola.

The FA announced their decision the afternoon before the final: Pep was facing fines and a possible dugout ban if he did not comply. In addition to the usual anticipation around a cup final, there was now a spotlight on how Guardiola would accessorise at Wembley.

Pep arrived with the yellow ribbon pinned to his shirt, not displayed visibly on his jacket. It was therefore covered during the match, although as the final whistle blew and Pep turned to hug Manel Estiarte, both men's yellow ribbons were clear for all to see.

In the run-up to match-day, a call had gone out via social media to the 35,000 travelling City supporters, asking them to wear a yellow ribbon in solidarity with the manager.

Pep Guardiola: "Seeing this makes me feel a sense of belonging and I'm very grateful. This is about something that's happening in another country and there's no reason why our fans should be involved. But they understand that there are people in prison and I can't thank them enough for this."

FA president Martin Glenn refused to back down and in fact complicated matters even further with his next comments: "You can't have, and we don't want, football equipment to display political symbols. It could be the Star of David, it could be the hammer and sickle, it could be a swastika, anything, like Robert Mugabe on your shirt: these are the things we don't want."

Not Mr Glenn's finest hour. The FA president subsequently apologised for including the Star of David in his comments, but didn't take back his reference to a swastika.

Pep remained equally intransigent: "If I've broken the rules then I accept my sanction. But I'm a human being first and a coach second. The FA knows that I'm going to continue to wear the yellow ribbon whether it's on display or not."

With the aid of Xavier Sala-i-Martín and City's legal team, Guardiola responded to the FA with a written explanation of his reasons for wearing the ribbon on his lapel, arguing that it represents "a humanitarian cause, not a political one".

He provided a list of similar symbols which represent important causes including: breast cancer (a pink ribbon), testicular cancer and domestic violence (a violet ribbon) and the terminally ill (a yellow flower), arguing that the yellow ribbon serves a similar purpose. It "represents a cross-cultural movement which transcends politics and the political beliefs of those who wear it".

The symbol "relates to the four people currently imprisoned without trial and the calls for them to be released". It does not, he insisted, represent any specific stance related to Catalan independence.

With rumours of an impending ban circulating, Pep became determined that his own actions should not affect the team. "Obviously the club comes first, before what I think," he said. In the end, he decided not to wear the ribbon in the dugout, the only place where it is specifically forbidden, but continued to display it at every press conference.

At Wembley, the City fans with the yellow ribbons pinned to their chests watched their team lift the first trophy under their Catalan coach. It was a landmark for him, and also for the goalkeeper deposed as first choice in the Premier League after Pep's first season: Claudio Bravo.

After a turbulent 12 months in England, the Chilean was exceptional when called upon in cup competitions and his saves paved City's path to Wembley.

The first big stop came at home against Wolves on October 24, 2017, in the fourth round of the competition. It was a hard-fought game with the Championship team holding City to a 0-0 draw through extra time. Wolves' talented young striker Bright Enokbhare brought three unforgettable saves from Bravo, who then denied both Alfred N'Diaye and Conor Coady from the spot to win the shoot-out 4-1.

Claudio Bravo: "That was my best performance of the season. Wolves battered us and they were through one-on-one a number of times. Last year they'd have ended in goals, for sure. This time I saved everything that came at me."

Against Leicester in the next round, and with fixtures piling up, Pep fielded a second-string team, with starts for Phil Foden, Brahim Díaz and Tosin Adarabioyo. Bernardo Silva opened the scoring and things looked good for City until Jamie Vardy – who had, along with Riyad Mahrez, started on the bench – put one away in the seventh minute of added time. Another half-hour of effort; another shoot-out.

Bravo was once more the hero, saving Mahrez's spot kick to give City the victory. Sevens months later, Mahrez would complete a long-planned transfer to City.

City's A-team were back in place for the final against Arsenal and, while the margin of victory was such that Bravo's shot-stopping was not the decisive factor, he was instrumental in the goal that put City on their way. The first goal appeared at first to be a break from the Guardiola playbook, but in fact was a training-ground routine. A long ball from Bravo to Agüero isolated the striker with Shkodran Mustafi. The striker shook off the German and before the covering defenders could reach him, he surged forward and looped the ball over David Ospina to give City the lead.

In the second half, City dominated. Vincent Kompany redirected an İlkay Gündoğan shot and then David Silva scored with a precise finish from inside the box. Silva put his left thumb in his mouth and raised his right hand heavenwards. That one was for little Mateo. He was swarmed by his teammates and the bench emptied to join in the celebration. It was one of the moments of the season for City.

Afterwards, celebrations had to be restrained because these teams would meet again, in the league, four days later. There was a small party for players, staff, families and friends in one of the function rooms at Wembley, where the Manchester City chairman, Khaldoon Al Mubarak, gave a business-like speech: he was delighted with Pep's first trophy, they had done well and should keep working hard.

Ferran Soriano was also low-key, thanking the players for everything they had done and telling them to have a good time at the party – and then start working on the club's next targets.

Pep also addressed the group and then the dancing began, with Pep's younger daughter Valentina plus Carla and Alejandra Álvarez (the children of Edu, the physio) leading the charge.

At the same time, the caravan of City fans had caused major tailbacks on the road to Manchester. One of their number, Noel O'Brian, had hired a minibus for a party of 10: seven adults, a teenager and two kids. They were stuck on the motorway, motionless for five hours. The kids slept through the night on the spare seats and the minibus crossed the Manchester city limits as the sun rose on Monday morning. O'Brian was due at work at 7am, but asked for a day off, to sleep. "The next time there's a Wembley final, we'll book a hotel and stay the night in London," he said.

One year on, that's exactly what happened: Noel and company splashed out for a hotel room in London for the trip to watch City defend the Carabao Cup.

To reach Wembley, they beat Oxford United, Fulham and – in a repeat of last year's shoot-out – Leicester in the quarter-final. Claudio Bravo was still recuperating from a bad tear in his Achilles tendon, so deputising for the deputy was Aro Murić. The young Kosovan had been on loan to NAC Breda, but the terms of his contract meant that City could call him back to Manchester in the event of injuries.

With Bravo facing surgery, Txiki Begiristain came up with the idea of recalling Murić after the 20-year-old had played only a single game for his Dutch club. Pep used him in the Carabao Cup, all the way to the final.

His signature performance came against Leicester. Kevin De Bruyne and Marc Albrighton scored the goals as a hard-fought 120 minutes of football ended with the teams level. After Harry Maguire and Gündoğan converted, Christian Fuchs uncharacteristically missed the target from the spot. Then Raheem Sterling's attempted Panenka floated over the bar. Murić then saved the next two Leicester kicks, getting his 6ft 6ins frame down low, first to his right to deny James Maddison, then the other way to keep out the penalty of Çağlar Söyüncü, setting up Oleksandr Zinchenko for the winning kick.

Murić had performed spectacularly, and so too did another of Begiristain's shrewd acquisitions: the 17-year-old Catalan central defender Eric Garcia, who produced a dazzlingly mature performance on his debut.

City's dismantling of Burton Albion (9-0 away and 10-0 on aggregate) meant that Murić had next to no work in the semi-finals. And as the final approached, the 20-year-old discovered the power of hierarchy, when he was told that Ederson would be in goal for the final, with Murić on the bench and Bravo, still early in his rehab process, watching from the stands.

Pep is a great admirer of Maurizio Sarri, as he said at the press conference before the final.

Sarri may have felt like he needed the support. The final came just a few weeks after City gave Chelsea their most brutal ever Premier League defeat: 6-0, at the Etihad. That game was followed by fierce speculation that Chelsea had run out of patience with their coach and the final could make or break Sarri's Stamford Bridge career.

"Sarri's situation is a bit different than my first year because in my case the club never doubted me," said Pep before the final. "It was never suggested by the media that [City] will sack me if I lose this or that game. I have always thought highly about Sarri."

The Catalan was also reluctant to take on an opponent his team had just humiliated. "When I won 6-0 in the Premier League I was delighted with the scoreline. Now that we're about to play them again, I'm much less happy."

On February 24, 2019, London enjoyed unseasonal temperatures of 18 degrees. Manchester City prepared to compete for the first trophy of the season, while back home in Manchester, United, under new manager Ole Gunnar Solskjær, hosted Liverpool in a game that would impact their progress toward another goal:

the retention of their league title. A United win would see City top the league with the same games played as Liverpool, but the match was notable only for the injury count. United lost Ander Herrera, Juan Mata and Jesse Lingard before half-time and Liverpool's Roberto Firmino lasted only half an hour. Liverpool survived the carnage with a 0-0 draw to top the league by a point.

The new standard set by City and matched by Liverpool was simple: no margin for error. Spurs' title challenge all but ended that same weekend, with a 2-1 defeat at Burnley.

Meanwhile, at Wembley, Chelsea had learned their lesson from the 6-0 mauling in Manchester. The game ended 0-0 after extra-time. City had 61 per cent possession, Chelsea produced seven shots on goal, none of them on target, while Guardiola's men got three of their 11 shots on target, all of them stopped by Kepa. City needed a penalty shoot-out to defeat a team they had blown away in their previous meeting.

After a cagey final, Begiristain said: "Playing that kind of game was their only option."

City's lead analyst, Carles Planchart, went into more detail: "Sarri corrected the tactics he'd used in our league game. He realised that it was too risky pressing us high, man to man, as we bring the ball out from the back. He saw that Chelsea didn't have that capacity and decided to defend deeper."

Planchart concluded that, this time, Chelsea caused City the kind of problems you'd expect from a Sarri side.

"If you analyse the data you'd see exactly what I mean about that Carabao Cup final. It's mad. Kanté and Jorginho ran 16 kilometres, whilst the most running by any City player was Bernardo, who covered 14 kilometres. Two kilometres less! That's huge. It tells you how hard it is to find space against Chelsea's midfield. You move, you circulate the ball, but they stick to you like glue. Chelsea's midfielders run more than, say, Liverpool's, but Klopp's team's great advantage is that they press as one unit.

They're all very strong. The three midfielders, the defenders are total beasts, their forwards are so intense – a couple of Chelsea's strikers don't have the same work rate or intensity off the ball."

Sarri's adjustments did not prevent City from lifting the trophy, but before that could happen, there was an unprecedented and startling pantomime played out in front of millions. In the final minute of extra-time, Sarri prepared to replace Kepa with Willy Caballero. The young Spaniard had been complaining of muscular problems for a while.

City had arrived at Wembley prepared to face Caballero in goal. Word had reached them, as football whispers will do, that Kepa was struggling with a muscular problem and City's analysts guessed that Caballero might start.

The Argentine is a former City player and knows his old teammates inside out: how they take penalties, who feels pressure, who he's got a good record against in training.

When Pep saw Caballero preparing to take over from Kepa before the shoot-out, he moved over to Mikel Arteta and whispered something. The pair did not look happy. They knew that in this situation, Caballero would be a much more dangerous prospect for their players.

Mikel Arteta: "We knew that Willy knows us really well and also how exceptional he is at saving penalties. Of course we also knew that there was nothing we could do about it. It wasn't our decision to make, but having him in goal would give Chelsea a real advantage. It's one of the things Pep always insists on when he talks to the players: we can only control the things that are in our power and we shouldn't waste even a moment's energy trying to control things that are out of our hands. Then, as it turned out, Caballero didn't come on."

Caballero had already warmed up indoors and was ready to take over in goal. The fourth official gave the go-ahead to make the substitution but, to the complete astonishment of his teammates, opponents, the 80,000 spectators and the millions watching on TV, Kepa flat-out refused to leave the field.

Sarri repeatedly insisted that the keeper did what he was told, but Kepa stood his ground and told him 'no' – three times. The substitution could not go ahead.

On the touchline, Sarri was incandescent with rage. He gathered his men around him just before the penalty shoot-out and berated Kepa at the top of his voice, until Antonio Rüdiger intervened and pulled him away.

Pep had told his men that he would only ask those who wanted to take a penalty to do so. At Anfield in October, he had insisted on Mahrez taking the penalty his team won in the 85th minute with the score at 0-0, only to watch his new signing miss the target.

Mikel Arteta: "We let them decide for themselves. In a final it's all about how confident you're feeling, how you've come into the match, how you've played, if you've taken one a couple of weeks ago and whether it went in or not. It's always better for them to take that decision. And I could immediately tell from their faces who was up for it and who wasn't. It's better not to force these things. If you can see someone's looking a bit doubtful, even if it's a player you think can handle it, it's better just to look the other way and not put him under pressure."

A show of hands decided who would take City's penalties. At this point Pep had just one instruction: "Choose a side and stick with it. No hesitation."

The coach thanked the whole team for their hard work and told them they were all going to score and that Ederson would make some saves.

As it turned out, the Catalan was pretty much spot on.

First up is Jorginho: Ederson dives to his left to make the save.

For City, Gündoğan, who reverses a fine shot past Kepa.

César Azpilicueta converts for Chelsea.

Agüero scuffs a side-footed penalty that rolls into the bottom-right corner, just beating Kepa's dive. He trots back to the group on the halfway line, all smiles.

Chelsea trail, but Emerson brings them level.

And when Sané's penalty is stopped by a fine diving save from Kepa, the score is 2-2 after three kicks each.

However, David Luiz, off a big run-up, smashes his shot against Ederson's left-hand post.

Bernardo Silva keeps his cool to put City in front again.

Eden Hazard has to score to keep Chelsea in it, and does so with an impish Panenka.

And so it's all down to Raheem Sterling. The forward's progress this season – tactical, technical and mental – has been phenomenal. This is about *cojones*. He steps up to take the last penalty of the final at Wembley and crashes it into the top-left postage stamp.

The entire squad races towards Sterling and Ederson to celebrate. Everyone, that is, except Aymeric Laporte, who, like Fernandinho, is now carrying an injury, and who heads over to Kepa, a good friend and former teammate at Athletic Bilbao.

The cameras catch Pep saying something to the hero of the hour, although nobody can make out exactly what. Sterling tells us later: "What did Pep say to me? He said he didn't watch it. He wanted to know where it went. I said: 'top bin.'"

Inevitably, post-match, everyone wanted to talk about the Kepa incident, but Sarri appeared at the press conference in conciliatory mood and attempted to play the whole thing down. "I understood he had cramp so I wanted to change him. Kepa was right, even if the way he conducted himself was wrong. Mentally he was prepared for the penalties. It was a misunderstanding."

Chelsea management, eager to draw a line under the incident, invited a trusted journalist to the dressing room to get the official line from the player and the club's press officers. Kepa explained that Azpilicueta, the Chelsea captain, had mediated between himself and Sarri, and that he had already apologised to the coach. Meanwhile, the other captains, who clearly shared the coach's view of the whole debacle, talked to the press. The following day the keeper learned that he would be fined a week's wages.

Over in the visitors' dressing room, the atmosphere was quite different: reggaeton boomed out and the traditional master of ceremonies, Sergio Agüero, was dancing, a scene that would find its way on to social media soon afterwards. Otherwise City's celebrations were relatively low-key.

Everyone was completely knackered. City had played six games in three weeks; several players were struggling with injuries and all of them were wiped out.

The party took place in the Three Lions gastro pub inside Wembley stadium. In attendance were every club employee who came down for the game, the board of directors, the players and 120 sponsors. A temporary stage was hastily erected for the evening – busy staff were relieved when the game went to extra-time and penalties, giving them more time to get everything ready.

Sky Sports' James Cooper was the evening's host and Manchester indie band The Blossoms provided the music. Ferran Soriano addressed the gathering. Khaldoon, the chairman, was also in attendance having almost missed the high point of the whole day. He arrived in the dressing room just after the Carabao Cup itself had been whisked away, but Anna Pala, City's events manager, ensured that the president got his photo with the trophy, surrounded by Pep, Soriano and the other directors.

For the players, the celebrations continued to differ from those at the same venue, 12 months earlier. Then, the Carabao Cup had represented a first trophy for many of them. Now it was a stepping stone, albeit a significant one, towards greater goals, and that shift in priorities was reflected in those men as they circulated around the room.

Things had changed a lot in Manchester. Over in Spain? Not so much.

A year before, Guardiola had been rebuked for wearing the yellow ribbon. Now the imprisoned Catalan politicians he had been supporting were being tried in Madrid's Supreme Court. There were 12 defendants in total, nine held on remand and three released on bail. The trial kicked off on February 12, as did protests in Catalonia: demonstrations, worker protests worthy of a general strike and barricades on Barcelona's main arteries.

Victory at Wembley gave Guardiola his 19th cup win from 23 finals. Seven had gone to extra-time and four to a penalty shoot-out, only one of which ended in defeat. In total, an outlandish success rate of over 83 per cent. It was also his third trophy as City manager; only Joe Mercer, with five, had won more.

Yet in all that time, Pep had never looked more exhausted than he did at the post-match press conference.

The squad headed back to Manchester that same night and Pep arrived home absolutely destroyed. He collapsed into bed and awoke the next morning disoriented, forgetting where he was for a moment. He struggled to get out of bed, but duty called. West Ham were in town in three days: Pellegrini, back at the Etihad.

As he headed off to the CFA, still worn out, Pep listened to the radio, as usual: the trial in Madrid was still ongoing.

THIRTY-ONE

WEMBLEY DREAMS

Pep Guardiola: "My first memories of English football were of the horrible pitches, the wind and rain, lots of high balls, loads of crosses into the penalty areas, elbows flying between strikers and centre-halves.

"Historically, they played that way in England partly because of the state of the pitches. They were so bad that you couldn't really do anything else. They didn't play on grass, just mudbaths."

On at least one day each season, however, English football exported a different image. For Guardiola, growing up in Spain in the late 1970s and early 80s, the only English football guaranteed to be broadcast was the FA Cup final, unless a Spanish team drew English opponents in Europe. "The cup final was always played at the old Wembley Stadium and that became the iconic image of English football for us. You'd sit there in front of the TV and dream."

For football fans the world over, the FA Cup and those thrilling Wembley finals are a huge part of the mystique that surrounds English football today. Marc Boixasa: "Pep and I both think that one of the best things about football here is that it doesn't matter if it's League One, League Two or Conference football, most stadiums will be full. The way fans live their football is what sets the game in the UK apart. People abroad get an idea of what it's like to experience that when they watch the FA Cup."

Over the last three years, the oldest football competition in the world has taken Pep's City out of the Premier League circuit on six occasions: to Huddersfield, who in 2016-17 were a Championship team, and to Middlesbrough, Cardiff, Wigan, Swansea and Newport. It's not always been an easy ride, but it has taken them from the humblest of football grounds to the cathedral of English football: Wembley Stadium.

Mikel Arteta: "In the FA Cup, it doesn't really matter which league your opponents are in. A team from the third division can give you as much of a fight as anyone else."

In his first three seasons in England, Pep experienced all the drama and despair the FA Cup can offer. Take Alexis Sánchez's extra-time winner in the semi-final in May 2017 – the goal that ensured Guardiola would end his first season at City without a trophy. Or their excruciating loss to Wigan of League One in February 2018, a game played on a churned up, muddy pitch where everything that could go wrong, did: Fabian Delph was sent off just before the interval, rival staff had a face-off in the tunnel at half-time and Sergio Agüero was involved in a confrontation with a Wigan fan during a pitch invasion.

Then in Pep's third season, it all came together. A stunning 6-0 win over Watford in the final gave City their fourth trophy of the season, but this one, in the view of some within the CFA, was made in Wales.

In the fifth round, City travelled to Newport County of League Two. Pep's global superstars would play at Rodney Parade, against a team whose total market value was placed at £70,000. At half-time, the game was goalless and even that was largely down to Ederson's brilliant diving save to keep out a header by Tyreeq Bakinson, a 20-year-old midfielder on loan from Bristol City.

The second half belonged to City, but even after goals from Leroy Sané and Phil Foden, Newport had their moment – a

Pádraig Amond goal that briefly opened the door on one of the all-time FA Cup stories. That door was firmly closed by another from Foden and a Riyad Mahrez strike.

Guardiola tends to give extra time to coaches from lower league clubs but in Newport things went to another level. It was not just Mike Flynn, the home manager, but his players and their families who mixed with the City staff and stars after the game.

The quarter-final, on March 16, 2019, took City back to Wales to face Graham Potter's Swansea, then mid-table in the Championship.

Head of analysis Carles Planchart recalls how Swansea threw City off balance by exploiting gaps in their defence to give them a shock 2-0 lead at half-time. "In three years [in England] Swansea have been one of the few teams who have been able to dominate us with positional play and circulation of the ball. They always play with courage and determination and are technically very good.

"We probably prepared more for that Swansea game than we have for some of our league matches. You need to do a lot of planning and preparation for Swansea because they're a side that always wants to play. From the start they were pressing us, one on one, chasing us. They wanted to do to us what we do to our opponents. They were constantly looking for space in the midfield, between our lines, something that's a big part of our game."

Pep Guardiola: "I didn't give them a row at half-time, although I know that's something journalists are always keen to hear about. I didn't need to, we weren't playing badly. It's true that whenever we let them get the upper hand, they punished us for it, but that's what I like about English football – you go up against a Championship team that's only halfway up the table and they produce fucking brilliant football."

In the second half Pep made some important changes, bringing on Sterling and Zinchenko for Sané and Delph and then Agüero for Mahrez in the 64th minute. Within minutes Bernardo Silva was curling the ball around Kristoffer Nordfeldt and into the back of Swansea's net. A Nordfeldt own goal from Agüero's penalty in the 77th minute drew City level before the striker produced a winning header in the 88th minute, which replays showed should have been ruled out for offside. Agüero was philosophical: "If I hadn't got that one I'd have got another."

Carles Planchart: "If you take another look at that game, Bernardo's goal celebrations, the way Gabriel and Kun hare after every ball that goes out – the little things that tell you that these guys are hungry. A team like that, with the kind of talent we've got, is usually going to come off best. You have to make the most of their desire to win. It's obviously not a guarantee of trophies but without it we'd never have done this well in so many competitions."

Swansea already had a special place in the story of Pep's City. In his first season, City played Swansea back-to-back, one a league game and the other in the Carabao Cup. With only three days between the two matches, Pep took the team to a golf resort near Cardiff and asked his staff to organise a barbecue (it would be the first of many barbecues that season, a particular favourite with the South American players).

Marc Boixasa: "That was the night it all came together for us. We'd brought the chefs with us: Mirko and Jean Luc. It was the first time the coaching staff had hung out with the kit men. Those of us who'd been at the club for a while knew what characters they are, but they excelled themselves that night: dancing, singing, telling jokes – Pep, Manel, Domé, Carles, all of them cracking up, asking each other, 'Where on earth did we get these guys from?' You could see the chemistry in the group that night."

City's journey to the 2019 FA Cup final continued with an uneventful 1-0 victory over Brighton in the semi-final, while Watford and Wolves played out a memorable tie in the other half of the draw. Wolves led right up to the 94th minute, when Troy Deeney converted a penalty to make it 2-2 and force extra-time. Watford's Gerard Deulofeu, a Catalan who started his career at Barça, scored his second goal of the game to set up a date with City.

May 18, 2019. Pep and his men are in London, preparing for the 138th FA Cup final and anticipating a game that could see them become the first English club to win a treble of the League Cup, the Premier League and the FA Cup (Pep adds the Community Shield to this haul, a major trophy in his eyes, the equivalent of the Supercopa in Spain). Only Ferguson's Manchester United came close, in 1994, when they lost to Aston Villa in the League Cup final before going on to win the league and FA Cup double.

The odds are in City's favour. They've won all of the last 10 head-to-heads, by an aggregate score of 32-6. But this is the first time in 35 years that Watford have made it to the FA Cup final and, as their supporters stream into Wembley, filling every one of their allotted seats, their hopes are high.

In the 11th minute, Watford counter-attack and Roberto Pereyra is put through one-on-one with Ederson, who blocks expertly with his legs. From then on, it's a demolition.

City put the final to bed with two first-half goals. The first is fired home by David Silva before his namesake Bernardo's perfect assist to the far post finds Gabi Jesus, who taps home for the second. Kevin De Bruyne comes off the bench 10 minutes after the break to score one and make another for Jesus. Raheem Sterling makes the scoreline even more emphatic with two more strikes. It's another record, equalling the biggest winning margin in the FA Cup final. Bury beat Derby by the same scoreline in 1903.

City are the first Premier League team to win 50 games in one season. Their 26 goals in the FA Cup was last achieved in 1945, when all stages of the competition except the final were home-and-away ties. Guardiola is only the eighth coach to win all three trophies, after Bill Nicholson, Don Revie, Joe Mercer, Kenny Dalglish, George Graham, Alex Ferguson and Jose Mourinho.

After the game, the BBC's cameras catch Guardiola talking to Sterling in impassioned terms. What may have looked like an ill-timed lecture turned out to be a constructive – if impulsive – analysis of the forward's second-half performance.

"I'd spoken to him at half-time and told him to change the way he was attacking Watford's goal. It was so he'd have a better chance of scoring. And he did exactly what I asked him to, so that's what we were talking about. Nothing more."

Domènec Torrent, who celebrated City's fourth title with his wife at their home in Manhattan, said: "That image of Pep lecturing Sterling, who has just scored two goals at the end of an extraordinary season, might look like a telling-off from the outside. But those of us who know Pep well understand that it's just his desire for perfection. It's the reason that this man's teams play like they do and win as much as they do."

THIRTY-TWO

SERGIO AGÜERO: THE LAW OF THE BARRIO

At a table inside Salvi's, a popular Italian restaurant in Manchester's Exchange Square, on January 19, 2017, sit Pep Guardiola, Sergio Agüero and the agent of the Manchester City striker. The following morning, a blurry mobile-phone photograph is published by the *Daily Mail.* A serious-looking Pep is leaning over the table. Agüero is partially hidden, leaning back in his chair. There have been rumours of discord between the incoming manager and his highest-profile player, rumours that have gathered pace since the arrival of Gabriel Jesus to contest the striker role in Pep's team. One glance at this image does nothing to banish them.

Agüero was a City legend before Pep arrived in England. He was on his way to becoming the club's greatest-ever goalscorer, including one that will live forever in the collective memory of the club and its fans: the final-day, 93rd-minute winner in May 2012 that won the league title for the first time in 44 years in the most dramatic fashion imaginable. His name is scrawled in ink across the neck of shaven-headed supporters; it adorns the back of more City shirts than any other. "Nobody is more marketable than Kun," explains Omar Berrada, right-hand man to City CEO Ferran Soriano.

However, as 2016 turned into 2017, not everyone at City was ready to have his name etched on to their skin. The knocks against Agüero had begun before Guardiola arrived, and only increased in volume in the early months of his reign: Agüero was lazy and his timekeeping was unpredictable; he did not press opposition defenders; he had become complacent; his diet wasn't right (too much red meat – a typical Argentine).

Pep wanted more from his star striker. Soon after taking over at City he told the media: "Agüero could definitely be contributing a lot more to our game, to the whole process. It would be great if he improved his use of the ball, keeping possession better. I can't do anything for him in terms of his performance in the box, because he's outstanding there. He's going to do a lot for us, but I'd like to help him become a better player."

Pep called the dinner meeting at Salvi's hoping to help Agüero understand his philosophy better, to tell him he wanted him to be the example for the rest of the team. Pep needed his No.10 to press more, keep the ball more determinedly when in possession and show the same work ethic as all of Guardiola's other players.

"We talked about loads of things," Agüero tells us when we meet him in the latter stages of season 2018-19, a long time after the dust has settled. "We kept postponing it and then, when we finally met up we talked about work for 20 minutes at the most. The rest of the meal we spent chatting about other stuff – family, life in general. But people got the wrong end of the stick and were saying that because I hadn't been playing much, I wanted to leave. The thought never entered my head. Sure, when Gabi [Gabriel Jesus] came I knew that I might lose playing time. But I didn't consider leaving. I decided to wait and see what happened and to speak to the club if it became necessary. But it never did, so I didn't have to speak to them."

However, before Pep took over at City, Agüero had been tempted by the chance of a transfer to Barcelona. His friend and Argentina teammate, Leo Messi, had asked the Catalan club to sign Agüero before Luis Suárez had joined Barça. Although Barcelona were willing to meet the €90m price tag City had placed on their star striker, the deal didn't go through. Due to Financial Fair Play regulations, City were limited to spending £60m during that transfer window and were not confident of replacing Agüero within that budget.

Then they recruited Jesus. The Brazilian had just been signed when Pep and Agüero met in Salvi's and the impact was immediate. Pep replaced Agüero with the talented Brazilian forward for three games. The new boy scored three goals and provided two assists, but then badly injured a toe in his fourth game.

Agüero found himself back in the starting XI, but for the first time in years, he was feeling the heat. There had been other contenders for the top spot over the years – most recently Wilfried Bony, Stevan Jovetić and Álvaro Negredo – but there was never any doubt who the ace was. Jesus' arrival had changed everything. The Argentine would have to up his game. Scoring goals was no longer enough.

Mikel Arteta puts the challenge that lay ahead of Agüero into context. "Do players have to adapt to Pep? There's really no other option. It's one of the secrets of his success. He gets people so focused and intense about the game that anyone who doesn't adapt is finished, out the door. It's impossible not to adapt. They all have do it."

"I had to adapt and do much more pressing," agrees Agüero. "We did a lot of work on that in training. I have to press the goalkeeper and centre-back. Maintaining the intensity like that is really tough for me and it was something I'd never done before. But I've become much stronger physically over the last few years and my game outside the box has improved. I just wasn't used to playing like that. I still do what I need to do when I've got the ball, but off the ball my positioning and pressing abilities have greatly improved and I move much more effectively.

"As a player I'm nothing like I was when I played for Independiente. I was a second striker back then. Then in Spain I learned to move differently. And now my game is totally different even from what I was doing five years ago at City. Total transformation. Pep asked me to try a new way of playing and I had to adapt to that. It wasn't easy, but I had no choice."

Sergio Agüero was born in Buenos Aires on June 2, 1988, the second child of Leonel and Adriana. Throughout his childhood, the family lived in some of the city's most impoverished neighbourhoods, his father getting what work he could to provide for his ever-growing family (five more children arrived after Sergio). Forced out of one home after another by looting, gang violence or sheer poverty, Leonel moved his family from Villa los Eucaliptos to González Catán, Florencio Varela and on to Quilmes. From one slum to another.

Although Agüero rarely shines a light on his humble beginnings, neither is it something he tries to hide. On the contrary, he's hugely proud of everything that his parents did to feed and clothe their kids, keep them safe and give them a good education, all the while making sure that football was at the centre of family life.

Sergio Agüero: "My mates all know where I grew up. I prefer not to go on about it but I know exactly how far we've come. I grew up very fast. The neighbourhood I was born in wasn't an easy place. It was pretty rough. I wasn't really aware of how bad it was, but later I understood why my parents were so worried all the time. It was the kind of place where you could be killed by a stray bullet. It was a scary place. But my parents managed to get us out of there and move the family to a better neighbourhood. They wanted to give us a better start.

"At that age I was only interested in playing football all day.

I was still very young when we moved. The new place wasn't far, just a few blocks away, nearer to the city centre, but it was definitely an improvement, a little quieter, a little safer. But I was only ever thinking about football.

"I remember playing constantly, from morning to night. For me it all passed really quickly but I realise now how tough it must have been for my folks. My mum and dad really sacrificed for us.

"Now that I'm an adult, I understand my parents' reactions so much better. My mum was always worried sick because I was out from morning to night. She used to give me hell when I got home: 'Didn't I tell you not to go out again!' As a kid I couldn't see what all the fuss was about, but now I realise how dangerous our neighbourhood was. There were a lot of bad people, guys with guns – anything could have happened. None of that mattered to me. I just wanted to play football."

Young Sergio started to play on the *potrero* – the waste ground – by his house, where two sticks in the ground made a goal. It was there that scouts from the Quilmes-based football club Loma Alegre first spotted him. During the week he would play in the streets around his home. And in the *barrio* the rules of street football applied.

"Getting kicked black and blue was all part of the game. You had to learn how to look after yourself. There was no referee to protect you, no spray markings for where the free-kick was or where the wall should stand. You held on to the ball any way you could. Running with the ball was a whole different concept for us. I'd be up against big, tough boys and I was always the youngest and smallest. But I learned how to survive."

Sometimes there was money to be won. "We'd play for the odd peso, although I made sure my dad never found out. We'd spend our winnings on treats, maybe buy ourselves an *alfajor* [a cake popular in Argentina]. You'd win a peso and you'd bet it on the next match, mainly because you were so desperate to keep playing. Then when you'd won another peso, you'd spend it on a *dulce de leche* [a dessert], put your remaining peso on the next game and so on. I was never really bothered about winning the peso. I just wanted to play football."

Agüero would play with his dad, a left-footed player who would tease his son about his comparative weakness on that side. Even now, when Agüero scores a goal with his left, he makes sure his dad hears all about it.

"My dad did so much for me. He had to run after me all day long. He used to take me to training and even occasionally borrowed a car to get me there, or he'd arrange for one of the other parents to take me. If he could, he always came with me on the bus at the weekend – no matter where the game was. If he couldn't make it, he'd make sure I knew exactly how to get there, which bus to take, the best route.

"He taught me so much: how to behave, how to conduct myself. I'm so grateful for all of that. I see kids coming up these days, the kinds of priorities they have. It's all about having the right boots, the right clothes – I listen to them and think: 'If my old man caught you talking like that...' He taught me about what really matters in life and what doesn't."

Agüero was nicknamed Kun when he was just two years old and it stuck. It was a family friend, Jorge Chetti, who came up with it. Young Sergio was a big fan of a Japanese cartoon whose main character was called Kum-Kum, about a kid in the time of cavemen who was always getting into trouble. Hearing the kid talking incessantly about his animated hero, Chetti began to call him Kum and it stuck. Sergio morphed the name into Kun. By the time he was 10, that's what everyone called him: his friends, coaches, opponents, family. When he registered as a professional footballer, that was the name he gave.

When journalist Eduardo González saw Agüero playing football in the streets around his home, he decided to put his parents in touch with Néstor Rambert and Ricardo Bochini of Independiente, on the outskirts of Buenos Aires. The club liked what they saw and signed him up, offering his father a job which allowed the family to move to a better neighbourhood.

The young striker went from strength to strength and, aged just 15 years, one month and two days, became the youngest footballer to play in the Argentinian premier division, breaking a record held by Diego Maradona, who would later become his father-in-law. Although now separated from Gianinna, he is father to their son, Benjamin, born in 2009.

Agüero's face lights up when he talks about his son, who lives in Argentina with Gianinna.

"Being a long-distance dad is tough and I struggled a lot with it at the start," he said. "When he was younger, Benja didn't want to come here because of the weather, it was too cold for him. Now he's really keen. He asks about all my games, about the Champions League and he's no longer bothered about the weather. He's really into football but it's difficult for him to play in Argentina. I'm not there to take him to training and his mum can't always do it. It's also really important to us that he doesn't grow up feeling pressured because of who his father and grandfather are. Far better that he grows up enjoying his football at his own rhythm.

"Right now he's into PlayStation and is just as happy playing with those toys. It's all very different from the way I grew up. Of course, we talk about football when we're together but, most of all, we just have a lot of fun. And that's the most important thing. Family is the centre of everything and the love you feel for your child – well, that's the best.

"I want him to understand and value everything he's got because life is tough. I could never have imagined the life I have now. I never expected to get this far. As a kid I dreamed of playing for a certain team, and I did it. Then it was all about getting goals. Then I made it to Europe really young. It all just seemed to happen without me really thinking about it. I moved to Madrid at 18 thinking that I'd be there for three or four years and then I'd go back to Argentina. I never dreamt that I'd still be in Europe 12 years later or that I'd end up living in Manchester for eight years. But I'm glad it's worked out like this and I'm proud of everything I've achieved."

The teenage Agüero became a phenomenon at Atlético Madrid. After scoring 100 goals in 230 games for *Los Colchoneros*, winning the Europa League in the process, Manchester City paid £35m for him in 2011. The transfer came the year before Txiki Begiristain took over responsibility for recruitment at City, but the director of football has since become the striker's greatest champion. Nobody can say a bad word about Agüero around him.

"Stats! Look at his stats! The boy's a forward and he does what he's supposed to: score goals. Just give me the damn stats! Never mind all the nit-picking, all your bullshit. Goals are what I'm talking about. He gets us goals. I don't see anyone better!"

Agüero is amused when we tell him what Begiristain, a talented forward in his day, says about him.

"Txiki and I get on brilliantly. He's a senior executive but he and I and Manel [Estiarte] have a really good laugh together. Txiki is like one of the lads."

Txiki Begiristain: "Kun is spectacular. This season [2018-19] he's better than ever. I think he's got over his worries about *la bestia* (the beast, Begiristain's nickname for Pep Guardiola). A lot of our forwards have the same fears when they start working with Pep. They know that they're going to have to work harder than ever. They know he's going to make them suffer.

"Pep's No.9s have tactical nous – it's not enough for them just to be focused on goals. The problem is that's what No.9s do. They score goals. They're usually obsessed about their stats."

Guardiola certainly asks a lot of his No.9s. He asks them to create superiority in the centre of the field, drop to the wing when needed, close down spaces as the opposition defenders bring the ball out and draw the opposition away in order to create passing space on the inside – and *still* get on the end of City's crosses like strikers are supposed to do. After a sticky start, Agüero now exemplifies that role. Despite this pivot in the middle of his eight years as City's starting forward, he has continued to knock down a series of individual records, while winning trophy after trophy as part of a team connected with more sophistication than any in Premier League history.

The goal that immediately cancelled Glenn Murray's opener for Brighton on the final day of the 2019 Premier League title race was Agüero's 21st in the league, matching his total from the previous season and placing him one behind the trio of players who shared the Premier League's Golden Boot, Sadio Mané, Pierre-Emerick Aubameyang and Mo Salah. He has hit 20 goals or more in each of the past five seasons, despite the change in his responsibilities on the pitch. As of summer 2019, his total of 164 league goals is a record for his club; as is his all-competitions total of 231.

Diego Maradona once reigned supreme at the San Paolo stadium, Napoli's passionate, volatile home. And it was there, deep in the sticky, broiling Italian south that Agüero became City's all-time top scorer when Leroy Sané set him up to stick the ball past Pepe Reina. City's third goal in a 4-2 win placed the Argentine ahead of Eric Brook, who played for the club between 1928 and 1939, scoring 177 goals in that period.

"I remember every goal I've ever scored," explains the striker. "I remember every detail of all the goals I've scored for City."

But which is his favourite? "My top goal is one I scored at home to Norwich in my first year with the club. There was a big crowd of players between me and the goal. I improvised a toe-poke, the ball nutmegged about three defenders and went in. That's the one I like best: I took the ball from Micah [Richards], back to goal, turned, saw that there was no room for a dribble and improvised that little poke of the ball which left them no time to block. I only saw it go through the legs of the first guy, but on the television it turned out that it nutmegged a couple of them. When I saw the replay I said to myself: 'That's the only way I could have scored that!'

"I also like scoring against United because I know what it means to our fans. The next day people will be out shopping or walking the dog or taking the kids to school, wearing their blue City shirt and so proud to have won the derby. I was exactly the same as a kid. When your team won, you'd be out wearing the colours. I know exactly how people here feel. That's why it feels so good to score against United."

Agüero is serious about his goals. Every time he scores, he keeps the shirt he was wearing. If he changes at half-time and scores in both, they both go into the trunk in which he stores them. Eventually, he intends to ship them all to his house in Madrid, in which he has installed a small museum to his career.

The change in Agüero has, like every other quantifiable performance metric, been recorded by the Manchester City analytics team. The medical staff have software that monitors the players as they train. Every metre run – long distances, sprints, jogging – is recorded. The data shows how many sprints a player performs, what top speed he hits, his rate of acceleration, his heart rate during each activity. A colour coding system then shows the intensity and power applied in each area of performance.

Fitness coach Lorenzo Buenaventura: "In Pep's second year here, Kun improved in every single area. There wasn't a single training session or physical test where he failed to improve on the previous season's stats. His work rate has been absolutely spectacular."

Sergio Agüero: "Pep makes sure all his players improve. He makes the best even better. It's just what he does. He won't leave you alone for a second – there are no off-days.

"Some of the young players have big ideas, but then they get complacent and mess up. With Pep, you don't get away with that. It doesn't matter what age you are – 20, 25, 30 – he wants you working to improve every single day. Everything he says is for your own good, although at the start I couldn't see that. But over time I realised that he was right. He can be very direct, but it's good that he's up front about things.

"People had told me good things about him before he came, that he was a good guy. Then, when he arrived, I was a bit taken aback by his intensity. It wasn't always easy to understand what he wanted. With Pep, it can feel like he's putting a lot of pressure on you.

"You start thinking 'I've got to play well' and only end up putting even more pressure on yourself. But I understood pretty quickly that it's just his way. It's how he is. He was the same in his second and third seasons here. That's Pep: super-intense."

Agüero recognises that there are two sides to the coach.

"I have a great laugh with him, he's really good fun, but there's no laughing when it comes to work. He's a real worrier, too. Just after we won the Carabao Cup, we were playing West Ham at home. That morning, I stroll into the CFA for a swim or a massage and I see Pep, pacing up and down his office, scratching his head and muttering to himself, obviously a bundle of nerves. And I think, 'What a state he's in.' He was so uptight. Okay, West Ham are tough to play and it was a difficult game but we had eight hours until kick-off. And it wasn't him who'd be playing, it was us! There was nothing he could do at that stage.

"He's brought his style of football here, improved ideas. Of course, it's happened before – City under Pellegrini or Arsenal under Arsene Wegner, years ago. But nobody has ever done what

Pep's done, playing the way we play. And that can only be good for the English game."

Mikel Arteta: "The way [Agüero] runs, his body language just seems to naturally suggest that he's too laid-back: diminutive stature, notable backside. But we got the message to him that if you win the ball back higher up and more often, then your goal total will go up. You can help the team. Not 25 flat-out pressing sprints every game. Give us two flat-out sprints, to press the opponents, and win the ball back. When we have the ball you just need to do what you've always done.

"His worth to the team is enormous. He's the destination for City's moves forward, breakaway or constructed. His timing and speed dictate much of what those behind him do with the ball. And perhaps Kun is the best finisher anywhere in the world. He tucks opportunities away with clinical precision. We'll probably never be able to find his equal."

A snapshot of the new Agüero: March 1, 2018: Arsenal at the Emirates. Four days after City beat the same opponent 3-0 in the Carabao Cup final, they repeat the scoreline in the league. Agüero is one of City's most decisive players, despite not scoring.

He puts the second on a plate for David Silva with a neat pass through a cluster of opponents; he drops deep, into midfield, to pick up the ball and offer passing options to teammates; his link-up play with Kyle Walker, Vinny Kompany and David Silva is terrific. The third goal stems from his unbelievable control, which takes him past his marker. Agüero sets up Kevin De Bruyne and Walker to weave their magic and when the ball is cut back, Leroy Sané arrives at Olympic-sprinter pace.

The player made other changes for season 2018-19: he dyed his hair blonde and came up with a new goal celebration, in which he raises his right hand with his thumb, index finger and pinkie up.

"It's all my brother Mauricio's fault," Agüero laughs. "He was on at me to change my goal celebration and told me to do this thing with my fingers. I forgot to do it and he started bugging me even more. I think it means 'I love you' in sign language.

"The hair was his idea too. I wasn't keen, but then he said that I didn't have the balls to dye it before a United game. That was like a red rag to a bull. The only problem is that now my son wants to copy me and there's no way I'm letting him go to school like that. Schools in Argentina don't look kindly on that kind of thing."

Another snapshot, this time from February 2019, a tough, anxious month for City as they fought hard to catch up on Liverpool and secure their first trophy of the year, the Carabao Cup. City lost to Newcastle away and then prepared to face four games in 13 days: Arsenal, Everton, Chelsea, and Newport County in the FA Cup. Agüero started both the Arsenal and the Chelsea games, producing a hat-trick in each.

After the Arsenal game, Pep said: "Sergio isn't just the three goals he scored. It's how he fought and worked back. He gave absolutely everything for the team."

Agüero has changed in other ways. In 2018, he took responsibility for organising the squad's Christmas party. And he went all-in. Having agreed the basics with the club, Agüero did the rest of the planning himself. He would arrive at the CFA every morning carrying a briefcase and after training would sit down with the administration staff, with two mobiles and a laptop in front of him. He told passing teammates: "As well as a player I'm now officially an events organiser for club parties and celebrations. I've got a double shift today. The club need me to multitask and from now on I'll be spending my afternoons organising parties."

Staff watched as Agüero negotiated with venues to get the best price for dinner and drinks. Such was the success of the party, his role was made permanent.

Agüero is an events manager then, as well as a transformed, dynamic presence at the top of Guardiola's winning machine. But there remains, too, something of the kid who grew up on some of the toughest streets in the world.

A final snapshot. The breakthrough moment of a record-breaking 2017-18 season comes on August 26, 2017, away to Bournemouth. Raheem Sterling scores in injury time and sprints over, closely followed by his teammates, to celebrate with the City fans. Some of them have climbed over the barriers to celebrate on the pitch, and Agüero catches sight of one over-excited City fan being manhandled by a cop. He sprints over to appeal on the guy's behalf, but receives a hard shove for his trouble. Kun faces up to the police officer, shoulder to shoulder with his normally laid-back teammate, Fernandinho – himself a product of the *favelas*. More pushing and shoving ensues and an official complaint about Agüero's conduct is made to the Dorset police. You can take the boy out of the *barrio* . . .

Sergio Agüero: "Sometimes the law of the *barrio* still applies – that same spirit, the same idea of fairness. I saw that they had got hold of one of our fans, four against one, and were practically smothering him. It was outright abuse. The guy couldn't breathe. Then this cop starts giving me a hard time, so I tell him to fuck off. Nothing more serious than that. It's the way I grew up and I can't help reacting like that. Back home there was a code: if there's a fight, and it's one on one, you stay out of it, but when it's one against four . . . That's how I grew up and it's something I still live by."

THIRTY-THREE

MAKING-OF MATCH: FULHAM 0 MANCHESTER CITY 2 MARCH 30, 2019

At first glance, a neutral observer would be forgiven for thinking the day was about Sergio Agüero. The striker scored his 27th goal of the season to seal a win that took City back to the top of the Premier League, and it provided an interesting point of comparison. This was Agüero's 228th goal for City in all competitions, matching the total that Thierry Henry scored for Arsenal (although Henry remained the leading foreign goalscorer in the Premier League). Agüero had reached Henry's mark having played 46 games fewer.

However, another towering figure from City's history most occupied the hearts and minds of the club, its fans and players: Bernard Halford, known as 'Mr Manchester City' – the heart and soul of the club for over 40 years.

Getting to Craven Cottage for the Fulham game was not easy. The London Underground had closed stations on the District Line from Earls Court onwards, meaning that City's 3,500 travelling fans, including Pep's wife Cristina and their kids, couldn't get off at the main stadium underground stop, Putney Bridge, and had to walk down Fulham Palace Road, or the Thames Path, from the Hammersmith stop.

When they reached their assigned stand, the famous Putney End, which butts on to Bishop's Park behind it, the City fans discovered around 1,500 red-and-black scarves which the club had sent a few days earlier and Fulham staff had graciously helped to distribute across the seating, in homage to Bernard, who had died during the night of March 26, aged 77, after a short battle with cancer.

Pep knew about Halford even before he signed for City, thanks to a profile article in *El Pais* newspaper in February 2015, and had enjoyed getting to know 'Mr City'. He had visited him in hospital the moment he heard about Halford's illness.

Pep Guardiola: "I was one year old when Bernard joined City. While getting to know him, he explained beautifully how things were back then, how City had evolved. In clubs like this, players and coaches come and go, but some special people stay for a lifetime. He's one of the guys who helped build our club, make it what it is, and so our fans naturally want to pay proper respects to him. When we play at home, against Cardiff, we'll try to make that match a homage to his memory and show how much we all loved him."

During the Fulham match, the travelling fans chanted Bernard's name, twirling their scarves in tribute to a man who perhaps invested more hours of his life in the club than any other.

Vincent Kompany: "Bernard is one of the reasons we're all here. He's been part of the fabric, part of the history of City for 47 years and he was part of everything which went before this current era of success. I'm certain that he'd have been honoured, hugely, to be remembered and celebrated in this way today. For everyone to hold a minute's silence at training on the morning we heard of his death was more than merited because he was vitally important to City across his life."

For Kompany and his fellow City veterans, David Silva and Agüero, Halford had been an important point of counsel and support. A man who'll be missed by them all.

In the corridors of the CFA, the sense of sadness and loss was palpable. Even relatively recently arrived players such as Ederson and Bernardo Silva took to social media to pay tribute.

"When you come into this world, in Manchester, you're either red or blue – I was born a Blue," Halford was fond of saying. "And that wasn't plain sailing. Schooldays as a City fan weren't easy by any stretch. We'd win a game one weekend and be relegated the next."

Born and bred in Chadderton, he was the son of a cotton mill worker at a time when that industry was the motor of Manchester. At school – St Gregory's in Ardwick – rugby was his game but, for the rest of his life, football was his passion. He often spoke with great nostalgia of his first sight of City in action, at Maine Road against Portsmouth. Just eight years old, he was taken to the game by his uncle.

"From Chadderton he and I had to catch three different buses in order to get there for a 12.30 kick-off."

That day was the dawning of a lifelong love affair. As a young fan, he lived through the few glorious highs, and the many painful lows, of the 1950s and 1960s.

After a short while working in the cotton industry, he joined Oldham Athletic as club secretary. By season 1972-73 Halford landed his dream job – he signed for City, initially in an administrative capacity. Then he was promoted to secretary, a vital post which he held for nearly four decades. His natural warmth and enthusiasm for the game made him a hugely popular figure across English football and, in 2006, he was inducted to the club's Hall of Fame – the only person to be given this honour without serving as either a player or coach.

Life as 'Mr Manchester City' was never dull. He saw 30 different first-team coaches, six owners, five relegations and five promotions. The good times were rich and varied. He was there when the club were in the third tier, and when they won three Premier League titles. He was there to see them lift the European Cup Winners' Cup in 1970, plus three more Wembley trophies. His mobile phone ringtone was Martin Tyler's famous *Agüeeeeeeeerooooo!*

They say that across all his 47 years at City, he only missed one match, away to Dortmund, after the death of his mother-in-law. "He loved the club. He gave them a bit of soul and he is as much a part of our history as the club's greatest players," said Noel Gallagher after Halford's death.

The scarves those fans whirled above their heads at Fulham, and which Pep and his players wore at the end of the match, were a graceful nod back to the one Halford wore when he became, until now, the only person other than a player or coach to lift the FA Cup at Wembley.

By 2011, in 39 years of working for City, Halford had seen them win just one trophy. The club told him that should they beat Stoke at Wembley and end a 35-year drought (since the 1976 League Cup final victory over Newcastle) he would be invited to lift the famous trophy.

Thanks to a Yaya Touré goal, City did just that and Mr Manchester City wore a red-and-black scarf to mark his moment of glory. "I was 69 years old and I lifted the FA Cup with 90,000 people at Wembley. Can you imagine? I remember sitting watching Stanley Matthews in 1953. Fifty-eight years later, it's *Alice in Wonderland.* It was an historic moment, perhaps the best day of my life," he recalled years later. He didn't know at the time that City had to work hard to convince the FA. Bureaucracy hasn't much time for sentiment, but they won the protocol battle, and then won on the pitch.

During those 40 years married to the club, Halford lived the joy and the pain as fully, as emotionally as any of the club's supporters. His toughest day, by his own admission, was January 5, 1980, in Halifax. "They were 92nd of the 92 professional clubs in England and they beat us. It was horrible. I'll never forget that day. It was even worse than when we were relegated against Luton in 1983."

His favourite player was Bobby Johnstone, the heart of the

Famous Five, to whom David Silva is often compared. Over the years Johnstone became one of his closest friends and was best man at Bernard's wedding to Karen.

Halford was also secretary to the Manchester association of ex-rugby players and president of Gregorians FC, the alumni team of his high school, for whom he raised funds throughout his life.

Back in the Putney End at Craven Cottage, the fans chanted 'There's only one Bernard Halford!'

Bernardo Silva and Agüero wrapped up the points with a goal apiece. City had 65 per cent possession and didn't give up a single shot on goal.

At the end of the game, Brian Kidd handed all the players and coaching staff red-and-black City scarves, so they could join the travelling fans in the Putney End in appreciation of a club legend.

His funeral procession departed from City's Etihad Stadium on April 10 for a ceremony which took place in St Mary's Presbytery in Failsworth, Manchester. But the 'goodbye' to Mr Manchester City began that day at the Putney End of Fulham's beautiful ground, on the banks of the Thames, when the fans showed their appreciation for one of the men who, for half a century, had given meaning to the club.

Fulham (5-4-1): Rico; Christie, Fosu-Mensah, Le Marchand, Chambers, Bryan; Ayite (Kebano 64), Zambo Anguissa, Cairney (Schürrle 70), Sessegnon; Babel (McDonald 88)
Man City (4-3-3): Ederson; Walker, Otamendi, Laporte, Zinchenko; De Bruyne (Fernandinho 75), Gündoğan, D Silva; B Silva, Agüero (Jesus 57), Sterling (Mahrez 88)
Goals: B Silva 5, Agüero 27
Bookings: Le Marchand, Christie
Referee: Kevin Friend
Attendance: 25,001

THIRTY-FOUR

PEP'S ROULETTE

The idea was raised over a staff lunch. Pep was looking for a new approach to squad discipline and one of his sports science staff mentioned Ralf Rangnick's roulette. Rangnick, sporting director at Leipzig, introduced the practice when he was in charge at Schalke 04, replacing fines with a series of chores related to the day-to-day running of the club. When a player broke the rules, he'd spin a customised roulette wheel and be allocated a task according to where the wheel stopped.

Pep had long doubted the value of fining multi-millionaires, which remains common practice despite the ever-increasing salaries of elite players. The funds raised would typically be used to pay an end-of-year bonus to lower-paid staff, or, as was the case at City, to make charitable donations. Pep doubted, however, that his super-rich players registered a relatively small deduction on their payslip, and associated it with a transgression in their workplace. It could just as easily be matchday tickets, replica jerseys or the use of a private plane.

He loved the idea of the wheel and asked Marc Boixasa, the team manager, to come up with an appropriate list of punishment-tasks. Boixasa turned in a list of 25, which Pep and Manel Estiarte narrowed down: paying for a team dinner, paying for a staff dinner, working in the kitchen, community work, a shift in the academy, joining the performance analysis team, working with the ground staff, helping out the kit crew and doing the laundry. There was also a 'teammates' choice' category where the dressing room chose the punishment, and an 'invite a friend' category where the guilty player nominates an innocent teammate to join him in the task. Guardiola and Estiarte added a 'lucky escape' option.

The following morning, as the first-team players arrived for work, there was a new addition to the dressing room: a roulette wheel, complete with blue-and-white triangles, mounted on a stand in the middle of the room. Pep explained: "No more fines. From now on, if you mess up you spin the wheel to find out what you have to do to compensate the team."

From that day on, the City players knew exactly who had broken the rules and what they had to do to make up for it. Talk on your phone in the massage room, duck out of commercial obligations or turn up late to breakfast or training and the consequences were immediate – straight to the roulette wheel.

There are those at City who are unlikely ever to have to spin the wheel – David Silva and outgoing captain Vincent Kompany, for example. Then there are others for whom laundry duties have become a part-time job. Sergio Agüero and Riyad Mahrez were frequent offenders, while Benjamin Mendy has spent so much time in the laundry that it has become his second home.

Completing these tasks also gives the players a sense of the hard graft that goes on behind the scenes at their football club. For Pep, the wheel has become a vital part of his efforts to create a sense of team spirit at all levels of the club. Having superstar athletes grafting alongside ground staff goes a long way to reinforcing the idea that everyone – not just the players – has a contribution to make to City's success.

Manel Estiarte: "Now they might have to spend an afternoon with the analysts, dissecting our opponents and it's a great chance to study say, the key strikers of the team we're playing in three weeks. They're starting to appreciate the amount of work done by technical staff, the groundsmen and the laundry staff."

THIRTY-FIVE

RAHEEM STERLING: CHANGING THE NARRATIVE

Another day at the CFA. Physios, medics and support staff are the first to arrive, followed by the players who troop in one by one. Music booms out of the dressing room as they get changed for training. Early bird Bernardo Silva is in first as usual and the jokes are already flying. Mostly at his expense. John Stones, Kyle Walker and Fabian Delph are having a good-natured but heated argument about something on the radio. Leroy Sané grabs the chance to pick De Bruyne's brain. David Silva is in business mode, talking with Vincent Kompany and Kun Agüero – a cabinet meeting of this team's senior figures. The kit men bustle about, handing out new kit; physios issue reminders of timeslots on the massage table or in the rehab swimming pool.

In the midst of it all, one man sits reading the Bible: the 24-year-old Londoner, Raheem Sterling.

Sterling has an unshakable faith in God and in the fact that his own talent is God-given. This is how he understands all that he has achieved, both as part of the City winning machine and also individually, named as the player of the year for 2018-19 by the English football writers.

Sterling's relationship with the press was not always like that. Kevin De Bruyne, in a piece with the *Players Tribune*, explained how the way Sterling was written about framed his early days at City, and how far removed the character portrayed in those stories was from the real Raheem. "Before I came to Manchester City, I didn't really know what to make of this Raheem Sterling guy. I had never met him, and from what I'd read about him in the English press, I thought he was going to be a very different character. Raheem and I have this strong connection, because we arrived at City around the same time, and there was a lot of negativity about us in the press. They said I was 'the Chelsea reject'. They said Raheem was this flashy guy who left Liverpool for money. They said we were difficult characters. Truthfully, I don't have many close friends – inside or outside of football. It takes me a really long time to open up to people. But over time, I got closer to Raheem, because our sons were born around the same time, so they would always play together. He couldn't be more different from what the tabloids were saying. This is the real truth: Raheem is one of the nicest, most humble guys I've met in football."

Pep Guardiola has trouble pronouncing Sterling's nickname 'Raz' and still calls him 'Rash' but the coach had no difficulty in spotting his latent talent from their very first training session together, despite the fact Sterling was not on his best form.

Sterling joined City the year before Guardiola left Munich, in July 2015, for a record £50m – at that time the highest fee paid for an English player. After a lacklustre first season, he joined England for their disastrous 2016 Euro campaign which saw them knocked out by Iceland in the last 16.

A disappointing first year followed by a disastrous summer. Enter Pep. City's football director, Txiki Begiristain, had signed Sterling specifically in anticipation of Pep taking over.

"He had a spark, a capacity to shake off markers. He's explosive and above all he's got that burst of pace which takes effective wide players to the goal line. Even then, it was also clear that he was a guy who loved to cut in, too."

Begiristain's football instincts were correct. Under the guidance of Pep and his team, Sterling has become a truly world-class player.

In his first season under Manuel Pellegrini, Sterling only managed six league goals and by the second half of the campaign had lost his place as a regular starter.

"The huge transfer fee was actually pretty detrimental in terms of his self-confidence, which is so important for any player. As things didn't come off for him you could almost see Raz fading away," explains Mikel Arteta, who was still playing for Arsenal at the time. The following year, Arteta joined Pep and Domènec Torrent at City and he began to work closely with Sterling.

"We wanted him much closer to the penalty area. It was like he was a bit scared of the goal. We wanted him to become the kind of player who would get us a goal every game, or even just missing two or three big chances. We wanted him constantly generating goal threat. And we wanted him to lose the fear. He needed to believe in himself, to believe that he could be the best."

The new regime had an almost immediate impact. Suddenly his head was up, he was running more than ever and, by Pep's second season, had formed one of the most lethal attacking forces in the history of the Premier League with Leroy Sané and Sergio Agüero, between them scoring 67 of the team's total of 140 goals.

First, however, the coaching team had to realign Sterling for his role on the right of Guardiola's trident. Mikel Arteta: "He'd picked up a few bad habits along the way. He'd played on the inside a lot or out on the left wing. When you move to the right wing, the direction and angle of possession coming to you is very different. When the ball reached him he really had his gaze fixed on it – rather than half-touch instinctive control and the vision of what's around him."

Sterling was static when he got the ball. Guardiola's solution was to try to turn him into City's version of Romario, the coach's old Barcelona teammate and a World Cup winner with Brazil in 1994.

Pep Guardiola: "In that Dream Team era, whenever I saw Romario with his back to the centre-halves I'd never give him the ball. But the instant I saw him on the half-turn with his shoulder dipping as if he wanted the ball fed into his right or left foot, I knew he thought he could explode away from his marker. In that instance I always hit the pass immediately. Every time. I'd learned that his vision meant he'd had one eye on the distance between him and the opposition goal and the other eye on where the ball was. If he opened up his body shape like that and I fed him the ball, the defender was automatically done for."

The key to this strategy was Sterling's acceleration. Guardiola's analysis staff compare their forward's explosive first steps to those of Leo Messi. While the Barcelona player doesn't possess a sprinter's speed over distance, his acceleration – combined with an intuitive sense of when to make his move – leaves defenders in his wake. Thus began the Romario-fication of Raheem.

The plan was that Sterling should make a habit of dropping slightly further away from his marker, or nearest opponent, when looking to receive possession, his body turned towards the goal. In that position, if he then gunned his extraordinary accelerator, the sprint was always to the danger area. Arteta: "If he's found a space about three metres off his defender but he's half-turned towards the goal then his sprint takes him much more quickly to a space where he can shoot and that's going to cause the rival much more damage. It's also a tactic, dropping off a little, so that your defender gets drawn into a position he mightn't want to be in. It leaves space behind him and Raheem can attack that space. If it's close to, or in the penalty area, they also have to hesitate before putting in a challenge."

Arteta is drawing on facts with his assessment. For example, in the 1-0 Champions League victory over Feyenoord in November

2017, Sterling pulled all of this together. He dropped off at the edge of the box, drawing his defender, Renato Tapia, with him and, with his back to goal, shunted a quick pass backwards to Gündoğan. The instant he released the ball, he swivelled and burst into one of his 0-60 sprints, into the space where Tapia had been. Gündoğan read the move, slid the one-two pass into that space. One-vs-one with the keeper, Sterling lofted it over Brad Jones for City's winning goal.

Sterling played increasingly on the left wing in season 2018-19, although Guardiola continued to move him around a lot. His partnership with Bernardo Silva went from strength to strength, meaning that Leroy Sané figured much less in the starting XI. The PFA Young Player of the Year won by Sané in 2018 went to Sterling in 2019, after he finished the season with a personal best of 25 goals and 18 assists from 51 games. By November 2018 City had seen enough to extend Sterling's contract through season 2022-23.

Yet Guardiola continues to see room for improvement. Take the coach's critique of him after the home game against Watford on March 9, 2019, in which he had scored a hat-trick by the 64th minute. "Sterling could do better. He didn't follow his full-back two times. He lost two, three or four balls which he has to avoid because he conceded counter-attacks. Of course, I am so glad in terms of what he has done, scoring three goals. The first half was not the best Raheem has done this season and we will work on that."

If Sterling changed gears on the pitch during season 2018-19, the same can be said of his life in the public eye. By the end of the season, his had become one of the most influential voices in the fight against racism.

At Liverpool, he was headbutted in the street and called the n-word. On December 16, 2017, as he got out of his car at City's training ground, a Manchester United supporter with a history of football-related violence, kicked and shouted racial abuse at Sterling. Then, during City's first league defeat of the season, against Chelsea on December 8, 2018, came a turning point.

During the first half, as Sterling leaned forward to pick up the ball in front of the Matthew Harding Stand, several home supporters were captured by cameras screaming obscenities at him, with one allegedly subjecting him to racist abuse. Chelsea suspended four fans from attending matches while they conducted an investigation into the alleged abuse. The following day, Sterling posted on Instagram drawing a correlation between the media's treatment of black footballers and "racism and aggressive behaviour" from the stands. As an example, he juxtaposed the *Daily Mail*'s coverage of two young players, one black (Tosin Adarabioyo) the other white (Phil Foden), buying homes for their respective mothers. While the headline on the Adarabioyo story read: 'Young Manchester City footballer, 20, on £25,000 a week splashes out on mansion on market for £2.25m despite having never started a Premier League match,' the headline on the Foden piece read: 'Manchester City starlet Phil Foden buys new £2m home for his mum.' Sterling concluded: "All I have to say is have a second thought about fair publicity and give all players an equal chance."

Sterling has a Kalashnikov tattooed on his right leg. The one that scores the goals and terrifies opponents. Not so long ago *The Sun* newspaper used the tattoo to attack the player. Just ahead of England's 2018 World Cup campaign, the newspaper published a photo of the tattoo under the headline: *Raheem shoots himself in the foot*. Sterling immediately defended himself on social media. "When I was two my dad was gunned to death. A long time ago I made a promise to myself that I would never touch a gun in my lifetime. I shoot with my right foot, so it has deeper meaning. And it's still unfinished."

Four months after the incident at Chelsea, on March 25, 2019, Sterling and his black teammates were subject to vicious racial abuse from the local fans during England's 5-1 away win over Montenegro. After scoring his country's fifth goal, Sterling ran to the opposing stand and celebrated by holding his ears. He posted the celebration picture on his Instagram after the match with the caption: "Best way to silence the haters (yeah I mean racists)."

The incident kicked off a huge debate in the UK media over how players should react to racist abuse. "I wouldn't personally agree with walking off. If you walk off they win," was Sterling's own view. By the end of season 2018-19, he told *The Times* that any club whose fans hurl racist abuse should have nine points deducted. "It sounds harsh, but which fan will risk racist behaviour if it might relegate their team or ruin their title bid?"

Sterling was born in Kingston, Jamaica, where he lived until the age of five. Three years after his father was shot, his mother brought him to live in England, looking for a better life. He grew up in Brent, in the shadow of Wembley, a tough, deprived area of north London, described by RightMove as one of the 10 worst places to live in the UK. Yet Sterling has great memories of his childhood and has never forgotten his old neighbourhood. He treated 550 kids from his old school to tickets for City's FA Cup semi-final against Brighton at Wembley and stepped in to save the local community centre in Stonebridge when it was put up for sale by the council.

When City played Newport in the FA Cup, he also took time out to meet a young fan, Ethan Ross, after the teenager's grandmother wrote to thank Sterling for his work against racism and explained that her grandson was coping with similar abuse.

"It was probably as heart-warming for me as it was for you to finally meet up, Ethan", Sterling wrote on Twitter after the meeting, telling the youngster to keep on fighting prejudice and report the incidents immediately.

Then in April, Sterling paid all the costs of Damary Dawkins' funeral after hearing that the 13-year-old Crystal Palace youth player had tragically died of leukaemia.

Sterling's forthright approach to combating prejudice has increased his marketability. Where once it was players like Sergio Agüero, De Bruyne and social media star Benjamin Mendy who attracted the big sponsorship money, now Sterling has joined them as a major commercial draw.

He gained control of the stories told about him at the same time as his productivity on the pitch began to reach new heights. He ended 2018-19 as the Football Writers' Association Footballer of the Year, a leading advocate in the fight against racism and one of the most dangerous forwards in Europe.

THIRTY-SIX

SPURS: A DRAMA IN THREE ACTS

April 19, 2019. The morning after the night before. Pep Guardiola is watching his players train, just hours after their agonising Champions League exit to Spurs on away goals. In one of the most dramatic finales in the history of modern football, his side appeared to have progressed to the last four of the competition after Raheem Sterling's 94th-minute goal, only for VAR to deny them, revealing Sergio Agüero to have been offside when the ball broke to him in the build-up. Pep – who had exploded in celebration, and then collapsed in something akin to grief – is still in shock, but something has caught his eye. Someone. Phil Foden.

The pride of City's academy is buzzing around the training pitch at the CFA, his infectious enthusiasm transmitting to his beleaguered teammates. Pep makes an instant decision. He will include Foden in the starting XI for the weekend's re-match with Spurs, in the league. If City are to keep Liverpool at bay and retain their title, this game would be vital.

Pep recalls: "He [Foden] radiated vitality that morning – some others around him were still in pieces, the team was hurt but he added an injection of bite, confidence, vitality which everyone around him needed."

The restoration process continues. Centre-half Aymeric Laporte, a tower of strength in the centre of City's defence all season, chose the Spurs tie to deliver his worst performance of the campaign. The defender was at fault for both of Heung-Min Son's early goals.

"I had the feeling that I could have done more," admits the French-Basque. "I knew I'd failed on a vital night. We were all buzzing when we went out to start the match, which only means that the way it ended fucked us off all the more intensely. I'm not the first to mess up, I won't be the last. You have to treat it as a lesson to learn from. Errors need to teach you as well as hurt you.

"I didn't speak with the manager the day after the Spurs game. If any of us makes a mistake we're only too well aware of it, there's no need for someone to point it out. Honestly, I think anyone talking to me about the things I did wrong would only have served to damage my morale even further. By then I was obsessed about getting Spurs back that weekend, putting things right – winning.

"I wanted to feel better again, to feel that I was still just as important to the team. That's the major difference with the Champions League. I can recall Premier League errors against United or Burnley, but they didn't carry the same level of punishment as a European knockout match."

Mikel Arteta sat down with Laporte. "We knew it was vital to raise Laporte's morale. There had been an impact. A defeat like that has to hurt, or else we aren't doing things right. But you can't let the effect reverberate. I talked to him to underline that every single player, no matter the level, tastes defeat. Everyone fails, everyone makes mistakes. I told him that I could show him footage of horrendous mistakes by centre-halves in Champions League and World Cup finals. The biggest names, too: Piqué, Ramos, Cannavaro, Maldini, even Beckenbauer. Top players committing errors in the worst scenarios. I told him that we wanted him to turn the page and get back to being what he'd been until that night – the best centre-half in the Premier League."

Guardiola's team selection during this period of the season is already planned, based on data analysis and the Catalan's own observations. Laporte had been scheduled to rest for the league match against Spurs, but Pep sees that moving his centre-back out of the team will appear to some as punishment for the errors in midweek. The plans are changed. Laporte will start against Spurs.

A couple of days later, Laporte is back at the scene of the crime and back at his imperious best. The highlight of his game is a providential interception as Son prepares to shoot past Ederson. A goal-saving intervention – and a 1-0 win for City.

When Txiki Begiristain was deployed to Uefa HQ in Lyon to attend the draw for the quarter- and semi-finals, nobody wanted Barcelona (Messi is always to be avoided) or Liverpool (familiarity doesn't breed contempt in the Champions League but it does make things complicated). For the same reason, when Spurs came out of the hat, while "it could have been worse" was a phrase used by some, there were no jigs of joy performed at the CFA. "Spurs always test you," was Carles Planchart's immediate verdict. "They make things difficult."

The images that last from the tie are from the Etihad – the breathless insanity of the opening exchanges; Fernando Llorente going up for Kieran Trippier's corner, nudging the ball into the net; a long VAR wait and then devastation for City. Agüero inching a hair beyond the last defender; Pep celebrating the goal that would take him to Amsterdam, the home of Cruyff; the cruel suspense of the VAR referral and then the heart-breaking reversal.

Yet perhaps the tie hinged on the first leg at White Hart Lane eight days previously, a deserved 1-0 win for the London team featuring a Kun Agüero penalty saved by Hugo Lloris.

Joan Patsy: "We lost the tie in the away match. For 14 straight matches, for three brutal months that season, from the defeat at Newcastle onwards, we played every single 90 minutes as if it were a cup final, except that match away at Spurs. From the outside it looked as if we were thinking: 'We can lose this one and we'll take it in the second leg.' The team didn't perform as if it were life or death. So we lost." After such a painful failure, everyone has a theory. Arteta's is different.

"We played to win, but by trying to control the ball and the entire first 90 minutes. We decided that, strategically, we didn't want a match of ebb and flow, toe-to-toe attacking, back and forwards. I think that we pretty much hit that objective – we won a penalty we could have led from, we created other chances, we definitely controlled the game overall and Spurs didn't really get through us very often. With retrospect, of course, it's easy to ask whether we could or should have done it differently. But I can say that we wouldn't have."

At the Lane, Pep chose an eyebrow-raising XI. "He out-Cruyffed Cruyff!" laughs Patsy, finally able to smile about it, months later. His old friend had a habit of picking a side full of surprise selections whenever his Dream Team played Madrid at the Bernabéu.

Guardiola's team was surprising, but with the benefit of Arteta's analysis, it's clear that some of the changes were made with the aim of controlling possession and position. Others seemed forced by circumstances. Fabian Delph was in the line-up because both Zinchenko and Danilo were carrying injuries. Benjamin Mendy had just reappeared in the team for the 1-0 win over Brighton in the FA Cup semi-final and his ongoing recovery required careful management. Pep recalls: "Fabian had looked in good form in training. Before making his return Mendy had been out five months. We decided pushing him into this match after playing against Brighton would have been too much too soon."

However, the relegation to the bench of both Kevin De Bruyne and Leroy Sané was harder to rationalise.

In the media conference which preceded the incredible second leg, Guardiola promised: "This time we'll push more players into and around their penalty area. Sometimes we've taken strategic decisions which not everyone understands. When we win we're geniuses and when we don't . . . But in the first match we had a plan and our players knew precisely why we'd taken every one of those decisions. The strategy was based on clear ideas and I think that we didn't do too badly in implementing it."

Most of the criticism was aimed at Guardiola for the decision to play two *pivotes* – or organising midfielders – in a tandem.

Pep Guardiola: "Football is a question of space and how to use it, it's a question of what your intentions are. If you use two inside midfielders then it's maybe to help the full-back or the single *pivote*. Because you always look to exploit space – make it and take advantage of it. If you use an extra man in midfield, you lose one up front, but you gain an extra element of control in the area where you most want it – above all, in supporting the left-back where we'd lost so many of the players who'd naturally start there. We decided to have Gündoğan there to help play the ball out from the back on the left side. Then it's a question of how the players interpret the space they've got, how to use it.

"With five at the back you can either call that an attacking or a defensive strategy. You can bring the ball out brilliantly with either two or three central defenders. Numbers and formations aren't the central point at all. The crucial thing is space, how to adapt to your opponent's movements and then to anticipate them and break into the spaces they leave."

By April 17 the 'Sold Out' signs had been plastered all over the ticket booths around the ground. In City's first ever Champions

League semi-final, under Manuel Pellegrini, having knocked out PSG, they faced Real Madrid at the Etihad. The stadium was packed that day, too, and had never been soldout since. Until now. It had prompted a song from the City supporters, to the tune of The Beautiful South's *Rotterdam (Or Anywhere)*: "We've been to Rotterdam and Monaco / Napoli and Rome / but we've still got blue empty seats / empty seats at home / empty seats at home."

Not tonight. Anna Palà and her events team ensured that there were either sky blue or white flags on every seat across the stadium. Nine sprawling crowd-flags with statements chosen by supporters' groups were passed above the heads of the crowd: *This is our city*; *The boys in blue never give up*; *We see things they'll never see*; *Loud proud loyal*; *Fight to the end*; *MCFC, Ok*; *Guardiola's Blue and White army*; *The best team in the land and in all the world*; *Blue Moon, you saw me standing alone*; and *MCFC, definitely Manchester* – this last one with the art and typography of an Oasis album.

Maybe the electrifying build-up plays some minor role in the volcano which erupts from the first whistle. Two teams built around the concept of control go haywire. It's 2-2 after 11 minutes. This is *not* supposed to happen.

Sterling puts City level on aggregate after four minutes. Heung-Min Son, in the seventh and 10th minutes, puts Spurs 2-1 ahead on the night. Laporte – a rock for City all season – is the guilty party each time. He has saved his worst game of the season for this night.

City need three. Just over sixty seconds later, Bernardo Silva scores and before the first half is even halfway over, Sterling makes it 3-2 on the night, 3-3 on aggregate and Spurs lead on away goals.

Complete footballing madness. But there's more on the way.

Just before the hour mark, Agüero scores, beating Lloris at his near post. Now it's City with one foot in the last four.

But it's a passing moment.

Just as will happen in the semi-final, Llorente comes on – this time before the break because Mo Sissoko is injured. Pochettino replaces his box-to-box midfielder with the Spanish target man.

City concede corners, pressure builds. Spurs throw men forward. Bubbling up from this cauldron of tension will be more than one all-or-nothing moment.

Another corner. Trippier's delivery from the left is terrific, dipping wickedly towards the front post. Walker can't get his head to it, but he and Toby Alderweireld are a combined presence sufficient to disturb Vincent Kompany. Llorente, who shares Basque nationality and an Athletic Club past with Laporte, not only gets in front of his old teammate but makes contact with the ball, which strikes part of his arm, then his hip and in it goes – Ederson is betrayed by the odd sequence of events.

The VAR officials invite the referee, Cuneyt Çakir, to re-watch what just happened. From the images he is shown he sees no infringements. No deflection off Llorente's arm. An angle from behind the goal clearly shows an accidental but decisive handball, and there will be much debate across the next 24 hours over whether or not the referee was shown this footage. The goal stands.

It is now 4-4 on aggregate and Spurs have the edge again due to the away goals rule. There are 17 minutes left, plus stoppages.

City hunt down a fifth goal – the one which can send them to Amsterdam. Spurs are tiring and swarmed. Christian Eriksen, pressed, exhausted, looking for a solution, attempts to seek out his keeper, Hugo Lloris, through a crowd. The back-pass isn't just a bad idea, it's what City have been trying to provoke. Fernandinho and De Bruyne harry him, Bernardo Silva gets a boot on to the Dane's tired pass and fate sends that deflection into Agüero's path. A little inside pass means that Sterling, now a 24-carat finisher, can fake a right-foot shoot for the benefit of

Alderweireld before cutting back the other way and shooting with his left, leaving Lloris spread-eagled, horrified and beaten.

Sterling continues his run to the corner. The rest of the team arrive, the substitutes arrive, it's a pile-up. Pep even strips off the grey hooded jersey he's been wearing all season.

The stadium erupts. Beer flies in the air. So do some supporters. The Etihad hasn't seen anything like it since Agüero scored against QPR to win the league.

This is football. *This* is the Champions League. *This* is City.

Spurs players are prostrate, it looks like some are already in tears.

Then: VAR. No whistle, no flag, but a word in the ear of Çakir from the officials in the studio and the world stops turning.

Bernardo Silva is the only one who's already alert to the danger. He's sniffed the idea that perhaps it was offside. The Portuguese hasn't wasted time joining the celebrating throng – now he's trying to influence the linesman. Silva knows there's a problem. Joan Patsy is nervous too and has already jogged down to the technical area – he's aware of what might be about to happen. Pep's eruption of relief and joy, shared by Arteta, Rodolfo Borrell and Manel Estiarte suddenly freezes. Patsy shouts to Estiarte – "VAR! It's going to VAR!"

A similar scene is unfolding in the normally tranquil directors' box. Like Silva, Begiristain is the only one who's held his celebrations in reserve because instinct tells him that City's predatory Argentine might have been offside. The Basque ex-winger, winner of this tournament under Cruyff in 1992, turns to Soriano and shares his concern.

Txiki Begiristain: "Honestly? I was sure. Kun was off from the moment Bernardo touched the ball and I guessed that video refereeing would disallow it. Is that cruel, or unfair? What's fair about football? We all make mistakes, the ref makes mistakes, players have good and bad days, we missed a penalty in the away match.

"My emotions were different. I felt that Pep didn't deserve to be out of the Champions League, that we really wanted to be playing in the Johan Cruyff Arena. We owed it to Johan, our professor, to take City there, but we were out, no further debate."

"I thought we were out," was Llorente's frank admission to us that night. "It was like dying and coming back to life."

Months earlier Pochettino had fessed up. He was VAR-sceptic. "Football's a sport where you've always tried to trick your rival – this move troubles me a bit, makes me worry that we are going to kill our sport in the form we've always loved."

By the City game his thinking had changed. "You need to trust in the VAR when it is against or for you. The decision to include VAR in football is going to change the game a little bit. I am pro the basis and trying to help the referees and maybe one year ago I was a little bit worried. Today my feeling is the same. When it is for you, you need to accept. When it is against you, you need to accept."

While the protagonists dissect the drama in the press room and mixed zones, the traditional get-together is underway in Pep's office. President Khaldoon, Soriano, Begiristain and Pep.

Ferran Soriano: "Pep took it worst, and that's quite normal in the circumstances. Khaldoon asked us to put the night in context, that we could still win four trophies in that same season. We've built an environment where nobody's going to lose their head, none of our fundamentals will be put at risk just because the team loses a match. The disappointment hurts, but it can last a day and then we have to get on with business. Losing an incredible quarter-final in that manner didn't indicate that any of the underlying ideas or work were off target and the president was fully aware of that."

All the same, Soriano, despite years in the football world, couldn't sleep that night. A phrase of Manuel Pellegrini's kept snagging in his mind. "When you win you're happy, but that slips away quickly because 'there's another game'. When you lose, the feeling of being completely pissed off can last months or years. In the end you try to learn that you can only feel that bad for 24 hours and then you move on, try to pick yourself up. It's an essential lesson to assimilate."

Soriano has his own way of trying to digest painful moments in life. And he's truly suffered those. One of his philosophies is that if something really bad happens it's healthy to really feel the suffering, and at times like these he draws on the teachings of a 3,000-year-old Jewish text offering guidance on dealing with grief.

"It's very specific and clear: it states that in the first week, you don't leave the house. The first month requires that you don't engage in playful or frivolous things – nothing festive. And during that first year of mourning you mustn't make fundamental decisions. But then the women-folk must come out of official mourning and not cry for whoever they've lost again. My compact version of that is that when things go against you, important, painful things like this, you must embrace the pain, make sure you really feel the loss – but then you have to shake it off. Otherwise the experience won't do you any good. It stays inside you and you brood."

Guardiola's practice is similar. The next day he barely spoke to anyone. By tea-time – after training – he was more himself again. By Friday things were pretty much back to normal. In the high offices, Soriano and Omar Berrada, City's chief operating officer, were knee-deep in big-picture strategy. The chance of a four-trophy season was a marker that things were still on track. The hard yards had been run and if Dame Fortune was looking the other way on a night when VAR's gaze was laser-like then who can affect that? They were confident in the consistency of their model. They were as business-like as they could be. But they had to accept that this was not business.

Ferran Soriano: "When I signed for City, I spoke in public a bit and said something that drew a bit of criticism. I was asked: 'What's the objective?' and I said 'a trophy per year.'

"I was drawing on what had happened when we were all at Barça. Did that mean I was demanding we won a trophy every single year? No. The idea, the objective was that if we had a season with no trophies, the next time we needed to win two.

"I think it's a true reflection of our ability and organisational aims. Look at the years we've had here and that's about the average we've achieved. Now, we'd all like to win everything, all the time. But if you take a step back and look long-term, who else in England has recently been winning a trophy per year? Nobody."

In Friday's press conference, Pep says: "Do you think that this doesn't hurt or that we have forgotten it? Well, no. And I don't want my players to forget what we went through. I don't want to see my players behave as if they're not affected by it. I want them to react to being wounded. What we went through on Wednesday in terms of emotion, or simply of life-experience, was incredible. We are fortunate to have lived through it. Over 65,000 people in their happiest state, then suddenly devastated. It will make us stronger."

It was just a prelude to what he told the team.

As soon as they took to the pitch for training, Pep was there.

"I'm proud of you. I know you feel like shit and you think it's not fair. Since when is football fair? I'm not being fair when I decide not to pick you. And I piss you off when I put you on the bench, so when you go out onto the pitch you show me that I'm wrong, right? Well, that's exactly what we're going to do now. Eat this fucking shit that we have to eat. Because we did everything to eliminate Spurs and they fucking beat us, we're out on our fucking arses. Now we just have to fight for everything we have left, stand up and fight for what we can still win. We can win two more trophies. And lads, let's go for them! I know you're going to do it because you're the best."

That Saturday, Spurs returned to the Etihad. And lost.

Foden got up on Saturday knowing he was starting. What he probably didn't imagine is that the next day he'd be splashed all over the sport sections of every newspaper.

In the fifth minute, Bernardo Silva crosses from the right towards Sergio Agüero at the far post. Agüero brilliantly cushions a set-up header into Foden's path and the kid nods the ball sweetly into the net.

City are back on their feet. They have a league to win.

THIRTY-SEVEN

PHIL FODEN AND THE TALENT FACTORY

Saturday, November 11, 2016. Wolverhampton's under-18s have been thrashed 6-1 by Manchester City. It's all everyone can talk about at the academy. Could this be the greatest generation of young players the club has ever seen? A few of today's performances suggest this might well be the case. Phil Foden, for example, one of the goalscorers: already an accomplished player at this level, a starter at the age of 16. Jadon Sancho, newly arrived from Watford, starts on the bench but comes on for the last 20 minutes and scores the sixth. Striker Joe Hardy scores a hat-trick. Midfielder Will Patching, an 18-year-old England international at under-16, -17 and -18 level, who is recovering from injury and therefore only plays a few minutes of the game, also makes his mark, producing a screamer from outside the box.

Within months of this game Hardy had left City to play for Brentford B. By 2019, Patching was relegated from the Football League with Notts County, having been cut by City the previous summer, as two of his former City teammates emerged as the stars of a new generation of English talent. Football can be brutal and for the elite, competition is fierce.

Brahim Díaz, a year older than Foden, was another of City's rising stars when Pep Guardiola arrived in Manchester. It was clear to the Catalan that the club's work to develop academy players, a priority since 2012, was beginning to bear fruit. There was an exciting future ahead for City and back in 2016, three names stood out for the new coach: Foden, Sancho and Díaz.

Pep Guardiola: "I saw this generation for the first time when they were just 16. Txiki had told me that we had talented kids coming up and wanted me to watch them in action. That same year we got them training with the first-team during the preseason. Phil, Sancho, Brahim – that was when their talent really showed."

After the first integrated session, Pep came off the field with a singular focus. He could see the potential in Brahim and Sancho, but he had fallen for Foden. "Did you see that kid in the centre of the field?" he asked his staff.

And yet, these days, of the three bright young stars who so impressed Pep that first summer, only Foden remains at City. In part, this is a consequence of a change in the recruitment strategy of elite clubs, who are now prepared to spend eight-figure sums to acquire teenage players who are yet to make a first-team appearance. The players are presented with an opportunity to sign a first-team-level contract and are frequently advised to do so. In other cases, a young player can see a clearer pathway to the first-team at another club, instead of facing down established internationals for a start at home.

In the summer of 2017, Sancho and Manchester City were deep in negotiations for his contract renewal. Pep and Txiki Begiristain were keen to hold on to the talented winger and made an offer of £30,000 per week, a club record for an academy player but reflective of the fact that he had been training with the first-team for a year. The player and his representatives seemed happy with the deal and the two parties shook hands. Sancho was staying and would be part of City's preseason tour of the US.

A few days later, everything had changed. Sancho was out of the US tour and refusing to train with City. The goalposts had moved. Sancho's representative had asked City to guarantee first-team football. With Sergio Agüero, Raheem Sterling, Leroy Sané, Bernardo Silva and Gabriel Jesus pushing for the same spots in Pep's team, that was an impossibility. Begiristain scolded the player: "We had a deal!"

City left for the States without Sancho. The player refused to attend training sessions. It was the end of the line.

Borussia Dortmund signed Sancho for £7m and he has since thrived in Germany. Sancho is now considered one of the best young players in the world. In 43 games with Dortmund until the end of season 2018-19, he scored 13 goals and provided 19 assists. At just 19, he is an established England international.

Should Sancho leave Germany, City have a contractual right to outbid any offer from a Premier League club, should they choose to.

Brahim Díaz was the next to go, although in very different circumstances. Aged 17, he joined the first-team for City's 2017-18 campaign but struggled to get playing time: 10 games, including five Premier League appearances (and so a league winner's medal), and a total of 190 minutes.

For Pep and his staff, that was an appropriate foundation and they had seen enough in the player's development to initiate contract renewal discussions 12 months ahead of schedule. However, Díaz, already frustrated at the lack of game time during the past season, saw the recruitment of Riyad Mahrez as a further blockade to the first-team.

The club suggested a loan to Girona. It worked for both clubs, but not the player. Díaz insisted on staying in Manchester to fight for his place.

However, after 15 minutes in the Community Shield plus three Carabao Cup appearances, Díaz clocked just 214 minutes in the first half of the season. Within that sample, the City fans saw a stunning performance against Fulham in the fourth round of the Carabao Cup, in which he scored two goals and received an ovation from the Etihad. As he left the pitch, he already knew that his days in Manchester were numbered. The winter transfer market was about to open and offers were rolling in. Real Madrid were the front-runner, with a £15m bid and an astronomical contract.

"We don't want him to go," Pep told the press. "But it's not our decision."

City could, of course, have insisted that Díaz stick to the terms of his contract, thus blocking his departure. But they understood his motivation to leave. Soriano met with Pere Guardiola (Pep's brother), who has represented the player since his early days at Malaga and agreed to change the terms of his contract so he could go. Brahim signed for Madrid, making 11 appearances before the end of the season and scoring one league goal.

Foden was born and raised in Stockport in a family of die-hard City fans. He joined City's academy aged seven and understands as much as any of his teammates the supporters who roar them on at the Etihad. He is one of them. He is a PR dream, but only because that backstory is in tandem with a phenomenal talent – one tailor-made for Pep's game.

Pep Guardiola: "One thing is very clear to us: Foden has a place in Manchester City's first-team because of who the club has put in charge. I'd be interested to see if a different kind of manager would have done the same, given him this chance to develop, or if they'd have loaned him out. Phil is a very special player."

On the preseason tour before the start of season 2019-20, Guardiola went further still. "He is the most talented I have seen as a player or manager."

Foden made his Premier League debut on December 16, 2017, 27 years to the day after Guardiola played his first game as a pro, for Barcelona. Foden ended that season with 10 appearances and a league winner's medal. The following year, he played 26 times, scoring seven goals. To begin with, his impact came in the cup competitions, but his moment arrived during the Premier League run-in.

Days after defeat by Spurs in the Champions League, the two teams were due to face off again in the league.

Guardiola's stars had been floored by the events of the second leg – the hangover was palpable at the CFA. Then Pep noticed Foden lighting up the darkness that engulfed the first-team squad at training.

In that moment, Pep made the decision to start the teenager against Spurs. Foden dominated the midfield, and scored the only goal of the match, a header after five minutes.

Post-match Bernardo Silva, who had been awarded man of the match, turned to Foden and, in front of the cameras, handed him the trophy. "Phil was the best. We won thanks to him."

Guardiola has attracted some criticism for failing to use Foden often enough. His absence from the team sheet for the away game of the League Cup semi-final against Burton Albion was met with incredulity in the press room of the Etihad.

Pep Guardiola: "I know how keen everyone is for Foden to play. I feel the same way. I understand why people keep asking, 'Why isn't he playing more?' But he's actually playing a lot and he's only 19. In England people sometimes expect too much of their young players. You see kids come up really fast and they end up paying for it. It's better to take things slowly. I don't like leaving him out of certain games, but I have to think of the whole squad. There has to be a balance. Phil understands that, although I know he'll demand more as time goes on. That's totally normal.

"He's competing with David Silva and Gündoğan. Silva is a club legend, perhaps the most important City player ever. And we wouldn't have won the league in 2019 without Gündo. He's been spectacular in midfield and is as good defensively as he is in attack. He passes brilliantly, supports our defence – he's superb.

Phil also has to compete with Kevin, Bernardo, Fernandinho – at this level you're always going to be up against elite players and he's only 19. He has to wait his turn."

And his turn will come. When news broke that David Silva will leave England at the end of season 2019-20, there were reports that City were interested in bringing in Isco as a replacement. Such a move was never considered.

Pep Guardiola: "We won't be signing anyone else for that position. When David Silva leaves, we know exactly who our new magician will be. He's here already, he's grown up with us, he's one of us. And he's going to be brilliant. One of the best players in the Premier League."

Foden is the poster boy for City's youth system, living proof that it can produce world-class players not just from the academy, but from the city itself.

Guardiola continued to include youth players in first-team training and the leading academy graduate to emerge during 2018-19 was Eric García. The Catalan defender was recruited from Barcelona in 2017 and made his senior debut the following season, during the pre-season tour. He played in three Carabao Cup games and big things are expected of him by the City staff.

Another Catalan, Adrián Bernabé, joined in 2018 and debuted with the first-team against Oxford in the Carabao Cup, aged just 18. Frenchman Claudio Gomes transferred from PSG the same year and played in the Community Shield and, briefly, in a cup game against Fulham. After Brahim's departure, talented attacking midfielder Ian Carlo Poveda got his chance to play in the Carabao Cup semi-final against Burton Albion. On the same day, midfielder Felix Nmecha made his debut.

However, if one name stands out amongst them all, it's Tommy Doyle. His grandfathers are Glyn Pardoe and Mike Doyle, two of City's all-time legends who between them played nearly 800 games.

When he comes to work at the CFA, Tommy walks down Doyle Lane, the street named after his grandfather. The junior model is an ambidextrous midfielder who can play as a *pivote* or attacking midfielder with a fierce shot and great passing ability. He's also a leader – the captain of the England under-18 team. "We have high hopes for him. We'll bring him in to train with us [in season 2019-20] and start the process of developing him," explained Pep, who was an academy graduate at an elite club himself. As such he knows that it takes time and patience to develop players in an environment when the pressure on the first-team to win is immense.

Doyle is one of 12 academy graduates who participated in City's Asia tour in the summer of 2018 (Foden joined them in the second half of the tour in Hong Kong after competing in the UEFA European Under-21 Championship). The club invest around £30m per year in the system that produced Foden, who has renewed through season 2023-24.

"We didn't give Phil Foden a new contract by accident," said Pep. "And I'll tell you this: he is the only player that cannot be sold, under any circumstances. The only one. Not for €500m. Phil's going nowhere. Phil is City."

THIRTY-EIGHT

14 WINS

Between January 29, 2019, when they lost at St James' Park and May 12, when they beat Brighton to retain their Premier League title, Man City won 14 consecutive league matches, dismissing Arsenal, Everton, Chelsea, West Ham, Bournemouth, Watford, Fulham, Cardiff, Crystal Palace, Tottenham, Manchester United, Burnley, Leicester and Brighton. They needed every one of those wins. City finished on 98 points, one ahead of Liverpool.

It was an incredible sequence but not a record-breaking one. Pep's City had set the mark at 18 victories the year before, with a winning streak that stretched from a 2-1 win over Bournemouth on August 26 to a 0-0 draw with Crystal Palace on New Year's Eve.

The problem was, on Merseyside Jürgen Klopp and his men were just as determined to win the battle for the title.

And this was not the only trophy in City's sights. There was the Carabao Cup. They lifted that a little under a month into their Premier League winning streak, but Chelsea took them all the way to penalties and the victory came at a cost: Fernandinho, forced off with a groin injury towards the end of normal time, would only complete one more full 90 minutes before the end of the season.

As spring bloomed, FA Cup fixtures added to City's already cluttered calendar. City's match against Manchester United had to be postponed to April 24, while Liverpool – knocked out by

Wolves in the third round – surged back to the top with a victory over Fulham.

Three days after the Carabao Cup final, February ended with a visit from Pep's predecessor, Manuel Pellegrini and his West Ham side. It was a tough, controversial game, decided by a Sergio Agüero penalty. As Liverpool thrashed Wolves 5-0 at Anfield, City struggled to keep pace. Despite controlling over 80 per cent of possession, the game was deadlocked until substitute Bernardo Silva won a penalty under a Filipe Anderson challenge. Agüero kept his head. Pellegrini, protesting the decision, came about as close as he ever gets to losing his. With 28 games played each, City were a single point behind Liverpool.

Next up, Bournemouth away and another 1-0 win, but once again, the trade-off threatened to derail City's run-in. John Stones and Kevin De Bruyne went down with injuries either side of the break and neither man could continue. De Bruyne's replacement was Riyad Mahrez, who ended a heroic resistance from Artur Boruc, the veteran Bournemouth keeper. With Liverpool idle, City went back to the top, having played an extra game.

Seven days later, on March 9, Raheem Sterling scored a 13-minute hat-trick against Watford at the Etihad. Going into the game, Pep had told Sterling to propel himself as close to the opponents' goal as possible – attacking from 'out to in' with the ball glued to his boot.

The first goal, though, should not have counted. The referee ignored an offside as the ball appeared to rebound off a Watford defender, but it was a clear error. Outside the press room, the two coaches discussed the matter at length, with Guardiola apologising to Javi Gracia about the nature of the breakthrough moment. "They'd worked so hard and played so well and then we go one up with that goal," he said.

He was justifiably proud of his own team's performance. "We demand a lot without giving them the rest-time they really require physiologically. No matter what happens this season they deserve my admiration."

After the Watford game came a 20-day international break and the players headed off to join their respective national teams. Guardiola was not happy. "You'll always have someone who's picked up some kind of injury and, because you don't see them for days, it can be difficult to re-establish the group dynamic. And you've maybe got just a couple of days to prepare for a decisive game."

City's next game was away to Fulham. Goals from Bernardo Silva and Agüero put City ahead and, although Liverpool were still in the lead, with one game in hand, Pep's team were gathering momentum and belief that they could retain their crown.

"Those first 20 minutes were incredible," said Pep. "Usually it's hard when we come back after an international break but the team were totally up for it."

After the game, Pep went to salute the fans and spotted his wife Cristina and the kids in the crowd, waving like mad. The passion and dedication of the travelling support is an aspect of English football that is different from Spain.

"It's one of the things I love most about playing in England," he said. "You go to Fulham, Burnley, Newcastle and you think to yourself, 'It's absolutely freezing and these buggers have come all this way for us.'

"I see it with my kids and their mates. They'll ask for tickets and I'll say, 'You want to go there?' And that's *exactly* what they want."

The City steamroller powered on. Cardiff were despatched in the Etihad in a brisk and efficient manner, with goals from De Bruyne and Sané. Then, on April 14, they headed to the capital and Crystal Palace – a 3-1 win that took them top.

As they made the trek back home from London, players and staff kept a close eye on the Liverpool-Chelsea game. If Chelsea could take something from Anfield, City would remain top. However, after a goalless first half, Mané and Salah had other ideas and Pep's men were displaced once more. With every passing fixture, the feeling grew stronger that this was going to the wire.

Assistant manager Mikel Arteta: "Tiredness began to creep in gradually. In that period we had Tottenham, the Champions League, and the FA Cup final just around the corner – we never seemed to stop and get a break, but we actually felt like we were getting stronger and stronger, because winning gives you that. It all felt a bit crazy."

Fitness coach Lorenzo Buenaventura: "There were days when a lot of the players spent more time on the massage table than on the training pitch. We could hardly spare any time for training because it was all recuperation."

Marc Boixasa, first-team operations manager: "You could feel the sense of absolute unity. Sometimes we played on Saturday but Liverpool's game was on the Sunday. Players would come in for training or a recovery session and then everyone would gather in the cafeteria to watch the Liverpool game together. We'd all be so hyped up and tense. Every foul, every throw-in, we'd all be on our feet, protesting, like fans in a pub. We all noticed the unbreakable bond that formed over those weeks and months."

Txiki Begiristain, director of football: "Pep was feeling totally confident and it was contagious. He had a thousand day-to-day decisions to make about away games, hotels, training plans, tactics, training sessions. He likes to oversee every detail. And that's what he continued to do. But he also has very capable people around him who know him well and can anticipate what he wants."

The win over Palace came between the two legs of the Champions League quarter-final against Spurs, with a league game against the same opponents following swiftly after that.

Before the dramatic, devastating second leg in Manchester, nobody could have predicted the aftershocks that Pep's players would have to deal with were they to keep their streak going in the league rematch.

"We were dead, but Phil Foden gave us the spark of intensity we needed that day," recalls Pep, who decided to include the youngster in his starting XI after seeing him at training on the Thursday after the second leg. It was Foden's header that decided the league game at the Etihad.

Now the run-in looked like this: Manchester United away; Burnley away; Leicester at home; Brighton away.

On April 24, City won 2-0 at Old Trafford, with David de Gea culpable for both goals, scored by Bernardo Silva and Leroy Sané. Once more the half-time score was 0-0, and once more City's control and patience paid off. All teams had now played 35 games and City had the edge by a single point.

"Managing those games was actually very easy," recalled Pep. "Your attitude is 'if we lose a single match, we lose the league'. It's pretty simple and it's a good way to approach a game. You can't afford a minute's relaxation."

Pep's mind was already on the Burnley game. A quintessentially English football side – tough, aggressive and stubborn. It would be a hard game, in every sense of the word.

Lorenzo Buenaventura: "Playing at Burnley is like going to the dentist."

Pep Guardiola: "I was utterly destroyed by the end of it. I felt like I'd played the whole 90 minutes myself."

They went to Burnley on Sunday April 28, the day Spain voted for its next president (Pep voted by mail).

Once more, the game was 0-0 at the break, and for the fourth time in the last nine Premier League matches, City won with the only goal. Agüero's winner set a couple of personal records. He became only the second player (after Alan Shearer) to have scored

20 goals in six different Premier League seasons. It was also the narrowest margin by which he has ever scored. His goal was allowed after the ball was judged to have crossed the line by 2.91 cm.

The goal, on 63 minutes, was a moment of relief and from then on City had a lot of opportunities to wrap it up. But they did not, and after they tried to run the clock down, Burnley won a free-kick, with 92 minutes gone.

Guardiola: "I almost had a heart attack. We had [Aymeric] Laporte and [Vincent] Kompany playing and I'd already put [Nicolás] Otamendi and [John] Stones on to help. Seriously, if I'd had John Terry, Carles Puyol and Rio Ferdinand there that day, I'd have thrown them on too, I'd have done anything, just to make it through those last few minutes. They hadn't had a single shot on goal the whole game and there's no way they were going to equalise with a long ball booted the length of the pitch into our area!"

Two games to go. The race would end in Brighton, but the visit of a resurgent Leicester under new manager Brendan Rodgers in the penultimate fixture now loomed.

Don't shoot Vinny! Don't shoot!

Vincent Kompany has attributed the quote to Sergio Agüero, but the Manchester City No.10 was not alone.

On the touchline, his manager, Pep Guardiola, was saying exactly the same thing. *Don't shoot.*

Raheem Sterling was ahead of his captain, thinking: *Don't shoot.*

Closest to Kompany, four yards to his left, Bernardo Silva feared the worst: *Just pass me the ball.*

Behind him, Oleksandr Zinchenko suspected that his mentor had lost the plot: *Don't do this Vinny, please don't do this, just pass the ball, that's it.*

The minority report came from Riyad Mahrez (who knows a thing or two about scoring from distance) and John Stones. Both were on the bench and had watched Kompany move upfield, his ambition growing with each stride.

Riyad Mahrez: "I was thinking, he has to shoot now."

John Stones: "I saw he had space and I thought he should have a shot."

Vincent Kompany cuts through the ball with his right foot, ripping a shot that swerves from left to right. Kasper Schmeichel, a goalkeeper whose heroism until that moment appears to be gradually nudging the Premier League title from Manchester to Liverpool, takes off once more, his arms outstretched, clawing at the air . . .

The day had started early. Breakfast at 9.30am sharp, followed by a 10.45 team meeting and a light training session at midday. Back to the canteen for lunch at 1pm before a mandatory afternoon nap. Another bite to eat at 4.30pm and then straight into the second team meeting of the day. With Pep's final instructions ringing in their ears, the players boarded the bus for the short journey (0.6 miles) to the Etihad ahead of the 8pm kick-off.

Two days earlier, Liverpool had looked like stumbling – fatally – before dramatically muscling their way past Newcastle with four minutes left. They went top by two points. Whatever happened between City and Leicester, the title would go down to the final day of the season. Win and Pep's team would be in control – victory at Brighton would mean the championship. Fail and Liverpool would have the upper hand.

"There was a huge tension [before Leicester]," admits Mikel Arteta. "The title was on the line. We'd gone over and over what our line-up should be and knew that Leicester would be tough opponents. We have a lot of respect for them – they beat us at the King Power Stadium and forced us to a penalty shoot-out in the Carabao Cup."

The title was on the line. No hype required. But for the captain, the stakes were even higher. Kompany had decided that he was leaving City after 11 years to be player-manager of Anderlecht, his first club. This would be his final game at the Etihad. He led his team on to the pitch for a game that would be decisive in their bid for back-to-back league titles, knowing that he would never do so again.

Kompany and Pep first met in the summer of 2016. The Belgian had been injured 10 minutes into the return leg of the Champions League semi-final against Real Madrid. After an operation in Barcelona, he was back in Manchester, recuperating.

The rest of the team weren't yet back for preseason training and Guardiola, newly arrived as manager, invited the captain to his office.

Vincent Kompany: "I remember it wasn't really a discussion about football – more of a presentation. Pep told me what he expected from his captains and filled me in on what he'd done in the past. I explained a bit about what he could expect here and reassured him that he'd find the locals friendly and up front. Manchester people like to say it like it is – to your face."

After that, Kompany regularly dropped into Pep's office. "I've gone in for a chat a few times. Usually because I'm not totally convinced about something and I want Pep to put my mind at rest. We'll debate it back and forth."

In Guardiola, Kompany found the perfect manager to feed his appetite for learning. He has spent hours talking over games with Pep and his coaching staff.

For the new manager, Kompany was a gift – a born leader, multilingual in an international dressing room, and a world-class defender. When fit.

Kompany's career has been punctuated by injuries and maximising his game time was one of Pep's challenges when he arrived. His concern was evident from the start: "My only wish for Vincent is that he stays fit and healthy," the Catalan said in 2016 when speaking about his captain for the first time. In the season before Guardiola arrived, Kompany had failed to play more than five consecutive games and was not fit enough to complete 90 minutes until April 2017.

Under Pep, the medical staff personalised every aspect of Kompany's preparation and care: his warm-ups; his diet; his training schedule. Kompany's blood was analysed regularly to monitor the quality of his muscle tissue and samples were sent to the University of Granada in Spain to guide changes to his diet.

Despite all that, Kompany played under 1,800 minutes of first-team football in each of his three seasons under Pep. It was an improvement on 2015-16, but by comparison Sergio Agüero played over 3,000 minutes in 2018-19.

Pep's efforts to increase Kompany's game time was driven by his phenomenal record when he had been able to play consistently. During his 11 years at City, Kompany was selected in the PFA team of the year three times. In 2012 he was voted their player of the year.

In the City dressing room, his value was even higher.

David Silva: "Who's going to give us lectures now? I think they could use him at the UN."

Instead, Kompany left City for Anderlecht, and the chance to combine the autumn of a storied playing career with his leadership skills and all he had learned under Guardiola. It is not difficult to imagine a Vincent Kompany team playing a game that is related to this City era.

"Pep made everything much easier," he said. "Playing the ball out from the back, passing, defending with space behind us – it all really suits me. You have to be ultra-accurate in your passing, but it's actually easier than you might think because knowing exactly where everyone is on the pitch gives you a huge advantage over the opposition. It's the easiest I ever found playing my position."

Kompany's thirst for education extends beyond football. He graduated with an MBA from Manchester Business School in December 2017, dedicating the achievement to his mother and offering some advice to those coming behind him: "You young athletes out there, stick with your education. If you want to be in charge of your own life, keep studying."

During his studies, Kompany would often read economics text books on the team bus or on flights. He was as likely to give his teammates investment advice after training as he was to issue tactical instructions during a game.

He captained them through their most spectacular era, winning four Premier League titles (2012, 2014, 2018 and 2019), four League Cups (2014, 2016, 2018 and 2019) plus two FA Cups (2011 and 2019).

And in his final game at the stadium that will not forget him, he signed off with a moment that was all his.

Don't shoot, Vinny!

"Everyone was saying that to me! But I've not come this far in my career to be told when I can and can't shoot", an ecstatic Kompany said later. "It's 15 years of top-level football and I always hear midfielders saying 'don't shoot, play the ball wide' – for 15 years! I said to them: 'One of these days I'm going to have a shot from outside the box and I'm going to score a goal and you're going to be really happy with that one.' And today it happened."

As Schmeichel lands on the turf, and the ball slides down the back of the net, Kompany races off to his right and slides down by the touchline. The crowd erupts. He is mobbed by his teammates.

Kompany is in tears after the match. He is joined by Caleb, the youngest of his three children, for a lap of honour, his personal goodbye to the fans who sing that "City loves you more than you will know" (to the tune of *Mrs Robinson*).

Afterwards, Pep tells his team that the league is theirs.

Mikel Arteta: "From then on Pep kept saying to us, 'We've done it, we've done it.' He just kept repeating it over the next few days – 'It's in the bag. It's in the bag. We still have one game left, but the title's ours.' He was so sure."

Kompany's goal means that City have scored in every home league game, a Guardiola trademark. The coach achieved the same with Barça at Camp Nou in 2009-10 and Bayern Munich at the Allianz Arena in 2015-16.

The day is special for Pep in another way: it is Valentina's 11th birthday and so also the anniversary of the day the then president of Barcelona, Joan Laporta, popped over to the maternity hospital to see the newborn and to offer Pep the top job at Barça, only to be told by the then B-team coach: "You wouldn't have the balls!"

Perhaps that is what they all thought, or hoped, about Kompany, as he strode upfield and cocked his right foot to shoot.

But he did. And in the aftermath, Gary Neville, commentating for Sky Sports, came up with a perfect line to capture the goal, the moment, the man.

"Where do you want your statue, Vincent Kompany?"

After Leicester, Pep was convinced they would be champions. On the way to Brighton for the final fixture, with everything riding on one last victory, the mood was completely different to the tension of the games against Leicester, or Burnley, or United or Spurs.

Pep Guardiola: "It was obvious. You could see it in their faces. They knew that they would not trip up. Even if Brighton scored first, however the game was going, however it began, we had this feeling. We all had this feeling that this wouldn't get away from us. I say that with all due respect to Brighton, but there are days when you just know you're going to win because you have to. Even if the other team is better. You know that that day, you're going to win. That's how it was."

Perhaps that was why Pep Guardiola's pre-match preparations were far less rigorous than usual – because of, not in spite of, the stakes.

Manel Estiarte explained: "All the players knew exactly what was on the line. They didn't need to hear it from us."

Pep Guardiola: "The fact that we'd worked together for three years by then made the tactical side of things much easier. They already know what you're asking them to do and they catch on immediately, almost anticipating the instructions you give them. And if we have to make the odd change here or there, they're immediately on board because they understand exactly why we do everything. They've already processed mentally what we want them to do and we don't even have to think about team motivation, quite the contrary."

The season-long battle with a mighty Liverpool side was almost over. Even with the Reds seven points ahead in January, City had refused to give up. Their belief became absolute, which perhaps explained why nobody seemed to bat an eyelid when, 27 minutes in, Brighton got a corner which Glenn Murray headed in at the near post. Brighton were 1-0 up, and Liverpool led at Anfield. As things stood, the title was Liverpool's.

Then Agüero slammed the ball home and City turned the screw. Laporte charged at a corner to head City in front just before half-time. Mahrez and İlkay Gündoğan started the party with two glorious strikes after the break. City were champions again.

In Manchester, 20,000 fans watched the game live inside the Etihad. The team made it back around midnight and the crowd was still there. Pep and Kompany led the festivities. A bashful David Silva practically had to be pushed out to enjoy his ovation.

It was time to party, but everyone had their own unique understanding of the term. City CEO Ferran Soriano, having joined the festivities in the tunnel, was back in work mode by the time he was in Manchester, busily making plans and setting up meetings. Begiristain and his wife didn't want the night to end and had to be dragged out at dawn. In the Bahamas, Domènec Torrent, assistant manager in Pep's first two seasons in England, and now in charge at New York City FC, celebrated his friends' success with his wife, Gemma.

Pep headed home with Cristina and Valentina in the early hours. Tired. Emotional. Happy.

In January, the task had been as clear as it was daunting: win 14 consecutive games to retain the league title. And they did it.

THIRTY-NINE

THE PHONECALL

June 1, 2019. Tottenham Hotspur 0 Liverpool 2.

Liverpool have just become European champions for the sixth time, winning a less-than-memorable final in Madrid with goals at either end of the match: the first a penalty from Mo Salah; the second another of Divock Origi's late-season cameos.

Pep Guardiola is watching on television. His City team edged out Jürgen Klopp's Liverpool at the end of an epic title race. On the big European nights, it is his rival who has repeatedly ended with that megawatt smile on his face.

If Pep arrived in England into a ready-made Guardiola v Mourinho storyline, then now, three years on, the narrative has changed. The duel that has crossed over from the continent into English football is not the one that produced the *Clasicó* wars of 2011 between Guardiola's Barça and José Mourinho's Madrid. Instead it is that of *Der Klassiker* during Pep's time at Bayern, when Klopp ran his great, counter-attacking Dortmund team.

Yet Pep's thoughts do not go to Klopp. Not immediately. He had skin in the game in Madrid. Guardiola picks up his phone and calls Lee Nobes, head of physiotherapy at Liverpool. At the start of the calendar year, Nobes was part of Pep's staff at Manchester City and he has been missed in the months since.

Pep Guardiola: "He's a brilliant guy, but there's always going to be interesting jobs elsewhere and everyone's free to make that choice. He'd been at City for a long time and wanted to try something new."

The two men chat for a while before it occurs to Pep that he might have a chance to congratulate the rival he has been wrestling with throughout the epic, thrilling season that has just ended.

"Is Klopp around?"

Nobes goes off to find the Liverpool coach and hands him the phone just before Klopp enters the post-match press conference. The schedule for the Champions League winning manager is tight, but he takes a minute to speak.

Pep Guardiola: "I just congratulated him on winning the title and for their spectacular season. And we both agreed we'd be back to kick some ass next year."

DEDICATION

DON'T LOOK BACK IN ANGER

May 22, 2017. 10.30pm. Pep Guardiola is at home watching a match on TV with his son, Màrius, when they hear an explosion outside. From the window, he can see people running down the steps of the Manchester Arena. Then his wife, Cristina, phones from inside the Arena, where she and their daughters have been attending an Ariana Grande concert. Something has happened. She's not sure what. She's trying to get out with the girls, Maria and Valentina. She lifts up Valentina and follows Maria, her eldest, who's making for the nearest exit. They make it outside. Safe. As soon as she gets a signal, she phones Pep. "We're out. We're okay. We're coming home." By this point, he is at the main door of the apartment building. Pep and Màrius meet them halfway and they all go home together: scared, shaken, in shock.

The facts begin to emerge. A 22-year-old man from the Fallowfield area, Manchester born and bred, has blown himself up in the foyer, close to the Victoria Station entrance. 22 people will later be declared dead and 166 wounded.

İlkay Gündoğan lives in the same building as the Guardiolas. He hears the noise and initially thinks it is kids carrying on, but when the police and the ambulance sirens start, he runs out into the street. He is met with a scene of horror. Young girls, clinging to each other, tears streaming down their faces. He bumps into Leroy Sané and David Quintana, City's first-team operations manager, who immediately phones Pep to check on the family's safety.

Then they become worried about Raheem Sterling, for whom Quintana had bought tickets for the concert. Sterling is not answering his phone. Then, out of nowhere, he appears on the street. The young Englishman decided not to go to the concert in the end and had been out to dinner when it all happened. He sends a message on the team's group chat as soon as he finds out. Some comfort for them all on Manchester's long night of loss and pain.

The people of Manchester, as warm and as strong as the bricks fired in the city's factories, respond with dignity. Two bouquets are left outside the church in St Ann's Square in the early hours following the attack. By mid-morning there are hundreds of bouquets which the police move to the centre of the square, under the statue of Richard Cobden, famous manufacturer, liberal statesman and possibly the farthest-travelled man of his age. The sea of flowers, soft toys and heart-shaped balloons continues to grow at the feet of the statue as thousands of people arrive each day to pay their respects. Pep and his family are among them.

A ceremony is held on May 25 in the square and a minute's silence is observed. Then, one woman in the crowd, Lydia Bernsmeier-Rullow, a Manchester-born poet and actress, spontaneously starts singing Oasis's *Don't Look Back in Anger*. She is very quickly joined by the rest of the crowd.

And so, Sally can wait
She knows it's too late as we're walking on by
Her soul slides away
But don't look back in anger
I heard you say

The song becomes Manchester's hymn, a tribute to the fallen and an expression of hope.

ACKNOWLEDGEMENTS

We moved to Manchester in 2016 and have followed every step of Pep's time at City since then – day after day, week after week, game after game. Beer after beer. Victory after victory.

This book, and all the encounters and events it recounts, is the product of everything we've witnessed during countless meetings (some of them accidental, most of them pre-planned) with the people featured – from hasty exchanges during lunch hours and tea breaks to long, fascinating conversations over dinner or beers, often lasting well into the night.

It is the product of all the interviews we've conducted with the executives and the technical and support staff of the CFA: Pep Guardiola, Ferran Soriano, Txiki Begiristain, Manel Estiarte, Omar Berrada, Vicky Kloss, Joan Patsy, Lorenzo Buenaventura, Domènec Torrent, Mikel Arteta, Brian Kidd, Carles Planchart, Xabier Mancisidor, Silvia Tremoleda, Edu Mauri, Edu Álvarez, Max Sala, James Baldwin, Marc Boixasa, Ana Leyva, Brandon Ashton, Michael Clitheroe, Ally Marland, Carlos Vicente, Anna Gil and Anna Palà.

To all of them we say a huge and heartfelt thank you.

Thanks, too, to those first team players who have given us so much of their time: Vincent Kompany, Ederson Moraes, Claudio Bravo, Aymeric Laporte, Oleksandr Zinchenko, İlkay Gündoğan, David Silva, Bernardo Silva, Leroy Sané and Sergio Agüero. It is their generosity that has allowed us to share their experiences with you.

Thanks also to Mike Summerbee and David Williams.

We'd also like to express our gratitude to Cristina Serra for her patience, kindness and generosity.

This book would not have been possible without the support of our fellow journalists, with whom we've shared the highs and the lows, plus the odd beer. We won't name them individually, but we want them all to know how much they are appreciated. We'll never forget you.

Thanks to Carlos Vicente, we couldn't have done this without you. To Xavi Heras, Edu Durán, Cesc Guimera and Rob 'Leo Messi' Pollard and Jonathan Smith who gave us so much help with the music. Our eternal thanks go to all of you and all the Manchester City staff for the patience you've shown us.

Special thanks to Màrius for your passion for football. It's been inspirational.

And to Florence and Bethany and Sir Ralph Abercromby, who introduced us to the Beautiful South's *Rotterdam*, which played night after night while we transcribed or wrote our stories, long before the City fans, away at Huddersfield, appropriated the song for their 'empty seats at home' chant.

We'd also like to mention the City Arms and their Titanic pints, the Sandinista, the Corbieres, the Castle (a special shout-out for Winston), Gulliver's, Night & Day (whose concerts have provided the soundtrack for this book), 42's, the Venue, the Soup Kitchen and the Wharf (so many happy memories of warm summer evenings), the Black Lion, the Pen & Pencil, the Shamrock Inn, the Abel Heywood, the Seven Brothers, Mr. Thomas's Chop House, the Lost Dene, the Brotherhood, Second City, the FAB in Portland Street (hats off to whoever who came up with that idea), the Dockyard, in Media City, where it all began, Mendizábal, with its table 25, and the bar of the Vilabella swimming pool, where we finished this book. And to Manu at Grindsmith. Brilliant coffee, mate!

To all the bartenders and baristas, the waiters and waitresses, to those who served and those who danced the night away, thank you.

Love and thanks to Amaia and Floren, for everything, to Néstor just for being there and to Jason Halligan for showing us a new way of living. To Juan, José Manuel and Elena, and all the team at Tapeo & Wine, thank you for feeding us, looking out for us and lending us your printer. To everyone at Tast, Miquel, Julià, Miquelet and Nil and others, sou molt grans (you're the best).

Huge thanks also due to David, Sam, Jon, Pol, Marta, Jose, Maks, Enric and Álvaro. David Quintana, you gave us the keys to the city and helped us more than anyone.

Thank you Gemma, Mercè, and Eva (love and kisses to Carla and Alejandra!) and to Ari, Ona, Nil and Nicola.

Lots of love to Larita Vilchez, for her cheerfulness and patience and for learning Catalan.

Thanks to Walter Oppenheimer for offering us his advice and support, his friendship and his sofa, to John Carlin for always picking up the phone and to Rafa Ramos for showing us the way.

To Louise and Graham Hunter, who have contributed so much more than just the translation of this book. For the drinks, the laughs and the great advice, many thanks guys!

Neil and Martin from BackPage and Pete from Polaris – your patience and guidance has been much appreciated, it got us over the line.

To NG for the gift.

And above all, a thousand thanks to Marta and Violeta for making it all possible and for being with me all the way. And Pol would like to express his thanks to his three best friends (and not just because of all the drinks they buy him).

Thanks Manchester

We love you.

Pol Ballús and Lu Martín, 2023

ABOUT THE AUTHORS

Luis Martín *is a legendary Spanish journalist who has written on La Liga and the national team since the 1980s. He worked with Pep Guardiola on the 2001 book La Meva Gent, El Meu Futbol (My People, My Football). He has lived in Manchester and Barcelona during Guardiola's time in England.*

Pol Ballús *is a young Spanish sportswriter who moved to Manchester shortly before Pep Guardiola landed in the Premier League, with a brief to cover the growing number of Spanish players in England. He has since developed close ties with the players and staff at City.*

ALSO AVAILABLE

ALSO AVAILABLE

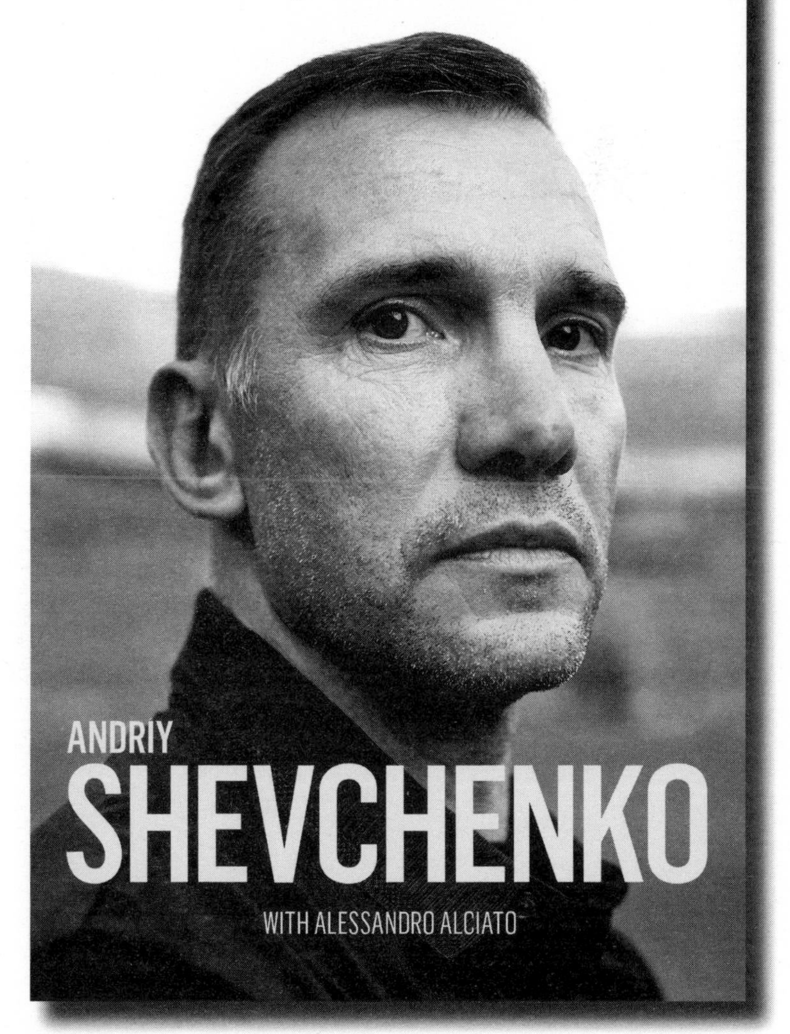